THE HUNDRED THOUSAND

SONGS OF *Milarepa*

Volume I

The life-story and teaching of the greatest Poet-
Saint ever to appear in the history of Buddhism.

SHAMBHALA   BOULDER & LONDON   1977

ཉ་བཅའི་བ་ལཱ་རང་སྐར་པ་ལ་ངུ་ལ་གྱགགག་ལ་
ལ་ཆི་ཅ་རཱུ

THE HUNDRED THOUSAND

SONGS OF *Milarepa*

Volume I

TRANSLATED AND ANNOTATED

BY *Garma C. C. Chang*

SHAMBHALA PUBLICATIONS, INC.
1123 Spruce Street
Boulder, Colorado 80302

© 1962 Oriental Studies Foundation

Originally published in cloth by
University Books, New Hyde Park, N.Y.

First complete paperback edition
published 1977 by Shambhala Publications, Inc.

ISBN 0-87773-095-4
LCC 76-55120

Distributed in the United States by Random House
and in Canada by Random House of Canada Ltd.

Distributed in the Commonwealth by
Routledge & Kegan Paul Ltd., London and Henley-on-Thames

Printed in the United States of America

To the memory of

My Guru

His Holiness, Lama Kong Ka

To my wife

Hsiang-hsiang

and

To my Brother-in-the-Dharma

Peter Gruber

without whom the publication of this

book would not have been possible

FOREWORD

MY FIRST meeting with the translator of this book goes back to the year 1947. We met in Darjeeling, a resort town in the foothills of the Himalaya Mountains. He had just come from Tibet, a distance which, though not far from Darjeeling, has to be measured in the number of days' travel by horses and yaks. Tibet was then a great mystery and source of curiosity to most people; the country was still closed to foreigners and only a few Europeans had been there. The barrier, however, was less stringent on the Chinese side. With this advantage, Mr. Chang had left China for Tibet in the late 1930's to search for Dharma and Enlightenment. He traveled extensively in the Kham region of Tibet and studied Buddhism in various monasteries for more than eight years. His fascinating and inspiring adventures in this "innermost part of Tibet" are a matter for another book. Because of his long years of study and practice in Tibet, his personal devotion and committment to Buddhism, and his first-hand experience of the lives of the Tibetan people, he is best qualified to translate this great Tibetan classic, *The Hundred Thousand Songs of Milarepa*, which, up to the present, has not appeared in complete translation in any Western language.

But what contribution has this book to make to a modern man, with no time to read, who has already been swamped in a *flood* of books? To answer this question, some relevant facts should first be reviewed.

If the average modern man is asked what he is living for, and what is the aim of his striving, he will probably tell you, with some embarrassment, that he lives "to enjoy life," "to support his family," "to have fun," "to make money," or "to achieve something meaningful and worthwhile." But in reality, we are all aware that no one seems to know exactly *what* he is living for. If he broods over the things surrounding him and the kind of world he is living in, he will soon become skeptical about the relevance of raising these questions. He cannot help but ask honestly, "Can we really know the right answers, do we have any choice over these matters, and after all, what difference will it make?"

In spite of the unavoidable resignation and bewilderment that the modern man feels, sooner or later he finds himself compelled to choose between two alternatives: he can either turn to religion with blind faith and hope, or turn to the world and "make the best of it." It is certain that men choose the former, not always because they are convinced of the truth of religion, but rather because doubt and despair have made their lives unbearable. On the other hand, they choose the latter, not because they have proved the untruth of religion, but because, in all likelihood, their spirits are deadened by pessimism and indifference. One fact, however, remains clear: in both cases the choice is made under the coercion of pain, sorrow, or despair.

It is common knowledge that an awareness of impending peril stirs men to act and to strive, that an awakening to man's limitations and helplessness in the face of the Universe, inspires him to pursue the "beyond" and the eternal. Thus both heaven and earth, Nirvāṇa and Saṃsāra, owe their births to human sufferings and despair. A thoughtful man must ask: "Is it really advantageous to lead a life without any suffering? Are not misfortune and grief prerequisites for spiritual awakening? From the ultimate viewpoint, are we, the sophisticated 'men-of-abundant-knowledge-and-possessions,' truly better off than the 'men-of-ignorance-and-scarcity' of olden times?" Let us think twice before we give an affirmative answer to these questions. Let us also ponder on some further ones: "Is it not true that science and technology, at their best, can alleviate but not eliminate the sufferings of men? Can plastic surgery, or the 'face-lift,' really make a miserable old woman happy? Does it really matter much whether or not we can defer our entrance into the grave for ten or fifteen years beyond schedule?" Many ingenious devices have been invented to conceal the unpleasant facts of life, and many gadgets have been created to gratify men's insatiable desires; but in the final analysis, what else have these contrivances brought us save their contributions to a fool's paradise for men to live in? Science, as some wise man has said, "makes major contributions to minor needs." Religion, whether or not it comes up with anything, at least is at work on the things that are truly important.

Deluded by material achievements and comforts, the majority of modern men are deprived of the opportunity and privileges of leading a rich spiritual life as their forefathers once did. In just reading a few stories of this great Tibetan classic, *The Hundred Thousand Songs of Milarepa*, we can readily find evidence that it was immeasurably easier for the "backward" Tibetans to contact the spiritual verities and to lead devotional lives than for their more "advanced" contemporaries. The reason for this is apparent: *They had much simpler minds and they led much simpler lives*. Being closer to the sheer *facts* of life uncloaked by camouflage and disguises, they had more opportunity to observe its sufferings and transiency; and in closer contact with Gurus and Saints they could draw more inspiration from them as

witnesses of the concrete results and rewards of a devotional life. But
the majority of modern men are deprived of these privileges, for they are
living in a civilization which a keen observer has wisely defined as
"one vast conspiracy against the spiritual life." And so the wave of
Karma keeps on rolling, and one is swept along by it regardless of his
unwillingness and dismay. No one is foolish enough to think that the
world will reverse itself and return to "the good old days"; what is
gone is gone. All one can do, perhaps, is to make use of the best that
the past has bequeathed us and apply it to the future and to the
"here and now." Any person, message, or action that may spark a
spiritual inspiration for men who must live in this age of spiritual un-
dernourishment should, therefore, be of great value to all concerned,
because they are what we need most, and what so rarely appear in
our time.

With this view in mind, Mr. Chang has spent many years in preparing the English translation of this great spiritual classic of Tibet,
the *Mila Grubum*, or *The Hundred Thousand Songs of Milarepa*, in
the hope of making it available to the people of the West.

What kind of a book is the *Mila Grubum?* An adequate answer to
this question is extremely difficult to make. Beyond doubt, it is one of
the greatest religious classics, ranking with the *Mahābhārata, the Ava-
taṃsaka Sūtra*, the Old and New Testaments, and the like. But at the
same time, it is far more — a different kind of book in its *own* right,
and no real parallel can be found in the literary field. Because of its
unique style, unusual setting, and comprehensive content, the *Mila
Grubum* is a book hard to introduce and to appraise in the ordinary
sense. Therefore, the best answer to the question, "What kind of a
book is this *Mila Grubum?*" should be given by the individual reader
himself through his own understanding and appreciation.

I can perhaps speak now for myself as to why, among the many
great religious classics, the *Mila Grubum* is a personal favorite. To
name just a few, I may say first of all that I found this book to be
an inexhaustible fountainhead of inspiration, an immense treasury of
spiritual teachings, a repository of yogic instructions, a guide on the
Bodhi-Path, and above all, an unfailing friend of the sincere devotee.
Secondly, it provides inside information on the religious life of the
Tibetan people — laymen, yogis, and monks alike — presenting a
vivid picture of their spiritual problems, strivings, and accomplishments.
In this book the profoundest ideas and teachings of Buddhism are revealed in sixty-one fascinating stories presented in simple language.
The reading, therefore, is extremely pleasant and interesting. Since
each story is an account of Milarepa's personal experience in a specific

situation, the messages and instructions given therein carry, inherently, an unusual persuasive power and charm which truly move one to greater conviction, wider consolation, and deeper insight. In addition, the *Grubum* contains clear descriptions and unequivocal evaluations of critical yogic experiences, including those of the most advanced stages, hitherto unrevealed in other scriptures.

If to evaluate the *Mila Grubum* is difficult, to praise it is even more so. Words, after all, may not be a good means of praise for a book of this kind. My sincere hope is that the readers may share with me, in silence and joy, a most rewarding experience in reading this beloved book of Tibet as millions of Tibetans once did, in the recent past and long ago.

PETER GRUBER

Oriental Studies Foundation
New York
September, 1962

A WORD FROM
THE TRANSLATOR

My Commentary, to be found in the Appendix under the title of "The 'Hundred Thousand Songs of Milarepa' — Its Origin, Background, Function, and Translation," was originally designed to serve as an Introduction to this book. But in order to encourage the general reader's direct contact with the text itself, I have transferred my comments to the Appendix — together with other material of particular interest to serious students and scholars. For them, it is strongly recommended that this Commentary be read first.

For readers who are not acquainted with the Tibetan literature, the actual sequence of the stories may not be the best way in which to read them. They follow each other in an interconnection which will be apparent enough to persons familiar with Tibetan literature; but the sequence may be more difficult to new readers. For them, I have starred certain representative stories in the Table of Contents, and recommend that they be read first. These will provide a cross-section of the three Parts into which the text is divided: Part One, stories concerned principally with Milarepa's subjugation and conversion of demons; Part Two, Milarepa's relationships with and instructions to his human disciples; and Part Three, miscellaneous stories that fall into no specific category.

The stories in this book cover a wide range of spiritual problems and their solutions in the light of Buddhist doctrine and of mystic and yogic experiences. For information on Milarepa's life and the central Teaching of Tibetan Tantrism, please see my Commentary in the Appendix.

Tibetan terms in the explanatory Notes are enclosed in parentheses and preceded by the letters "T.T.", denoting that these are Tibetan transcriptions as rendered in the English alphabet.

I wish to express my sincerest gratitude to the Bollingen Foundation for its generous grant, which has made possible the completion of this work; to Mrs. Dorothy C. Donath and Mr. Gerald Yorke for their most helpful editorial suggestions and assistance; to Miss Toni Schmid of the Statens Ethnografiska Museum, Stockholm, Sweden, for her kind permission to use an illustration from her beautiful book, The

Cotton-clad Mila, as our frontispiece; to Dr. W. Y. Evans-Wentz, Miss Natasha Rambova, Mr. Peter Gruber, and Miss Gwendolyn Winser, for their constant encouragement and aid; and to my wife, Hsiang-hsiang, for the typing of the entire manuscript and for her unfailing help and interest throughout the translation of this book.

GARMA C. C. CHANG

CONTENTS

VOLUME I

APPENDIX

INDEX 703

PART ONE
MILAREPA'S SUBJUGATION AND CONVERSION OF DEMONS

THE TALE OF RED ROCK
JEWEL VALLEY

Obeisance to all Gurus

ONCE the great Yogi Milarepa was staying at the Eagle Castle of [Red Rock] Jewel Valley,[1] absorbing himself in the practice of the Mahāmudrā meditation.[2] Feeling hungry, he decided to prepare some food, but after looking about he found there was nothing left in the cave, neither water nor fuel, let alone salt, oil, or flour. "It seems that I have neglected things too much!" he said, "I must go out and collect some wood."

He went out. But when he had gathered a handful of twigs, a sudden storm arose, and the wind was strong enough to blow away the wood and tear his ragged robe. When he tried to hold the robe together, the wood blew away. When he tried to clutch the wood, the robe blew apart. [Frustrated], Milarepa thought, "Although I have been practicing the Dharma[3] and living in solitude for such a long time, I am still not rid of ego-clinging! What is the use of practicing Dharma if one cannot subdue ego-clinging? Let the wind blow my wood away if it likes. Let the wind blow my robe off if it wishes!" Thinking thus, he ceased resisting. But, due to weakness from lack of food, with the next gust of wind he could no longer withstand the storm, and fell down in a faint.

When he came to, the storm was over. High up on the branch of a tree he saw a shred of his clothing swaying in the gentle breeze. The utter futility of this world and all its affairs struck Milarepa, and a strong feeling of renunciation overwhelmed him. Sitting down upon a rock, he meditated once more.

Soon, a cluster of white clouds rose from Dro Wo Valley[4] far away to the East. "Below this bank of clouds lies the temple of my Guru, the great Translator Marpa,"[5] mused Milarepa, "At this very

1

moment He and His wife must be preaching the doctrines of Tantra, giving initiation and instruction to my brothers. Yes, my Guru is there. If I could go there now, I should be able to see Him." An immeasurable, unbearable longing for his teacher arose in his heart as he thought despairingly of his Guru. His eyes filled with tears, and he began to sing a song, "Thoughts of My Guru":

In thoughts of you, Father Marpa, my
    suffering is relieved;
I, the mendicant, now sing you a fervent song.

Above Red Rock Jewel Valley, in the East,
Floats a cluster of white clouds;
Beneath them, like a rearing elephant, a
    huge mountain towers;
Beside it, like a lion leaping, looms another peak.

In the temple of Dro Wo Valley rests a great
    seat of stone;
Who is now enthroned there?
Is it Marpa the Translator?
If it were you, I would be joyful and happy.
Though limited in reverence, I wish to see you;
Though weak in faith, I wish to join you.
The more I meditate, the more I long for my Guru.

Does your wife, Dagmema, still dwell with you?
To her I am more grateful than to my mother.
If she is there I will be joyful and happy.
Though long the journey, I wish to see her,
Though perilous the road, I wish to join her.
The more I contemplate, the more I think of you;
The more I meditate, the more I think of my Guru.

How happy I would be could I join the gathering,
At which you may be preaching the Hevajra Tantra.[6]
Though of simple mind, I wish to learn.
Though ignorant, I long to recite.
The more I contemplate, the more I think of you;
The more I meditate, the more I think of my Guru.

You may now be giving the Four Symbolic
    Initiations[7] of the Oral Transmission;[8]

If I could join the gathering, I would be
    joyful and happy.
Though lacking merit, I wish to be initiated—
Though too poor to offer much, I desire it.
The more I contemplate, the more I think of you;
The more I meditate, the more I think of my Guru.

You may now be teaching the Six Yogas
    of Nāropa;[9]
If I could be there, I would be joyful and happy.
Though short my diligence, I have need for
    learning;
Though poor my perseverance, I wish to practice.
The more I contemplate, the more I think of you;
The more I meditate, the more I think of my Guru.

The brothers from Weu and Tsang may be there.
If so, I would be joyful and happy.
Though inferior my Experience and Realization,
I wish to compare mine with theirs.
Though in my deepest faith and veneration
I have never been apart from you,
I am now tortured by my need to see you.
This fervent longing agonizes me,
This great torment suffocates me.
Pray, my gracious Guru, relieve me from this
    torment.

No sooner had Milarepa finished than the Revered One, the Jet-sun[10] Marpa, appeared on a cluster of rainbow clouds resembling a robe of five colors. With an ever-increasing [celestial] radiance suffusing his countenance, and riding a lion with rich trappings, he approached Milarepa.

"Great Sorcerer,[11] my son, why with such deep emotion," he asked, "did you call to me so desperately? Why do you struggle so? Have you not an abiding faith in your Guru and Patron Buddha? Does the outer world attract you with disturbing thoughts?[12] Do the Eight Worldly Winds[13] howl in your cave? Do fear and longing sap your strength? Have you not continuously offered service to the Guru and to the Three Precious Ones[14] above? Have you not dedicated your merits to sentient beings[15] in the Six Realms?[16] Have not you yourself reached that state of grace in which you can purify your sins and achieve merits? No matter what the cause, you may be certain that

we will never part. Thus, for the sake of the Dharma and the welfare of sentient beings, continue your meditation."

Inspired by this sublimely joyous vision, Milarepa sang in reply:

When I see my Guru's countenance and hear his words,
I, the mendicant, am stirred by the Prāṇa in
      my heart.[17]
In remembrance of the teachings of my Guru,
Respect and reverence arise in my heart.
His compassionate blessings enter me;
All destructive thoughts[18] are banished.

My earnest song, called "Thoughts of my Guru,"
Must surely have been heard by you, my teacher;
Yet am I still in darkness.
Pray, pity me and grant me your protection!

Indomitable perseverance
Is the highest offering to my Guru.
The best way to please Him
Is to endure the hardship of meditation!
Abiding in this cave, alone,
Is the noblest service to the Ḍākinīs![19]
To devote myself to the Holy Dharma
Is the best service to Buddhism—
To devote my life to meditation, thus
To aid my helpless, sentient fellow beings!
To love death and sickness is a blessing
Through which to cleanse one's sins;
To refuse forbidden food helps one to attain
Realization and Enlightenment;
To repay my Father Guru's bounties
I meditate, and meditate again.

Guru mine, pray grant me your protection!
Help this mendicant to stay ever in his hermitage.

Exalted, Milarepa adjusted his robe and carried a handful of wood
back to his cave. Inside, he was startled to find five Indian demons
with eyes as large as saucers. One was sitting on his bed and preaching, two were listening to the sermon, another was preparing and
offering food, and the last was studying Milarepa's books.

Following his initial shock, Milarepa thought, "These must be magical apparitions of the local deities who dislike me. Although I have been living here a long time, I have never given them any offering or compliment." He then began to sing a "Complimentary Song to the Deities of Red Rock Jewel Valley":

> This lonely spot where stands my hut
> Is a place pleasing to the Buddhas,
> A place where accomplished beings dwell,
> A refuge where I dwell alone.
>
> Above Red Rock Jewel Valley
> White clouds are gliding;
> Below, the Tsang River gently flows;
> Wild vultures wheel between.
>
> Bees are humming among the flowers,
> Intoxicated by their fragrance;
> In the trees birds swoop and dart,
> Filling the air with their song.
>
> In Red Rock Jewel Valley
> Young sparrows learn to fly,
> Monkeys love to leap and swing,
> And beasts to run and race,
> While I practice the Two Bodhi-Minds[20]
>   and love to meditate.
>
> Ye local demons,[21] ghosts,[22] and gods,
> All friends of Milarepa,
> Drink the nectar of kindness and compassion,
> Then return to your abodes.

But the Indian demons did not vanish, and stared balefully at Milarepa. Two of them advanced, one grimacing and biting his lower lip, and the other grinding his teeth horribly. A third, coming up behind, gave a violent, malicious laugh and shouted loudly, as they all tried to frighten Milarepa with fearful grimaces and gestures.

Milarepa, knowing their evil motives, began the Wrathful Buddha Meditation and recited forcefully a powerful incantation.[23] Still the demons would not leave. Then, with great compassion, he preached the Dharma to them; yet they still remained.

Milarepa finally declared, "Through the mercy of Marpa, *I have already fully realized that all beings and all phenomena are of one's own mind. The mind itself is a transparency of Voidness.*[24] *What, therefore, is the use of all this, and how foolish I am to try to dispel these manifestations physically!"*[25]

Then Milarepa, in a dauntless mood, sang "The Song of Realization":

> Father Guru, who conquered the Four Demons,[26]
> I bow to you, Marpa the Translator.
>
> I, whom you see, the man with a name,
> Son of Darsen Gharmo,[27]
> Was nurtured in my mother's womb,
> Completing the Three Veins.[28]
> A baby, I slept in my cradle;
> A youth, I watched the door;
> A man, I lived on the high mountain.
>
> Though the storm on the snow peak is awesome,
> I have no fear.
> Though the precipice is steep and perilous,
> I am not afraid!
>
> I, whom you see, the man with a name,
> Am a son of the Golden Eagle;[29]
> I grew wings and feathers in the egg.
> A child, I slept in my cradle;
> A youth, I watched the door;
> A man, I flew in the sky.
> Though the sky is high and wide, I do not fear;
> Though the way is steep and narrow, I am not afraid.
>
> I, whom you see, the man with a name,
> Am a son of Nya Chen Yor Mo,[30] the King of fishes.
> In my mother's womb, I rolled my golden eyes;
> A child, I slept in my cradle;
> A youth, I learned to swim;
> A man, I swam in the great ocean.
> Though thundering waves are frightening,
>   I do not fear;
> Though fishing hooks abound, I am not afraid.
>
> I, whom you see, the man with a name,
> Am a son of Ghagyu Lamas.
> Faith grew in my mother's womb.
> A baby, I entered the door of Dharma;

A youth, I studied Buddha's teaching;
A man, I lived alone in caves.
Though demons, ghosts, and devils multiply,
    I am not afraid.

The snow-lion's paws are never frozen,
Or of what use would it be
To call the lion "King"—
He who has the Three Perfect Powers.[31]

The eagle never falls down from the sky;
If so, would that not be absurd?
An iron block cannot be cracked by a stone;
If so, why refine the iron ore?
I, Milarepa, fear neither demons nor evils;
If they frightened Milarepa, to what avail
Would be his Realization and Enlightenment?

Ye ghosts and demons, enemies of the Dharma,
    I welcome you today!
It is my pleasure to receive you!
I pray you, stay; do not hasten to leave;
We will discourse and play together.
Although you would be gone, stay the night;
We will pit the Black against the White Dharma,[32]
And see who plays the best.

Before you came, you vowed to afflict me.
Shame and disgrace would follow
If you returned with this vow unfulfilled.

Milarepa arose with confidence and rushed straight at the demons in his cave. Frightened, they shrank back, rolling their eyes in despair and trembling violently. Then, swirling together like a whirlpool, they all merged into one and vanished.

"This was the Demon King, Vināyaka[33] the Obstacle-Maker, who came searching for evil opportunities," thought Milarepa. "The storm, too, was undoubtedly his creation. By the mercy of my Guru he had no chance to harm me."

After this, Milarepa gained immeasurable spiritual progress.

This story relates the attack of the Demon King Vināyaka; it has three different meanings, and hence may be called either "The Six Ways of Thinking of My Guru," "The Tale of Red Rock Jewel Valley," or "The Story of Milarepa Collecting Wood."

NOTES

1 The Eagle Castle of Red Rock Jewel Valley (T.T.: mChoṅ.Luṅ. Khyuṅ. Gi.rDsoṅ.). Although "mChoṅ" usually means to leap or jump, here it seems better to translate it as "Gem," or "Jewel" — the other meaning of the word.

2 Mahāmudrā (T.T.: Phyag.rGya.Chen.Po.), meaning the "Great Symbol," is the practical teaching of Śūnyatā (Voidness). Śūnyatā is the principle that stresses the non-existence of the "substance" of all beings, which is the most important doctrine of Mahāyāna Buddhism as well as of Tibetan Tantrism. According to some Tibetan scholars, the Mādhyamika (Middle Way Doctrine), is a teaching of Śūnyatā in its general form, while Mahāmudrā is a teaching of Śūnyatā by which one can actually put the Mādhyamika principles into practice. Mādhyamika is often referred to as the "Theory of Voidness," and Mahāmudrā, "The Practice of Voidness."

At this point a few words on "Voidness" may be helpful. When we say "That house is empty," we mean that it contains no occupants; but Buddhist "Voidness" *does not mean absence*. When we say, "That whole block is now empty," we mean there were houses in the block before, but none exist now; but Buddhist "Voidness" *does not mean extinction*. Voidness is difficult to define and describe. We can say a great deal about what Voidness is *not*, but very little about what it *is*. Voidness denotes the relative, flowing, undefinable, and ungraspable nature of all things. Philosophically it represents the illusory and dream-like nature of phenomena; psychologically it signifies a total liberation from all bondage.

The Whispered Transmission School (Ghagyuba, T.T.: bKah.rGyud.Pa.) and the Old School (Ningmaba, T.T.: rÑiṅ.Ma.Pa.) in Tibet, regard Mahāmudrā as the highest and most important of all the teachings of Buddhism. But the Yellow School (Gelugba, T.T.: dGe.Lugs.Pa.) does not entirely agree with this view.

Mahāmudrā is, in many ways, very similar to Chinese Ch'an (Zen.) See the translator's "Yogic Commentary" in "Tibetan Yoga and Secret Doctrines," 2nd ed., W. Y. Evans-Wentz, Ed., Oxford University Press, London, 1958.

3 Dharma: This term, most frequently employed in Buddhist literature, has two common usages: to denote the teaching of Buddha, sometimes translated as the Law or Doctrine; and to denote being or objects. Here it is used in the former sense.

4 Dro Wo Valley: the location of Marpa's temple.

5 Marpa the Translator was Milarepa's teacher. He was a great scholar as well as a great yogi, who founded the Oral, or Whispered Transmission School (Ghagyuba) of Tibet.

6 Hevajra: a Sanskrit name; its Tibetan equivalent is dGyes.Pa.rDor.rJe. To help readers who are not familiar with the Tibetan words, many equivalent Sanskrit names and terms are also used in the translation and Notes.

7 The Four Symbolic Initiations (T.T.: dWaṅ.bShi.): The first initiation is called "The Initiation of the Vase." The person who has taken it is allowed to practice Mantra Yoga. The second is called "The Secret Initiation," and gives the initiate the privilege of practicing Prāṇa Yoga. The third is called "The Wisdom Initiation," and allows the initiate to practice advanced Prāṇa Yoga. The fourth is called "The Symbolic Initiation," and confers the privilege of practicing Mahāmudrā Yoga. These four initiations embrace almost all the major teachings of Tibetan Tantrism.

8 The Oral Transmission (T.T.: bKah.rGyud.Pa.), is translated in this book

in several different ways: Whispered, or Oral Succession, Transmission, or Lineage. This School (the Ghagyuba) in its early period, stressed the Yoga practice and tradition — including secrecy by transmitting the teachings orally. Later, when it grew into a large monastic Order, this tradition was partially lost.

9 Naro Chu Dru (T.T.: Naro.Chos.Drug.): The Six Yogas of Nāropa are as follows: (1) Heat Yoga, (2) Dream Yoga, (3) Illusory Body Yoga, (4) Bardo Yoga, (5) Yoga of Transformation, and (6) Yoga of Light.

10 Jetsun (T.T.: rJe.bTsun.): A Tibetan term of reverence and respect given to religious leaders, saints, and great teachers.

11 Great Sorcerer: Milarepa's nickname. See Milarepa's Biography. "Tibet's Great Yogi, Milarepa," W. Y. Evans-Wentz, Ed., Oxford University Press, London, 1951.

12 Disturbing thoughts, Nhamdog (T.T.: rNam.rTog.) is a very frequently used term in Buddhist literature as well as in this book. Nhamdog has many meanings, the most common one being "disturbing thoughts" or "flowing thoughts." This constant flow of thoughts never stops, though men may not be aware of its existence. To curb and halt this unceasing thought-flow is a prerequisite for the attainment of Samādhi. Nhamdog also means wild thoughts, wrong judgements, fantasy, whims, imagination, impulse, and so forth.

13 Eight Worldly Winds or Dharmas (T.T.: Chos.brGyad.): the eight "winds," or influences, which fan the passions, i.e., gain, loss; defamation, eulogy; praise, ridicule; sorrow, joy. This term is also translated in this book as "Eight Worldly Desires."

14 The Three Precious Ones, or the Three Gems: the Buddha; the Dharma; and the Saṅgha. Buddha is He who has attained Perfect Enlightenment, Dharma is His teachings, Saṅgha the enlightened Buddhist sages.

15 Sentient beings: a term for mankind and all living beings, for whose benefit Dharmic training is undertaken and to whom all merits are dedicated.

16 Six Realms, or Six Lokas: the six Realms in Saṃsāra, i.e., the Realms of Hell, of Hungry Ghosts, of Animals, of Asuras or Non-men, of Mankind, and of the Heavenly Beings.

17 Heart-Prāṇa or Heart-Wind (T.T.: sÑiñ.Rluñ.; pron.: Nin Lung): It is believed that most visions seen and emotions felt in meditation are caused by Prāṇa from the Heart Center.

18 Destructive thoughts: non-Dharmic thoughts, or thoughts which are against the Buddhist teachings.

19 Dākinīs (T.T.: mKhah.hGro.Ma.): female sky-travelers, or goddesses. Dākinīs are female deities who play very important roles in performing various Tantric acts.

20 The Two Bodhi-Minds (T.T.: Byañ.Chub.Sems.gÑis.): These are the Mundane and the Transcendental Bodhi-Minds (T.T.: Kun.rDsob. [and] Don.Dam. Byañ.Chub.Gyi.Sems.); or the Bodhi-Mind-as-a-Wish (sMon.Pa.Byañ.Chub.Gyi. Sems.) and the Bodhi-Mind-as-a-Practice (sPyod.Pa.Byañ.Chub.Gyi.Sems.). Bodhi-Mind is perhaps the most important term which symbolizes and represents the central spirit, idea, and principle of Mahāyāna Buddhism. Because of its manifold meanings and usages, Bodhi-Mind (Skt: Bodhicitta; T.T.: Byañ.Chub.Sems.) is extremely difficult to translate. Bodhi-Mind can perhaps be roughly described as the wish, vow, aspiration, and realization of the noble idea of bringing oneself and all sentient beings to the state of great perfection — Buddhahood. The following are a few examples of the variance of this term in denoting the different aspects of the Bodhi-Mind:

(1) Bodhi-Mind-as-a-Wish: the wish, vow, or aspiration to deliver all

sentient beings from all suffering, and to bring them to the state of Buddhahood.

(2) Bodhi-Mind-as-Practice: the aspiration, determination, and practice of all meritorious deeds in the light of Dharma, which include the Six Pāramitās, and other Bodhisattvic practices.

(3) Mundane Bodhi-Mind: the Bodhi-Mind of a person who has not yet realized the truth of Sūnyatā (Voidness).

(4) Transcendental Bodhi-Mind: the Bodhi-Mind of a person who has realized the truth of Sūnyatā (Voidness).

(5) Bodhi-Mind, as "borrowed" by Tantrism, is used to denote the essence of the positive and negative energy, i.e., seed or semen (T.T.: Tig.Le.)

Bodhi-Mind is sometimes translated in different contexts as Bodhi-Heart, Heart-for-Bodhi, Enlightened Mind, and the Great Compassionate Mind.

21 Lit.: Jung Bo (T.T.: hByuń.Po.): a type of Tibetan demon.

22 Lit.: Non-men (T.T.: Mi.Ma.Yin.): the general term for demons, ghosts, Asuras, or heavenly beings.

23 Powerful incantation (T.T.: Drag.sÑags.): a potent Mantra or spell to dispel demons and obstacles. It includes mantras, mudrās, visualization, and other ritualistic practices.

24 According to Mahāmudrā, the nature of mind can best be described as being the Illumination-of-Voidness, or the Illuminating-Void (T.T.: gSal.sToń.). It teaches that the primordial nature of mind is not only "void" in its essence, but is also an illuminating self-awareness embodied in the Void.

25 Lit.: " . . . how foolish I am to try to dispel these demons and trouble-makers outwardly."

26 Four Demons: the four major hindrances that impede one's spiritual progress are figuratively called "The Four Demons." They are: the demons of illness, of interruption, of death, and of desires and passions.

27 Darsen Gharmo: the name of the snow lioness. See first song of Story 4.

28 Lit.: Completing the Three Nādīs. These are the three mystic Channels in the human body — the Right, the Left, and the Center. The Right Channel (T.T.: Ro.Ma.rTsa.; Skt.: Pingalā Nādī), is said to correspond to the solar system; the Left (T.T.: rKyań.Ma.rTsa.; Skt.: Idā Nādī) to the lunar system; the Center Channel (T.T.: dBu.Ma.rTsa.; Skt.: Suṣumṇā Nādī) to Unity. Tibetan scholars have given many differing opinions and explanations regarding these three mystical Channels. A single clear-cut definition or description of them is very difficult.

29 Lit.: The King-bird Eagle (T.T.: Bya.rGyal.Khyań.) or the Gāruda bird.

30 Nya Chen Yor Mo (T.T.: Ña.Chen.Yor.Mo.): the King of all fish, according to Tibetan legend.

31 The translator is not certain as to what these three legendary "perfect powers of the lion" found in Tibetan folklore may be. However, they do imply three superior qualities of this animal.

32 The Black Dharma is black magic; the white Dharma, the teaching of Buddha.

33 Vināyaka (T.T.: Bi.Na.Ya.Ga.): A particular class of demon. According to some sources, it is another name for "Gaṇêśa" or for "Gāruḍa."

2

THE JOURNEY TO LASHI

Obeisance to all Gurus

O NCE, when the great Master of Yoga, Jetsun[1] Milarepa, was staying in the Jewel Valley hermitage, he thought, "I should obey my Guru's order to go to Lashi Snow Mountain and practice meditation there," and set out for that place.

Milarepa approached Nya Non Tsar Ma, the gateway to Lashi Snow Mountain, where the people of Tsar Ma were holding a drinking party. In their talk, someone asked, "Do you know that at the present time there lives a great yogi called Milarepa? He always dwells alone in the snow mountains, in remote and uninhabited places, observing an ascetic discipline which none except the perfect Buddhist can attain. Have you ever heard of him?" While they were thus praising the Jetsun, Milarepa arrived at the door. A beautiful girl named Lesebum, decked with rich ornaments, greeted him there, asking, "Who are you and where do you come from?" "Dear hostess," Milarepa replied, "I am the Yogi Milarepa, who always dwells in unknown places in the mountains. I came here to beg food." "I will gladly give you some," said the girl, "but are you really Milarepa?" He replied, "There is no reason why I should lie to you." The girl, delighted, immediately rushed back into the house to spread the news. She called all the revelers, saying, "You were talking about that celebrated yogi who lives so far away. He is now standing at the door."

Everyone rushed to the door, some making obeisance to the Jetsun, others asking him various questions. All became aware that he was the actual Milarepa. Then they invited him in, paid him great respect and reverence, and gave him food.

The hostess, a rich young girl named Shindormo, extended her hospitality to the Jetsun, and asked, "Revered one, may I ask where you are going?" Milarepa replied, "I am on my way to Lashi Snow Mountain to practice meditation." The girl then said, "We hope you will grant us the boon of staying in Dreloon Joomoo and blessing this

11

place. We will provide all the food you need without any effort on your part."

Among the guests was a teacher called Shaja Guna, who said to Milarepa, "If you would be kind enough to remain here in Dreloon Joomoo, the valley of ghosts, it would help you and would also help us. I shall try my best to serve you." A layman exclaimed, "How wonderful it would be if we could have the great Yogi staying with us! I have a fine cattle farm, but the demons and ghosts are becoming so bold that they actually appear [even in the daytime]! They are so vicious that even I do not dare to go near the place any more. I beseech you, in your kindness and grace, to vist my farm very soon." All the guests then made obeisance to the Jetsun, begging him to go to the farm.

Milarepa replied, "I will go there at once—not because of your farm and cattle, but in obedience to my Guru."

"We are satisfied as long as you have promised to go," they declared. "Now, let us prepare the best food and arrange for your departure."

Milarepa then said, "I am accustomed to solitude . . . I dwell in a hermitage and need neither companionship nor good food. But please accept my gratitude for your thoughtfulness in offering it. First, I should like to go to the farm alone. Afterwards, you may come and see what has been done."

When Milarepa arrived at the foot of the mountain, the Non-men created frightful hallucinations to harass him. The path to the top of the peak, which seemed to reach to the sky, quaked and tossed. Angry thunder rolled, jagged lightning struck all around, and the mountains on both sides trembled and shifted. The river suddenly became a raging torrent and burst its banks, turning the valley into a vast lake, in later years called Demon Lake. Milarepa arose and made a gesture, and the flood at once subsided. He went on to the lower part of the valley. The demons shattered the mountains on both sides, and showers of tumbling rocks fell like heavy rain. Then the Hill Goddess created for the Jetsun a path like a running snake along the range, a track later called Hill Goddess Path [or Ḍākinī's Ridge]. This subdued all the lesser demons, but the greater and more powerful demons, angered by their failure, gathered round the end of Hill Goddess Path to unleash a new attack. Milarepa concentrated his mind, and made another mystic gesture to subdue them. Suddenly all the evil visions disappeared. A footprint was impressed in the rock where Milarepa had stood.[2] He had gone only a few steps when the whole sky cleared. In an exalted mood, he then sat down at the top of the hill; he entered the Samādhi of Mercy,[3] and an immeasurable compassion toward all sentient beings arose in his heart. Because of this, Milarepa

experienced great spiritual growth and inspiration. Later, the place
where he sat was called the Hill of Mercy.

Milarepa then went to the bank of the river [lit.: Good River],
where he practiced the Flowing-River Yoga [Samādhi].[4]

On the tenth day of the autumn moon of the Fire Tiger Year, a
demon from Nepal called Bha Ro, leading a vast demonic army
which filled the earth and sky in the valley of Good River, came to chal-
lenge Milarepa. The demons shifted the mountains and threw them
down upon the Jetsun, and attacked him with thunderbolts and a rain
of weapons. They screamed at him, abusing him with threats: "We'll
kill you! We'll tie you up and chop you into pieces!" and on and on.
They also appeared in hideous and dreadful shapes to frighten him.

Sensing the evil purpose of the demon army, Milarepa sang "The
Truth of Karma":

> I take refuge in all gracious Gurus,
> And pay homage to them.
>
> Through mirages and illusions,
> You pernicious male and female devils
> Can create these fantastic terrors.
>
> You pitiable Ah Tsa Ma demons,[5] hungry ghosts,
> You can never harm me.
>
> Because your sinful Karma in the past
> Has fully ripened,[6] you have received
> Demonic bodies for this life.
> With minds and bodies so deformed,
> You wander in the sky forever.
>
> Driven by the fiery Kleśas,[7]
> Your minds are filled with hostile and
>   vicious thoughts.
> Your deeds and words are malignant and destructive.
> You screamed, "Kill him! Chop him! Beat him!
>   Cut him up!"
>
> I am a yogi who is devoid of thoughts,[8]
> Knowing that there is no such thing as mind.
>
> Walking valiant as a lion,
> Actions fearless as the brave,

My body merges with the body of Buddha,
My words are like the true words of the Tathāgata,
My mind is absorbed in the Realm of Great Light.[9]
I see clearly the void nature of the Six
    Groups.[10]
A yogi, such as I, ignores the abuse of
    hungry ghosts!

If the Law of Cause and Effect is valid,
And one commits the deeds deserving of it,
The force of Ripened Karma[11] will drive him down
Into the miserable Path
Of suffering and grief.

It is distressing and woeful that you
    ghosts and demons
Should not understand the Truth![12]
I, the plain-looking Milarepa,
Now preach to you the song of Dharma.

All sentient beings who live by nourishment
Are my fathers and my mothers!
To afflict those to whom we owe gratitude
Is indeed senseless and foolish!

Would it not be a happy and a joyous act
If you were to renounce your vicious thoughts?
Would it not be a blessed and joyful thing
If you were to practice the Ten Virtues?[13]
Remember this and ponder its meaning,
Exert yourselves and carefully consider it.

The demons then scoffed at Milarepa: "Your rambling talk will
not deceive us. We refuse to cease our magic and set you free." They
then multiplied their supernatural weapons and increased the force of
their demonic army to afflict him. Milarepa pondered awhile and then
said, "Hearken to me, you army of demons! By the grace of my Guru
I have become a yogi who has fully realized the Ultimate Truth. To
me, the afflictions and obstructions caused by demons are the glories
of a yogi's mind. The greater such affliction, the more I gain in the
Path of Bodhi.[14] Now listen to my song of 'The Seven Adornments'":

I pay homage to Marpa the Translator,

I, who see the ultimate essence of being,
Sing the song of [Seven] Adornments.

You mischievous demons here assembled,
Lend your ears and listen closely to my song.

By the side of Sumeru,[15] the central mountain,
The sky shines blue o'er the Southern Continent;[16]
The firmament is the beauty of the earth,
The blue of heaven its adornment.

High above the Great Tree of Sumeru[17]
Shine radiant beams from sun and moon,
Lighting the Four Continents.
With love and compassion, the Nāga King[18]
      wields his miraculous power:
From the immense sky, he lets fall the rain.
Of the earth, this is the adornment.

From the great ocean vapors rise,
Reaching the vast sky.
They form great clouds;
A causal law governs the transformations
      of the elements.

In midsummer, rainbows appear above the plain,
Gently resting upon the hills.
Of the plains and mountains,
The rainbow is the beauty and adornment.

In the West, when rain falls in the cold ocean,
Bushes and trees flourish on the earth.
To all creatures on the Continent,
These are the beauty and adornment.

I, the Yogi who desires to remain in solitude,
Meditate on the Voidness of Mind.
Awed by the power of my concentration,
You jealous demons are forced to practice magic.
Of the yogi, demonic conjurations
Are the beauty and adornment.

You Non-men, listen closely and hearken to me!

Do you know who I am?
I am the Yogi Milarepa;
From my heart emerges
The flower of Mind—Enlightenment.
With a clear voice[19] I sing this allegory to you,
With sincere words I preach the Dharma for you,
With a gracious heart I give you this advice.
If in your hearts the Will-for-Bodhi[20] sprouts,
Though you may not be of help to others,
By renouncing the Ten Evils,[21]
Know that you will win joy and liberation.
If you follow my teachings,
Your accomplishments will increase greatly;
If you practice the Dharma now,
Everlasting joy will at last enfold you.

Most of the demons were converted by the song, becoming faithful
and respectful to Milarepa, and the evil conjurations ceased. They
said, "You are indeed a great yogi of marvelous powers. Without your
explanation of the Truth, and the revelation of your miraculous powers, we would never have understood. Henceforth, we will not trouble
you. We are also most grateful for your preaching of the truth of Karma.
In all frankness, we are of limited intelligence and limitless ignorance.
Our minds are steeped in a morass of stubborn habitual thoughts.[22]
Pray, therefore, teach us a lesson profound in meaning, great in profit,
and simple in comprehension and observation."

Milarepa then sang "The Song of the Seven Truths":

I make obeisance to you, Marpa the Translator.
I pray that you grant me increase of Bodhi-Mind.

However beautiful a song's words may be,
It is but a tune to those
Who grasp not the words of Truth.

If a parable agrees not with Buddha's teaching,
However eloquent it may sound,
'Tis but a booming echo.

If one does not practice Dharma,
However learned in the Doctrines one may claim to be,
One is only self-deceived.

Living in solitude is self-imprisonment,
If one practice not the instruction of the
    Oral Transmission.
Labor on the farm is but self-punishment,
If one neglects the teaching of the Buddha.

For those who do not guard their morals,
Prayers are but wishful thinking.
For those who do not practice what they preach,
Oratory is but faithless lying.

Wrong-doing shunned, sins of themselves diminish;
Good deeds done, merit will be gained.
Remain in solitude, and meditate alone;
Much talking is of no avail.
Follow what I sing, and practice Dharma!

Faith in Milarepa was further aroused in his listeners, and they paid him great respect. They made obeisances and circumambulated[23] him many times. Most of them then returned to their homes. But the leader of the demons, Bha Ro, and some of his followers still would not depart. Once again they conjured dreadful visions to frighten Milarepa, but he countered them with the song in which the truth of good and evil is told:

I bow at the feet of gracious Marpa.

Are you pernicious demons still in an angry mood?
Your bodies through the sky can fly with ease,
But your minds are filled with sinful habitual thoughts.
You bare your deadly fangs to frighten others,
But you may be sure, when you afflict them,
You are only bringing trouble on yourselves.

The Law of Karma never fails to function;
No one escapes from its ripening.[24]
You are only bringing trouble on yourselves,
You hungry ghosts, confused and sinful!
I feel only sorrow and pity for you.

Since you are ever sinning,
To be vicious is natural to you.
Since the Karma of killing binds you,

You relish meat and blood for food.
By taking the lives of others,
You are born as hungry ghosts.

Your sinful deeds led you
To the depths of the lower Path.
Turn back, my friends, from this ensnaring Karma,
And try to attain true happiness which is
Beyond all hope and fear!

The demons scoffed: "Your skillful impersonation of a preacher who
knows the Doctrine thoroughly is most impressive, but what conviction have you gained from the practice of Dharma?"

Milarepa replied with "The Song of Perfect Assurance":

Obeisance to the perfect Marpa.

I am the Yogi who perceives the Ultimate Truth.
In the Origin of the Unborn, I first gain assurance;
On the Path of Non-extinction, slowly
    I perfect my power;
With meaningful symbols and words
Flowing from my great compassion,
I now sing this song
From the absolute realm of Dharma Essence.

Because your sinful Karma has created
Dense blindness and impenetrable obstruction,
You cannot understand the meaning
Of Ultimate Truth.
Listen, therefore, to the Expedient Truth.[25]

In their spotless, ancient Sūtras,
All the Buddhas in the past, repeatedly
Admonished with the eternal Truth of Karma—
That every sentient being is one's kinsman.
This is eternal Truth which never fails.
Listen closely to the teaching of Compassion.

I, the Yogi who developed by his practices,
Know that outer hindrances are but a shadow-show,
And the phantasmal world
A magic play of mind unborn.

By looking inward into the mind is seen
Mind-nature—without substance, intrinsically void.
Through meditation in solitude, the grace
Of the Succession Gurus and the teaching
Of the great Nāropa[26] are attained.
The inner truth of the Buddha
Should be the object of meditation.

By the gracious instruction of my Guru,
Is the abstruse inner meaning of Tantra understood.
Through the practice of Arising and
    Perfecting Yoga,[27]
Is the Vital Power engendered
And the inner reason for the microcosm realized.
Thus in the outer world I do not fear
The illusory obstacles.

To the Great Divine Lineage I belong,
With innumerable yogis great as all Space.

When in one's own mind one ponders
On the original state of Mind,
Illusory thoughts of themselves dissolve
Into the Realm of Dharmadhātu.[28]
Neither afflicter nor afflicted can be seen.
Exhaustive study of the Sūtras
Teaches us no more than this.

The chief and subordinate demons then offered their skulls[29] to Milarepa, made obeisance, and circumambulated him many times. They promised to bring him a month's supply of food, and vanished like a rainbow in the sky.

The next morning at sunrise the demon Bha Ro brought from Mon many richly clad female ghosts and a numerous retinue. They carried jeweled cups filled with wine, and brass plates heaped with many different foods, including rice and meat, which they offered to the Jetsun. Promising henceforward to serve and obey him, they bowed to him many times and disappeared. One of the demons, called Jarbo Ton Drem, was the leader of many Devas.

Through this experience, Milarepa gained great yogic improvement. He remained there for a month, spirited and joyous, and without the pangs of hunger.

One day, [when the month had passed,] Milarepa recalled a place in Lashi renowned for its good water, and decided to go there. On the way, he came to a plain dotted with flourishing tamarisks. In the middle of the plain rose a large rock with a projecting ledge above it. Milarepa sat upon the rock for a time; many goddesses appeared, bowed to him, and served him with desirable offerings. One of the goddesses also left two footprints on the rock, and then disappeared like a rainbow.

As Milarepa proceeded on his way, a host of demons assembled and conjured visions of huge female organs on the road to shock him. Then the Jetsun concentrated his mind and exposed his erected male organ with a gesture. He went farther, and passing an apparition of nine female organs, reached a place with a rock shaped like a vagina standing in its center—the quintessence of the region. He inserted a phallic-shaped stone into the hollow of the rock, [a symbolic act][30] which dispersed the lascivious images created by the demons. The place was later called Làdgu Lungu.

When Milarepa reached the middle of the plain, the demon Bha Ro returned to welcome him. He prepared a preaching seat for the Jetsun, gave offerings and service, and asked him for the Buddhist teachings. Milarepa lectured him comprehensively on Karma, and the demon then melted into a huge rock in front of the seat.

Milarepa, in a very joyous state, remained on the central plain for a month, and then journeyed to Nya Non Tsar Ma. He told the people there that the plain had indeed been infamous until he had conquered its demons and transformed it to a place suitable for the practice of Dharma. He also told them he wanted to return there to mediate as soon as possible. After this, the people of Nya Non had deep faith in Milarepa.

This is the story of "The Journey to Lashi."

NOTES

1 Meaning the "Revered One." See Story 1, Note 10.

2 Tibetans believe that spiritually enlightened beings should be able to perform out-of-the-ordinary, or miraculous, deeds. To leave a footprint or handprint in hard material, such as rock, was considered a proof of a yogi's occult powers, and accomplishments. Much evidence of this belief can be found in Tibet.

3 Samādhi of Mercy: According to Buddhism, Samādhi is merely a mental state of deep concentration. It can be applied or utilized for any religious purpose. How-

ever, the power of Samādhi enables the yogi to accomplish almost all the spiritual wishes he may have. Here Samādhi is applied to the expansion and perfection of love or mercy. In other words, the Samādhi of Mercy is a deep and pure conscious state in which the purest love is brought to consummation.

4 Flowing-River Yoga [Samādhi] (T.T.: Chu.Wo.rGyun.Gyi.rNal.hByor): In this Samādhi the yogi experiences his identity with the flow of the Universe, yet he transcends it. He never withdraws from the flow, nor does he intend to ignore it; he is in it, but not bound by it. This Samādhi is the active or dynamic aspect of Mahāmudrā Yoga.

5 Ah Tsa Ma Demons (T.T.: A.Tsa.Ma.): a Tibetan name for Indian demons.

6 Ripened Karma (T.T.: rNam.sMin.Gyi.Las.; Skt.: Vipāka Karma) may be translated as "fully ripened Karma," or "the Karmic force that ripens in different lives." The Law of Karma says that usually a deed brings not merely one, but many, effects. For example, if a man commits murder, he will be punished by his conscience, by the law, by the ruin of his reputation and life, and so on. But this is not all. The force of Karma has not yet been exhausted. In a future incarnation, or incarnations, the murderer will be subjected by this mysterious Karmic force to shorter lives and much sickness; or he will be prone to rebirths in times and lands where there are frequent wars and perils. This force, the Karma that ripens in different lives, seems to be the most fundamental and mysterious aspect of the Buddhist doctrine.

7 Fiery Kleśas: These are the strong desires and passions that cause all the pains and distresses of Saṃsāric life.

8 Devoid of thoughts: An accomplished yogi should have freed himself from *all* thoughts or conceptualizations, be they simple or complex, good or evil, monistic or dualistic . . . , then he is said to have acquired the Wisdom of Equality or Non-discrimination.

9 The Realm of Great Light is the realm of primordial Buddhahood. The term "Light" should not be treated in its literal sense as denoting luminosity. It is actually beyond description and attribution. Free and universal clarity, devoid of the slightest clinging or attachment, perhaps can best be described in words as "Great Light."

10 Six Groups (T.T.: Tsogs.Drug.): the Six Consciousnesses and the Six Sense Objects. The Six Consciousnesses are: consciousness of eye, ear, nose, tongue, body, and discernment (mind). The Six Sense Objects are: color or form, sound, smell, taste, touch, and dharma (being).

11 See Note 6.

12 This sentence could also be translated " . . . should not understand the Immanent Truth."

13 The Ten Virtues: These are the antitheses of the Ten Evils. See Note 21.

14 Path of Bodhi: the Path that leads to Buddhahood. This is the practice of the Bodhisattva, as taught in Mahāyāna Buddhism.

15 Sumeru: The legendary center of the Universe, an idea borrowed by the Buddhists from the Hindus, and believed by some modern scholars to represent a place in the Himālaya Mountains.

16 Southern Continent: In Buddhist legends, the earth on which we live is the Southern Continent. There are four continents in this universe, floating in a sea: Northern, Eastern, Southern, and Western. In the center of these four continents stands the great mountain, Sumeru.

17 The Great Tree of Sumeru: This refers to another Buddhist legend: From the bottom of the ocean grows a tree which reaches to the top of Heaven. The

Asuras, who live in the ocean, quarreled and fought with the beings in Heaven over the ownership of this tree.

18 The Nāga King is the Dragon who controls rainfall.

19 Milarepa is said to have had a very fine singing voice. See his Biography, "Tibet's Great Yogi, Milarepa," edited by W. Y. Evans-Wentz, Oxford University Press, 1951.

20 Or, Mind-for-Bodhi, Heart-for-Bodhi, or Bodhi-Mind (Skt.: Bodhicitta; T.T.: Byañ.Chub.Sems.): "Bodhi" refers to the state of the realization of Buddhahood. "Mind-for-Bodhi" is the desire to attain such realization; but usually, this term implies more than just the wish; it also implies the vow to serve and save all sentient beings through meritorious deeds and spiritual practices, including the Six Pāramitās. "Bodhicitta" is a term of many connotations. It not only refers to the wish or "heart" for Buddhahood and the practices that lead toward it, but in many cases it refers to the intuitive wisdom with which the Ultimate Truth — the Dharmakāya — is realized. "Bodhicitta," therefore, can be translated as Bodhi-Mind, Mind-for-Bodhi, Heart-for-Bodhi, or, THE MIND OF BODHI, depending on how it is used in different contexts. See Story 1, Note 20.

21 The Ten Evils: killing, stealing, adultery, cheating, double-talk, coarse language, talking nonsense, covetousness, anger, and perverted views.

22 Habitual thinking or thought (T.T.: Bag.Chags.): the force driving sentient beings in Saṃsāra. See Story 4, Note 11.

23 Circumambulation: In paying homage to the Buddha, the Dharma, the Guru, or any revered monk, Buddhist disciples were in the habit of circling or walking around the person or object of veneration three times in a clockwise direction and then making obeisance. This custom, however, has died out in many Buddhist countries today.

24 Karma-Ripening or in some cases, Ripened Karma (T.T.: rNam.sMin.): See Note 6.

25 Expedient Truth (T.T.: Drañ.Don.): Because individuals and groups differ in their dispositions and capacities, it is not advisable to give the highest teaching to all. Expedient teachings that lead one *toward* the Final Truth are needed for the majority. These expedient teachings, however, are in principle in accord with, and in practice conducive to, the Final Truth. Thus they are also known as "Expedient *Truths*." It is in this light that the Mahāyāna Buddhist evaluates the various teachings from different schools and religions.

26 Nāropa: Marpa's teacher.

27 Arising and Perfecting Yoga (T.T.: sKyed.Rim.Dañ.rDsogs.Rim.): In the Anuttara Tantra (the Highest Division of Tantra) there are two main practices:
    (1) The teaching of the "Successive Steps toward Creation" (T.T.: sKyes. Rim.), which may be translated as the "Arising, or Growing Yoga." It is a teaching and practice of identifying oneself with Tantric Creation.
    (2) The teaching of the "Successive Steps of Completion, or Perfection" (T.T.: rDsogs.Rim.), may be translated as the "Perfecting Yoga." This is the advanced type of Yoga practice in which one identifies oneself with the Ultimate Perfection, or the great Nirvāna.

28 Dharmadhātu: The Absolute Universality, or the Truth of Totality.

29 Offered their skulls: According to Tantric tradition, offering his skull is the most solemn pledge that a demon or ghost can make. It symbolizes the complete surrender of his body and soul to whomsoever his oath has been made.

30 The meaning of this passage in the text is esoteric and therefore obscure; it may thus be subject to different interpretations. This is a free translation.

THE SONG
OF THE SNOW RANGES

Obeisance to all Gurus

Jᴇᴛsᴜɴ Milarepa's reputation for conquering malignant demons and ghosts grew as a result of his visit to the region of Lashi Snow Mountain. All the people of Nya Non village became his patrons and rendered him service and offerings. Among them was a lady named Wurmo, who with deep faith earnestly sought the teachings of the Dharma. She had a young son called Joupuva, whom she decided to offer to Milarepa as a servant when the boy grew up.

Milarepa was invited to stay at Nya Non Tsar Ma by the villagers, and while there was attended by his patroness, Shindormo. The Jetsun stayed in the village for some time, but soon became severely depressed by the worldliness of everyone. Indicating his unhappiness, he told the villagers that he wanted to return to Lashi Snow Mountain.

The villagers then cried, "Revered One! It is simply for our own sake and not for the welfare of other sentient beings that we ask you to remain in our village this winter and teach us. You can conquer evil demons at any time. Next spring everything will be ready for your journey." Venerable Dunba[1] Shajaguna [a priest] and Shindormo were especially earnest in their petitions: "The winter is coming, and you will meet too much difficulty and hardship on the snow mountain. Please postpone your departure until later."

Disregarding their repeated supplications, Milarepa made up his mind to go. "I am a son of the Nāropa Succession," he said. "I do not fear hardships and raging storms on the snow mountain. For me to remain permanently in a village would be far worse than death. My Guru Marpa also commanded me to avoid worldly distractions and to remain in solitude to pursue my devotions."

Then the villagers of Tsar Ma quickly prepared provisions for him;

before leaving, he promised to see those who would come to him for instruction in the Dharma during the winter. Dunba Shajaguna, Shindormo, and four others, monks and laymen, carrying drink for the farewell party, accompanied the Jetsun. They crossed a hill and came to a small plateau.

Taking with him flour, rice, a piece of meat, and a cut of butter, Milarepa set out alone for the Great Cave of Conquering Demons, where he intended to reside.

On their way home, the six disciples encountered a terrible storm on the far side of the mountain, so blinding they could hardly find their way. They had to summon all their strength to struggle against it, and only reached the village after everyone had retired for the night.

The snow fell for eighteen days and nights, cutting off communication between Drin and Nya Non for six months. All of Milarepa's disciples assumed that their Guru must have died in the storm and, in his memory, held a sacramental feast.

In the Month of Saga [part of March and April], the disciples, carrying axes and other tools, went to search for the Jetsun's corpse. Just short of their destination, they sat down to take a long rest. In the distance they saw a snow-leopard yawning and stretching as it climbed up on a big rock. They watched it for a long while, until it finally disappeared. They were quite sure they would not find the Jetsun's corpse, as they firmly believed the leopard had killed him and eaten his body. They murmured, "Is it still possible to obtain some remnants of his clothes, or hair?" The very thought of this made them cry out in agonized grief. Then they noticed many human footprints beside the leopard's tracks. Afterward, the narrow path where the vision of the leopard [or tiger] had appeared became known as "The Tiger and Leopard Path." [Having seen this phantasm of the leopard], the villagers were very mystified. They thought, "Could this be a conjuration of a Deva or ghost?" In bewilderment, they approached the Cave of Conquering Demons, and, hearing Milarepa singing, they asked themselves, "Is it possible that passing hunters have offered food to the Jetsun, or that he has acquired some left-over prey, so that he did not die?"

When they reached the cave, Milarepa chided them: "You laggards, you reached the other side of the mountain quite a while ago. Why did it take you so long to get here? The food has been prepared for a long time and must be cold. Hasten yourselves and enter!" The disciples were overjoyed, and cried and danced happily. Swiftly they rushed up to the Jetsun, bowing down before him. Milarepa said, "Now is not the time to discuss this; now it is time to eat." But they first made obeisance to him, greeting him and asking after his health. Then they looked round the cave and saw that the flour which they had given him earlier was still not used up. A dish of barley, rice, and meat stood ready. Dunba Shajaguna exclaimed to the Jetsun, "Indeed, it is dinner-time for us, but surely you must have known that we were coming." Milarepa replied, "When I was sitting on the rock, I saw you all resting on the other side of the pass." "We saw a leopard sitting there," said Dunba Shajaguna, "but we did not see you. Where were you then?" "I was the leopard," Milarepa answered. "To a yogi who has completely mastered Prāṇa-Mind,[2] the essence of the Four Elements is perfectly controlled. He can transform himself into whatever bodily form he chooses. I have shown you my occult powers of performing supernormal acts because you are all gifted and advanced disciples. However, you should never speak of this to anyone."

Shindormo said, "Jetsun, your face and body seem to glow with even more health than last year. The paths on both sides of the mountain were blocked by snow, and no one could get through to bring you food. Were you fed by divinities, or did you find some animal killed by wild beasts? What is the secret?"

Milarepa replied, "Most of the time, I was in the state of Samādhi, and hence required no food. On feast days, many Ḍākinīs[3] offered me food in their Tantric festival gatherings. Occasionally, I ate a little dry flour on the tip of a spoon, as I did yesterday and several days ago. At the end of the Month of the Horse, I had a vision that all of you, my disciples, surrounded me and offered me so much to drink and eat that for many days afterward I felt no hunger at all. By the way, what were you doing at the end of the Month of the Horse?" The disciples counted back and found that it was the date on which they had held the sacramental feast for the Jetsun in the belief that he had passed away. Milarepa commented, "When worldly men make charitable offerings, it is surely helpful to their Bardo[4] state. However, it is still better and more useful to realize the Bardo of Here-and-Now."[5]

The disciples earnestly besought Milarepa to come down to Nya Non, but he refused, saying, "I am enjoying my stay here very much; my Samādhi also shows improvement. I want to remain, so return without me!" But the disciples countered, "If the honored Jetsun does not come down with us this time, the people of Nya Non will blame us for leaving him alone to go to his grave. Then abuse and curses will be heaped upon us." Wurmo cried, "If you do not come, we will either carry you down or sit here until death overtakes us." Milarepa could not resist their insistent appeals and, forced to yield, agreed to go with them.

The disciples then said, "Maybe the Dākinīs do not need you, but the disciples in your Succession certainly do. Now let us show the Dākinīs how we can conquer the snow without snowshoes."

The next morning they all left the cave and set out for Nya Non. Shindormo went ahead to bring the villagers the good tidings that the Jetsun was still alive and was returning to them.

[As they neared the village] Milarepa and his disciples came to a huge flat rock shaped like a platform, upon which the farmers threshed their wheat. By then the news of his arrival had spread. Men and women, adults and children, old and young, all flocked to the Jetsun, gazing at him, embracing him, crying with great emotion, asking after his well-being, greeting him reverently, and making obeisance to him. In reply to them, Milarepa, with the snowshoes still on his feet and resting his chin on a headstick sang:

> You and I—patrons, patronesses, and old Milarepa,
> Under the blessed canopy of this auspicious sky,
> Meet once more before our worldly lives
>   have passed away.
> I sing in answer to your questions on my welfare.
> Listen closely, and pay heed to my song!
>
> At the end of the Tiger Year
> Before the Rabbit Year began,
> On the sixth day of Wa Jal,
> A sense of renunciation grew within me.
> To the remote Lashi Snow Mountain
> Came Milarepa, the anchorite, who
>   clings to solitide.
> It seems that sky and earth agreed; between,
> A wind which tears the skin was sent;
> The rivers ran and torrents surged;
> Black clouds swept in from all directions;
> The sun and moon were shut in darkness;
> And the Twenty-eight Constellations[6]
>   were fixed.
> The Milky Way was pegged,
> And the Eight Planets[7] were tied by an
>   iron chain.
> The firmament was wrapped in fog;
> In the mist, snow fell for nine days and nights.
> Then more and more for a further eighteen
>   nights and days.

The snow fell, big as bags of wool,
Fell like birds flying in the sky,
Fell like a whirling swarm of bees.
Flakes fell small as a spindle's wheel,
Fell as tiny as bean seed,
Fell like tufts of cotton.

The snowfall was beyond all measure.
Snow covered all the mountain and even
    touched the sky,
Falling through the bushes and weighing down the trees.
Black mountains became white,
All the lakes were frozen.
Clear water congealed beneath the rocks;
The world became a flat, white plain;
Hills and valleys were leveled.
The snow was such that even evil-doers
    could not venture out.[8]
Wild beasts starved and farmyard creatures, too,
Abandoned by the people in the mountains,
Pitiful, hungry, and enfeebled.
In the tree-mists famine struck the birds,
While rats and mice hid underground.

In this great disaster I remained in utter
    solitude.
The falling snow in the year's-end blizzard
Fought me, the cotton-clad, high on Snow Mountain,
I fought it as it fell upon me
Until it turned to drizzle.
I conquered the raging winds—
Subduing them to silent rest.
The cotton cloth[9] I wore was like a burning
    brand.

The struggle was of life and death,
As when giants wrestle and sabers clash.
I, the competent Yogi, was victorious—
I set a model for all Buddhists,
An example for all great yogis.

My power over the Vital Heat[10] and the
    Two Channels was thus shown.

By observing carefully the Four Ills[11]
    caused by meditation,
And keeping to the inward practice,
The cold and warm Prāṇas became the Essence.
This was why the raging wind grew tame,
And the storm, subdued, lost all its power;
Not even the Devas' army could compete
With me. This battle I, the Yogi, won.

A faithful son of Dharma in a tiger skin,
I have never worn a coat of fox-fur.
Son of a giant, I have never
From the wrathful run.
Son of a lion—of all beasts the king—
I have ever lived in the snow mountains.
To make a task of life is but a joke to me.

If you believe what this old man tells
Hearken to his prophecy:

The teaching of the Practiced Succession[12]
    will grow and spread afar;
A few accomplished beings will then appear on earth;
The fame of Milarepa will spread throughout the world.
You, disciples, in the memory of man
Will abound with faith;
Fame and praise of us
Will be heard in aftertimes.

To answer your concern for my health,
I, the Yogi Milarepa, am very well indeed.
And how are you, dear patrons? Are you all
    well and happy?

    The Jetsun's happy song so inspired the villagers that they danced and sang for joy, and Milarepa, in a merry mood, joined in. The great stone platform on which the dance was held became impressed with his foot- and hand-prints, as if they had been carved in it. The center of the platform sank, forming a small basin with irregular steps; thenceforth the platform, formerly called "White-Stepped Rock," became known as "Snowshoe Rock."
    Then the villagers escorted Milarepa to the village of Nya Non Tsar Ma, and gave service and offerings to him. The patroness Lese-

bum said, "Revered One, nothing could give us greater joy than to learn that you are alive and have returned safely to our village. Your countenance is more radiant than ever, and you are energetic and spirited. Is this because the goddesses made offerings to you when you were in solitude?"

In answer, Milarepa sang:

I bow down at the feet of my Guru Marpa.

The gift of blessing is bestowed by the Ḍākinīs;
The nectar of Samaya[13] is abundant nourishment;
Through faithful devotion the organs of sense are fed.
Propitious merits are thus garnered by my disciples.

The immediate Mind has no substance;
It is void, less than a smallest atom.
When seer and seen are both eliminated,
The "View" is truly realized.

As for the "Practice" — in the Stream of Illumination,
No stages can be found.
Perseverence in Practice is confirmed
When actor and acting are both annulled.

In the Realm of Illumination,
Where subject and object are one,
I see no cause, for all is Void.
When acting and actor disappear,
All actions become correct.

The finite thoughts[14] dissolve in Dharmadhātu;
The Eight Worldly Winds bring neither hope nor fear.
When the precept and the precept-keeper disappear,
The disciplines are best observed.

By knowing that the Self-mind is Dharmakāya[15] —
Buddha's Body absolute —
By an earnest, altruistic vow,
The deed and doer disappear.
Thus the glorious Dharma triumphs.

In answer to his disciples' questioning,
This is the happy song the old man sings!

The falling snow enclosed
My house of meditation;[16]
Goddesses gave me food and sustenance;
The water of Snow Mountain was the purest draught.
All was done without effort;
There is no need to farm when there's no
        demand [for food].
My store is full without preparation or hoarding.
By observing my own mind, all things are seen;
By sitting in a lowly place, the royal throne
        is reached.
Perfection is attained through the Guru's grace;
This bounty is repaid by Dharma practice.
Followers and patrons here assembled,
Give your services with faith.
Be happy, all, and gay.

Dunbar Shajaguna made obeisance to Milarepa, saying, "It is indeed wondrous and pleasing to learn that so much snow did not harm the Jetsun, and that we, your disciples, were able to return with you safely to the village. What a joy that all the disciples could see their Guru! We will be deeply grateful and happy if you preach the Dharma on your meditative experiences this winter, as an arrival-gift to us."

Milarepa, in answer to Shajaguna's request and as an arrival-gift to the disciples of Nya Non, sang the song of "The Six Essences of Meditative Experience":

Obeisance to my Guru with the Three Perfections.

This evening, at the request
Of my disciples Shajaguna and the Patron Dormos,
I, Milarepa, tell what I experienced when meditating,
I who ever dwell in the remote fastnesses.

The pure vow made this congregation possible;
The pure precept of Dharma united me and my patrons.
My sons! What you have asked, will I,
The father, present as my arrival-gift.

I renounce the world, and have lamented for it.
I, Milarepa, came to Lashi Snow Mountain
To occupy alone the Cave of Conquering Demons.

For six full months, the experiences of meditation
    grew;
I now disclose them in this, the song of the
    Six Essences.

First come the Six Parables of Outer Appearance;
Second, the Six Inner Misconducts,
Which one should carefully consider;
Third, the Six Ropes which bind us in Saṃsāra;
Fourth, the Six Ways through which Liberation
    is achieved;
Fifth, the Six Essences of Knowledge
Through which one attains confidence;
Sixth, the Six Blissful Experiences of Meditation.

If one does not commit this song to memory,
No impression is left upon the mind.
Heed carefully, then, my explanations.

If there be obstacles,
It cannot be called space;
If there be numbers,
It cannot be called stars.
One cannot say "This is a mountain,"
If it moves and shakes.
It cannot be an ocean
Should it grow or shrink.
One cannot be called a swimmer
If he needs a bridge.
It is not a rainbow
If it can be grasped.
These are the Six Outer Parables.

The limits of the definite
Limit understanding.
Drowsiness and distractions
Are not meditation.
Acceptance and rejection
Are not acts of will.
A constant flow of thought
Is not Yoga.
If there be East and West,[17]
It is not Wisdom;

If birth and death,
It is not Buddha.
These are the Six Inner Faults.

Denizens of Hell are bound by hate,
Hungry ghosts by misery,
And beasts by blindness.
Men by lust are bound,
By jealousy, Asuras,
And Devas in Heaven by pride.
These Six Fetters are the Obstacles to Liberation.

Great faith, reliance
On a wise and strict Guru,
Good discipline,
Solitude in a hermitage,
Determined, persevering
Practice, and meditation—
These are the Six Ways that lead to Liberation.

The Original Inborn Wisdom[18] is
The sphere of primordial [depth].
Without "exterior" or "interior" is the sphere
    of Awareness;
Without brightness or darkness is the sphere
    of Insight;
Omnipresent and all-embracing is the sphere
    of Dharma;
Without mutation or transition is the sphere
    of Tig Le;[19]
Without interruption is the sphere of Experience.[20]
These are the Six Unshakable Realms of Essence.

Bliss rises when the Vital Heat is fanned,
When air from the Nādīs[21] flows in the
    Central Channel,
When the Bodhi-Mind[22] flows from above,
When it is purified below,
When white and red meet in the middle,
And the joy of leakless body satiates one,
These are the Six Blissful Experiences of Yoga.
To please you, my sons and followers,
I sing this song of the Six Essences,

Of my experiences last winter when meditating.
May all at this delightful meeting
Drink the heavenly nectar of my song.
May everyone be gay and full of joy.
May your pure wishes be fulfilled.

This is the silly song sung by this old man;
Do not belittle it, this gift of Dharma,
But with joyous hearts stride forward
On the Path of the Blessed Doctrine!

Shindormo cried, "Jetsun! Most Precious One! You are like unto the Buddhas of the past, present, and future. The opportunity to serve you and to learn from you is a rare privilege. Those who do not have faith in you are indeed more foolish than the animals."

Milarepa replied, "It may not be so very important for a person to have faith in me. It does not matter much either way. But if you have a precious human body and have been born at a time and place in which the Buddhist religion prevails, it is very foolish indeed not to practice the Dharma." Milarepa thus sang:

At the feet of the Translator Marpa, I
    prostrate myself,
And sing to you, my faithful patrons.

How stupid it is to sin with recklessness
While the pure Dharma spreads all about you.
How foolish to spend your lifetime without meaning,
When a precious human body is so rare a gift.
How ridiculous to cling to prison-like
    cities and remain there.
How laughable to fight and quarrel with your
    wives and relatives,
Who do but visit you.
How senseless to cherish sweet and tender words
Which are but empty echoes in a dream.
How silly to disregard one's life by fighting foes
Who are but frail flowers.

How foolish it is when dying to torment
    oneself with thoughts of family,
Which bind one to Māyā's[23] mansion.
How stupid to stint on property and money,

Which are a debt on loan from others.
How ridiculous it is to beautify and deck the body,
Which is a vessel full of filth.
How silly to strain each nerve for wealth and goods,
And neglect the nectar of the inner teachings!

In a crowd of fools, the clever and sensible
Should practice the Dharma, as do I.

The people in the assembly said to Milarepa, "We are deeply grateful for your songs of wisdom. But we can never emulate your indus-
try and intelligence. We can only try to avoid the foolish things you
have cited. Our only wish is for the privilege of your continued pres-
ence, that the living may give their service and obtain instruction
from you, and that the dead, too, may be saved through your grace."
Milarepa replied, "In obedience to the order of my Guru, I have
been meditating on Lashi Snow Mountain. I may stay here for a time,
but I can never stay here as you worldly people do. Disrespect, and
not goodwill, would result if I were to remain among you. He then
sang:

Obeisance to Marpa the Translator.

May all my patrons and patronesses here assembled
Have immutable faith, and pray to me with
    sincerity unfeigned.

If one stays too long with friends,
They will soon tire of him;
Living in such closeness leads to dislike and hate.
It is but human to expect and demand too much
When one dwells too long in companionship.

The belligerence in human nature leads to
    broken precepts;
Bad company destroys good deeds;
Honest words bring evil when spoken in a crowd;
To argue the right and wrong only makes more foes.

To cling to sectarian bigotry and dogma
Makes one vicious and more sinful.

An obligatory response to the offerings of
    the faithful ever causes evil thoughts.

To enjoy the Food of the Dead[24] is sinful
    and dangerous.
The offerings of worldly beings are low and worthless.

Companionship itself causes contempt;
From contempt hate and aversion grow.

The more houses one owns, the more one
    suffers at the time of death.
These sufferings and lamentations are indeed
    intolerable,
Especially to yogis who dwell in solitude.

I, Milarepa, am going to a quiet hermitage,
    to live alone.
Faithful patrons, your endeavor to amass
    merits is wonderful;
My patrons and patronesses, it is good
To make offerings and to serve your Guru.
I confirm my wish to meet you soon,
And see you many times.

The patrons all said to Milarepa, "We never tire of hearing your instruction and preaching; it may be that you have tired of us. No matter how warmly we entreat you to remain here, we know it will be in vain. We only hope that from time to time you will come to visit us from Lashi."

The villagers then offered Milarepa many provisions and other goods, but he did not take them. All the people were inspired with veneration and paid him deep respect. In a mood of great delight and happiness, the villagers strongly confirmed their unshakable faith in the Jetsun.

This is the Song of the Snow Ranges.

NOTES

1 Dunba (T.T.: sTon.Pa.): a high priest who is versed in Buddhist scriptures and proficient in giving spiritual instructions to Buddhist followers.

2 Prāṇa-Mind: According to Tantric teaching, mind and Prāṇa manifest as

two aspects of a unity. Mind is that which is aware; Prāṇa is the active energy which gives support to the awareness. He who masters the mind automatically masters the Prāṇa, and vice versa. The aim of any system of meditation is to control or master the Prāṇa-Mind. An accomplished yogi is one who has mastered his Prāṇa-Mind.

3 See story 1, Note 19.

4 Bardo (T.T.: Bar.Do.): the intermediate state of existence between death and rebirth. According to Tibetan Buddhism, this very important state is like a crossroad, the fate and fortune of one's rebirth depending much upon it.

5 The Bardo of Here-and-Now: From the viewpoint of Tantric teachings, the state of Bardo is not confined to the state after death. This very life itself is a state of Bardo. The person in physical existence, as we know it, goes through the same experiences as in Bardo, only in more "substantial fashion." To a Bardo-dweller, it is the person in physical existence who seems to be in Bardo, whereas the two states of life and death are actually correlative and similar.

6 The Twenty-eight Constellations (T.T.: rGyu.sKar.Ñer.brGyad.; lit.: the twenty-eight running stars): They are the constellations through which the moon passes in her revolution round the heavens.

7 The Eight Planets (T.T.: gZah.brGyad.) refer to the Sun, Moon, Mars, Mercury, Venus, Jupiter, Saturn, and Rāhu (see Story 4, Note 1).

8 The snowfall is sometimes so heavy in Tibet that all activity stops. Thus, even if one wants to do evil things, one is prevented.

9 Cotton cloth: The Tantric yogi who practices Heat Yoga is not supposed to wear furs — he wears only simple cotton clothing even in a cold country like Tibet.

10 Vital Heat, Dumo (T.T.: gTum.Mo.): the "mystic" heat produced from the Navel Center in Tantric meditations. It is one of the most important practices of Tibetan Tantrism. See "The Six Yogas of Nāropa," in Evans-Wentz' "Tibetan Yoga and Secret Doctrines," 2nd ed., Oxford University Press, 1958. See also the translator's "Teachings of Tibetan Yoga."

11 The Four Ills: the sicknesses that are caused by the unbalancing strength and activity of the Four Elements — earth, water, fire, and air — in the yogi's body.

12 The Practiced Succession (T.T.: sGrub.brGyud.): another name for Ghagyuba, the School of Marpa and Milarepa. The reason for this nomenclature is due to the spirit and tradition of this School which emphasizes Yoga practice and actual experience, rather than scholastic investigation. This tradition differs sharply from the traditions of the Yellow (Gelugba) and Gray (Sajyaba) Schools of Tibet.

13 Nectar of Samaya: Samaya implies the Tantric precepts. He who observes these precepts receives grace and blessings, a necessary nourishment for spiritual growth.

14 This can also be rendered as: "thoughts of a limitative pattern" (T.T.: Phyogs.Chahi.rTog.Pa.). The patterns of thought of sentient beings are of a limited or finite nature. When one realizes the truth of Voidness (Sūnyatā), the limitative patterns of thought are fundamentally transformed. Using Buddhist terminology, they "dissolve" into the Dharmadhātu — the absolute, universal, and interpenetrating state of all the different aspects of existence in the light of the Void.

15 Dharmakāya: the "Body of Truth," which is ultimate, formless, omnipresent, and yet without any attributes.

16 When a yogi is preparing to meditate over a long period, he will mark lines on the ground around his dwelling, outside of which he will not go. In this case Milarepa did not have to make any marks, as the snow itself was deep and heavy enough to confine him.

17 East and West: If the very idea of *direction* still exists, then there is no Wisdom, because direction implies a limitation and differentiation, while Wisdom transcends both.

18 T.T.: lHan.Cig.sKyes.Pahi.Ye.Çes. This term is translated in this book as the Original Inborn Wisdom, or as Innate, or Inborn Wisdom. Its literal translation should perhaps be the Coemergent, or Simultaneously Born Wisdom, implying that it is within one at all times. However, for convenience sake, Innate, or Inborn Wisdom is used.

19 Tig Le (T.T.: Thig.Le.; Skt.: Bindu): This term has many meanings, such as "the dot," "the solid one," "the essence," etc. It is also used to signify male semen or female "blood," which represent the Life-Essence of physical bodies. Here Tig Le implies the essence or immutability of Absolute Truth.

20 Sphere of Experience: The yogi, in all activities of daily life, whether walking, eating, sleeping, talking, or the like, never loses the feeling or "sensation," of his yogic experience.

21 The Nādīs (Roma and Junma): the mystical left and right Channels (see Story 1, Note 28).

22 Bodhi-Mind (or Bodhi-Heart) here means Tig Le.

23 Māyā means delusion or illusion. The phenomenal world is considered by Buddhism to be a dream, a phantasm, a magic shadow play, a reflection — in short it has only an illusory existence and not a real one.

24 Food of the Dead: The Tibetan Lamas believe that to accept offerings from relatives of the deceased person on his behalf incurs a great responsibility. Once the "Food of the Dead" is taken, the Lama is responsible for liberating the "soul" from sufferings and dangers. Therefore, in Tibet, to receive the offering for the dead is considered a very serious matter.

CHALLENGE FROM
A WISE DEMONESS

Obeisance to all Gurus

ONCE Milarepa stayed in Nya Non [for a short period]. The people there besought him to remain but he would not consent, and, in compliance with his Guru's order, went to Riwo Balnbar and practiced meditation in a cave near Linba. To the right of his seat there was a cleft in the rock. Late one night, Milarepa heard a cracking sound from the crevice. He got up from his seat and looked around. But as he saw nothing, he thought it must be an illusion, and so returned to his bed-seat. Suddenly, a great beam of light shone out from the crevice. In the midst of the light appeared a red man on a black deer led by a beautiful woman. The man gave Milarepa a blow with his elbow accompanied by a suffocating wind, and then disappeared. The woman became a red bitch, who immediately caught Milarepa by the foot. Milarepa realized that this was an apparition conjured by [the she-demon] Draug Srin Mo, so he sang the following song to her:

I make obeisance to Marpa, the gracious one.

You, malignant Draug Srin Mo of Linba Draug,
　　you sinful female ghost
Appearing in a vicious conjured form,
In your contempt you come looking for a
　　chance [to harm me].
I do not deceive in tuneful song:
I sing only honest words and truth.

In the midst of the blue sky,
The blessing of moon and sun brings affluence.

From the marvelous Palace of Heaven
    shines the ray of light
By which all sentient beings are illumined and seen.
[I pray] the planet Chamju[1] will not rival
The sun and moon as they circle the Four
    Continents.[2]

In the Eastern Quarter, on the top of Snow Mountain,
Darsen Gharmo, the snow lioness, brings prosperity;
She is the queen of beasts,
And never eats spoiled meat.
When she appears on the horizon
Do not afflict her with a storm!

In the South, amid the forest trees,
The mountain tigress, Dagmo Ridra, brings prosperity;
She is the champion of all wild beasts,
    gallant and invincible.
When she walks on a narrow and dangerous path,
Do not ambush her in a hunter's trap!

In the West, in the Ma Päm ocean, blue and vast,
The Dogar Nya [White-bellied Fish] brings
    prosperity;
She is the supreme dancer of the water-element,
In a marvelous way she rolls her eyes.
When she seeks delicious food,
Do not harm her with a fish-hook!

In the North, above the wide Red Rock,
Shajageubo, the great vulture brings prosperity;
She is the queen of birds.
Wondrous indeed, she never takes the
    lives of others.
When she seeks food on the top of the
    three mountains,
Do not trap her in a net!

In the cave of Linba where the vultures live,
I, Milarepa, bring prosperity.
I aim at my own and others' welfare,
Renouncing a worldly life.
With an enlightened mind,[3]

I strive for Buddhahood in one lifetime.
Diligent and undistracted I practice Dharma.
Draug Srin Mo, pray do not afflict me!
Pray hearken to this song with five
    parables and six meanings,
The song with rhythm, the song like a golden string.

Pitiable Draug Srin Mo! Do you understand me?
To commit evil Karma is a heavy sin.
Should you not take heed of this sinful Karma?
Should you not control your harmful thoughts
    and vicious heart?
If you do not realize that all things are
    merely of the mind,
The endless apparitions of Nhamdog⁴ will
    never cease.
If one realizes not that the Mind-Essence is void,
How can one dispel the spirit of evil?
You sinful demon hag! Do not afflict me!
Harm me not, and return to your own abode!

Instantaneously she disappeared. However, still holding his foot, she
replied to Milarepa:

Oh, you gifted son of the Dharma,
The one alone who has courage and fortitude,
The yogi who treads the Path of the Cemetery,⁵
The saintly Buddhist who follows the ascetic way,
Your song is the Buddha's teaching,
More precious than gold.
To exchange gold for brass is shameful.
Should I not atone for the sins I have committed,
All that I have ever said will be a lie.

For an answer to the Song of Karma
Which you have just sung to me,
Hearken closely to my allegories.

In the midst of the blue sky,
Shines the light of sun and moon
Through which prosperity to earth is brought.

As you have just said,

Rays from the Measureless Palace[6] of the Gods
Dispel the darkness in the Four Continents,
While moon and sun circle the Islands Four,
With ease they give out beams of light;
Were they not dazzled by their glowing rays,
How could Rāhu afflict[7] them?

In the East, where towers the crystal snow mountain,
Darsen Gharmo brings prosperity;
She is the queen of beasts;
She commands them as her servants.
When she appeared on the horizon,
The hurricanes and storms would not have
　　afflicted her
Had she not become too proud and arrogant.

In the South, amid the dense forest trees,
The mountain tigress brings prosperity;
Champion is she of all the beasts.
With pride she boasts of conquests with her claws;
When she comes close to a narrow and dangerous path,
She shows off her pride with great hauteur.
Were she not flaunting her delusive stripes
　　and smiles,
The hunter's trap would never catch her.

In the Western Quarter, in the depth of the
　　blue ocean,
The White-bellied Fish brings prosperity;
She is the dancer in the water element.
She claims to be the seer of great gods.
Because of her gluttony, she searches for
　　delicious food.
Had she not used her illusive body
To search for human food,
How could the fish-hook harm her?

In the North, above the wide Red Rock,
The vulture, queen of birds, brings prosperity.
She is the Deva[8] of birds, who dwells among
　　the trees.
She proudly claims that she disposes of all the birds.
When she searches for blood and flesh to eat,

She flies over the three mountains.
If she swooped not at her prey,
How could the bird net catch her?

In the vulture-dwelling Rock, you,
    Milarepa, bring prosperity.
You claim that you are doing good, both
    for yourself and others.[9]
With the flowering of the perfect Bodhi-Heart,
    attentively you meditate;
Your ambition is, in one life, to become Buddha.
Your hope is to save sentient beings in the
    Six Realms.[10]
When you were engrossed in the practice of
    meditation,
The powerful force of your habitual-thoughts
    arose,[11]
It stirred your Self-mind and aroused delusory
    discriminations.
If in your mind the discriminating thought,
    "Enemy," had ne'er arisen,
How could I, Draug Srin Mo, afflict you?

You should know that from one's mind alone
Comes the evil of habitual-thinking.
What is the use of my following your guidance
If you have not realized the Mind of Suchness?[12]
You had better go your own way, while I go mine.

He who does not realize the mind's voidness,
Can never be exempted from the influence of evil.
If one knows the Self-mind by oneself,
All obstacles and difficulties become one's aids.
Even I, Draug Srin Mo, will then gladly be
    his servant.
You, Milarepa, still have wrong ideas,
You have yet to pierce into the Self-mind's nature,
You have yet to penetrate to illusion's root.

When Draug Srin Mo finished her singing, Milarepa was much impressed with her cleverness. He appeared to be very pleased [and somewhat surprised] to hear such expressions from a demoness, and, in answer to her, replied with a song, "The Eight Parables of Thinking":

Yes! Yes! What you have said is true, true indeed.
Oh! You vicious Draug Srin Mo,
It is hard to find words truer than these.
Although I have traveled far and wide,
Never have I heard a song so beautiful.
Even should one hundred great scholars assemble here,
No better illustration could they give.
You, a specter, have sung good words;
They are like a rod of gold,
Which strikes into my very heart.
Thus the Heart-air,[13] the Dharma-clinging[14]
      are dispelled;
The darkness of my ignorant blindness is
      thus illumined;
The white lotus of wisdom blossoms thus;
The lamp which brightens self-awareness[15]
      is lit;
And mindfulness of awareness is fully liberated.

[In observing that] this mindfulness is liberated
I stare upward at the great blue sky,
I realize completely the empty nature of being;
Of palpable existence,
No anxiety or fear have I.

When I look at the sun and moon
I realize their nakedness, the radiance of
      Mind-Essence;
Of distraction and drowsiness,[16] no fear have I.

When I gaze at the top of the mountains,
I clearly realize the immutable Samādhi;
Of change and flow I have no fear.

When I look down at the flowing river,
I fully realize the running nature of all flux;
Of the wrong view of Non-cause, I have no
      fear or misgiving.

When I contemplate the rainbow-like [illusions
      of existence]
I clearly realize the identity of Form and
      Voidness;

Of the nihilistic and realistic wrong-views[17]
    I have no fear.

When I see the shadows and the moon-in-water,
I fully realize the self-radiance of Non-clinging;
Of subjective and objective thoughts,[18]
    I have no fear.

When I look inwardly to the self-aware mind,
I clearly see the light of the inner lamp;
Of ignorant blindness, I have no fear.

When I hear what you, sinful spirit, have sung,
I fully realize the nature of self-awareness;
Of the obstacles and difficulties, I have no fear.

You, specter, are indeed eloquent in speech!
Do you really understand the nature of mind
    as you have said?
Look at the ugly birth of a hag-specter which
    you have merited!
You do nothing but vicious and evil deeds.
This is caused by your Dharma-ignorance and
    disregard of morality.
You should heed more diligently
The evils and sufferings of Saṃsāra.
You should thoroughly renounce the Ten
    Evil Actions![19]
A yogi, lion-like, I have neither fear nor panic.
You, sinful demon, should not think my
    joking words are true.[20]
I was only making fun of you.
Oh spirit! You have mocked me this evening!
But may we follow the legend of the Buddha
    and the Five Demons,[21]
And may the perfect Bodhi-Mind arise in you!
With your pure vow, combined with my compassion,
May you become one of my disciples in the
    future life.

Moved by his reply, a full faith in the Jetsun blossomed in Draug
Srin Mo's heart. She released Milarepa's foot and sang with a sweet
voice:

It is by virtue of the stock of Merits[22]
That you, oh gifted Yogi,
Are able to practice the Dharma
And remain alone within this mountain solitude!
Your merciful eyes keep watch o'er all beings
    in compassion!

I follow the Lineage of Bedma Tutrin[23]
And have heard the rosary of precious
    words in the holy Dharma.
Though I have listened to much preaching,
And attended great congregations,
Still my craving and clinging are excessive.

I lead to goodness those who observe the Dharma;
I show the right Path to gifted Buddhists.

Although my intention is friendly and my
    motive good,
Food must be sought to support this depraved body.

I roam the earth in this evil form,
Desiring blood and flesh for food.

I enter into the soul of whomsoever I encounter;
I incite the hearts of maidens, pretty and
    charming;
I madden with lust the blood of young men,
    strong and handsome.
With my eyes, I amuse myself watching all
    the dramas;
With my mind, I instigate cravings in all nations;
With my body I incite people to excitement
    and restlessness.

My home is at Linba,
My residence is in the Rock.

These are the things I do,
This is my sincere reply and honest
    self-confession.
These are the words of greeting for our meeting,

This is the evidence of my faith in you,
    and of my offerings.
Singing this song of honesty,
Let us be inspired and happy.

Milarepa thought, "This demon's earnest inquiry must be well answered, and her pride subdued." He then sang:

Hearken, hearken closely, you depraved hag.
The Guru is good, but the disciple is bad.
Those who have only heard and read the
    teaching of the Dharma,
Merely grasp at words.
They do not understand the real Dharma.
Eloquent and convincing as their words may sound,
There is neither use nor value in them.

Deceitful sayings and empty talk help not
In cleansing the defilements of one's mind.

Because of your evil *habit-propensities*
    formed in the past,
And your vicious doings in the present,
You have violated the Precepts and your Vows.[24]
By force of these transgressions,
You were born as a lower form of woman.
Your body wanders in the wretched haunts
    of cannibals;
Your talk is self-cheating and deceiving;
Your mind is saturated with thoughts of
    afflicting others.

It was because of your disregard of the
    Law of Karma,
That an ugly body in an inferior birth was taken,
Should you think now upon the vices of Saṃsāra,
You would confess your guilt, and promise to
    do good.

Like a lion, I do not fear;
Like an elephant, I have no anxiety;
Like a madman, I have no pretension and no hope.
I tell you the honest truth.

To make trouble and afflict me
Will only bring more sorrow on yourself.

Make a vow toward the pure Dharma.
Make a wish to be my disciple in the future.
Oh, you confused, depraved hag,
Think on these words with care!

Draug Srin Mo now appeared visibly as before, and with honesty she sang:

Of the Holy Buddhas of the Three Times,[25]
The Buddha Vajradhara is the chief;
He also is the Lord of the wondrous Doctrine.
The arising of Bodhi-Mind is indeed remarkable.

You may call me a depraved hag, but I do
        have great Merits.
True understanding arose when I heard your
        warning.
At first I swore to obey my Guru's instructions,
I studied and learned the holy Dharma.
But then I indulged myself, committing evil deeds.
With vicious passions[26] burning wildly,
        unbearably in my heart,
I was born in the ugly form of a she-demon.
I meant to help all sentient beings,
But again and again the results were evil.

You came, great Yogi, at the beginning of last year;
Staying alone in the cave, you meditated in
        solitude.
Sometimes I like you, but sometimes I do not!
It is because I like you that I came tonight;
It is because I do not, that I seized your foot.
I now repent this evil deed.

Hereafter, this wretched hag will renounce
        her wrong-doings;
With all her heart she will practice the Dharma;
She will serve Buddhism as best she can.
From now on, with the cool shade of the
        tree of grace,

Please protect her from the Five Poisonous
    Cravings.[27]

I, the depraved woman with ugly form,
    take refuge in you,
And rely on the instructions you have given.
I herewith renounce my malicious intentions.
From now until the time I achieve Buddhahood,
I swear to protect the yogis, and befriend
    all who meditate.
I will serve and assist the followers
Of the Doctrine, the observers of the Precepts.
To advanced yogis and the Dharma, I shall be
    an honest servant.

Thereupon, Draug Srin Mo swore before Milarepa that in the future
she would never harm anyone. She also took an oath to protect all
who meditate. In order to guide Draug Srin Mo, Milarepa then sang:

I am the venerable one who has renounced Saṃsāra;
I am the noble son of my Guru;
In me are stored the precious teachings;
A Buddhist with great sincerity and devotion am I.

I am the yogi who perceives the essence of being;
I am like a mother to all sentient beings;
I am a man who has courage and perseverance,
The holder of the spirit of Gautama Buddha,
The master of the Heart-aspiring-to-Bodhi.

I am the one who always adheres to kindness;
With great compassion I have subdued all
    evil thoughts.
I am the one who stays in the cave of Linba,
Who practices meditation without distraction.

Do you think you are happy now? You confused,
    wretched hag!
If you have not found happiness, it is your
    own fault.
Beware! Your clinging-to-Ego[28] is greater
    than yourself;

Pay heed! Your emotions are stronger
    than yourself.
Oh, specter, your vicious will is far
    wickeder than yourself;
Your habitual-thought is more characteristic
    than yourself;
Your ceaseless mental activity[29] is more
    frantic than yourself!

To maintain the existence of a ghost,
Only brings about mischief;
To understand the non-existence of a ghost
Is the way of Buddha;
To know that ghost and Reality are one
Is the way to Liberation.
Knowing that the ghosts are all one's parents
Is the right understanding;
Realizing that the ghost itself is Self-mind
Is glory supreme.

You will be emancipated from all fetters
If you realize the truth that I have stated;
This is my instruction to you, demoness!

To become my disciple you must observe the
    precepts.
Violate not the rules of Vajrayāna,[30]
Debase not the great Compassion,
Afflict not the body, word, and mind of Buddhists.
If you ever violate these rules.
You can be assured of plummeting to
    the Vajra Hell![31]
Recite these important rules three times;
Remember their meaning and practice them.

Let us now make a wish, and may the boon
    come quickly to you!
With the peerless Bodhi-Heart, inconceivably
    great, may you have great happiness.
In your future life,
May you then become my chief disciple,
Oh, woman of Dorje Semba.[32]

After Draug Srin Mo had taken the oath before the Jetsun, she made obeisances to him and also circumambulated him many times. She swore that thereafter she would obey all his orders. Then she disappeared like a rainbow, vanishing into the sky.

In the meantime, the day was dawning, and the sun shone. After a while Draug Srin Mo returned, bringing with her brothers, sisters, and a retinue, all with handsome faces and dressed in their best, to see the Jetsun. They made many offerings to him.

Draug Srin Mo said to Milarepa, "I am a sinful ghost. Forced by evil Karma, I was caught in a low form of birth; driven by evil habit-ual-thoughts, I influenced others, also, to become evil. I pray you to forgive me. Evil intention made me do you mischief. I entreat you to forgive me for what I have done. Hereafter I will obey your orders strictly and try to be your honest servant. Be gracious, and tell us of the supreme Truth that you have realized." In making this request Draug Srin Mo sang:

> Oh, thou! Thou [great one]! The son of
>   great heroes!
> Having amassed numerous merits,
> You have become a gifted person;
> Belonging to a distinguished Succession,[33]
> You are endowed with Waves of Grace.[34]
>
> You are the one who meditates with great perseverance,
> Who with endurance stays alone,
> Who industriously practices the deep teachings.
> To you there are no devils and no obstacles!
>
> Through realizing the microcosm of the
>   inner Channels and Prāṇas,
> You can work great miracles.
>
> We and you are in harmonious relationship.
> Our pure wishes in previous lives brought
>   about our meeting.
> Though I have met numerous accomplished saints,
> Only through you have I received grace and guidance.
> I, a hag-specter, speak with sincerity!
>
> The expedient truth of Hīnayāna[35] may
>   be illusive;

It is indeed hard to subdue the passions
    due to Karma!
One may talk eloquently about the Dharma,
But talk is of no avail when suffering
    and misery come.
That kind of Guru who strays from the Dharma,
Will not help himself, and merely incurs hatred.

You! The Incarnation Body of Buddha[36]
    in the Three Times,
Realize the immutable truth of Dharmata.[37]
With the inner teaching, you practice the
    quintessence of Dharma.
In this blessed place where grew the Ultimate
    Enlightenment,
We, Draug Srin Mo and her retinue,
Pray you to elucidate for us the teaching
    of the Innermost Secret.
Pray! Grant us the secret words of Vajrayāna,
    the truth of the Ultimate;
Pray! Teach us the great illuminating Wisdom,
Pray! Grant us the radiance of the Light!

By hearing the immutable Truth, the profound
    Secret Doctrine,
One will not fall into the lower path.
By practicing the teaching of the Secret Doctrine,
One will not wander in Saṃsāra's paths.
Without hiding and concealment,
We pray you to unfold to us the Truth complete.

Milarepa then said, "From what I can see now, not all of you
are able to practice the highest teaching of the immutable Truth. If
you insist on learning the Inner Teaching you must swear with your
life and pledge a solemn oath."

Thereupon, Draug Srin Mo swore an oath that henceforth she would
follow all the orders of the Jetsun, and that she would serve and assist all Buddhists. In answer to her questions, Milarepa sang a song,
"The Immutable and Real Dharma on the Twenty-seven Vanishments":

To the secret Buddha with a human body,
To the incomprable Translator, Marpa,
    my father Guru,

At your feet I bow, oh Gracious One!

I am not a singer who wishes to display his art,
But you, specter, entreat me to sing and sing again.
Today I will sing to you of the Ultimate Truth.

Thunder, lightning, and the clouds,
Arising as they do out of the sky,
Vanish and recede back into it.

The rainbow, fog, and mist,
Arising as they do from the firmament,
Vanish and recede back into it.

Honey, fruit, and crops grow out of the earth;
All vanish and recede back into it.

Flowers, leaves, and forests,
Arising as they do out of the earth,
Vanish and return back into it once more.

The ripple, tide, and flux,
Arising as they do from the great ocean,
Also vanish and into it return.

Habitual-thinking, clingings, and desires,
Arising as they do from the Alaya Consciousness,[38]
All vanish and return to the Alaya.

Self-awareness, self-illumination, and self-liberation,
Arising as they do from the Mind-Essence,
All vanish and dissolve back into the mind.

Non-arising, Non-extinction, and Non-description,
Arise from the Dharmata
And all return to it again.

Phantasms, hallucinations, and visions of demons,
All are produced from Yoga,
And all go back and vanish into it again.

Should one cling to the reality of visions,[39]
He would be confused in his meditation.

If he knew not that all obstacles
Reveal the Void, the manifestation of Mind,
He would be misled in his meditation.
The very root of all confusion
Also comes out of the mind.
He who realizes the nature of that mind,
Sees the great Illumination without coming
    and going.
Observing the nature of all outer forms,
He realizes that they are but illusory visions
    of mind.
He sees also the identity of the Void and Form.

Moreover, to meditate is an illusory thought;
Not to meditate is illusory, too.
It is the same whether or not you meditate.

Discrimination of "the two"[40] is the
    source of all wrong views.
From the ultimate viewpoint there is no
    view whatsoever.
This is the nature[41] of Mind.
The teaching of observation of
The Dharma-nature is illustrated through
    the simile of space.
You, Draug Srin Mo, should look into the
    meaning of beyond-thoughts;
You should enter the non-distracted realm
    in meditation;
You should act naturally and spontaneously,
Ever conscious of the Essence.

Beyond words is the Accomplishment, free
    from hope and fear.
I have no time to sing for fun, chatting with
    empty words.
Oh, spirit! Think of the auspicious Dharma.
Ask little, do not raise so many questions;
But be relaxed and sit at ease!

I sing as you requested;
These are my mad words.[42]
If you can practice them,

You will eat the food of Great Bliss[43]
when hungry,
And drink the Nectar[44] when thirsty.
Then you can help yogis by your actions.

Whereupon Draug Srin Mo and her retinue were overwhelmed with devotion for the Jetsun, making obeisances and circumambulating him many times. They cried, "Revered One, we are indeed deeply grateful to you!" and disappeared like a rainbow, vanishing into the sky. From then on, they obeyed the orders of Milarepa; they served yogis, never afflicting them, and became their good friends.

This is the story of [Milarepa's meeting with] Draug Srin Mo at the cave of Linba.

NOTES

1 The Planet Chamju (or Rāhu) (T.T.: Khyab.hJug.): a legendary planet which was supposed to be malignant to the destinies of mankind, and was known for continually wreaking vengeance on the sun and the moon.

2 Four Continents: See Story 2, Notes 15, 16, and 17.

3 An enlightened mind — the Bodhi-Heart, or Bodhi-Mind (Skt.: Bodhicitta; T.T.: Byan.Chub.Sems.): This most important and frequently used term in Mahāyāna Buddhism signifies the fundamental spirit, doctrine, and philosophy of the Mahāyāna. Among the meanings and applications of this term, two are most significant: first, the vow and action of liberating all sentient beings from suffering and bringing them to Buddhahood; and second, the direct realization of the Ultimate Truth. To signify these different aspects of Bodhicitta, Bodhi-Heart, Bodhi-Mind, enlightened heart or mind, etc., are alternatively used in this book. See Story 1, Note 20.

4 Nhamdog (T.T.: rNam.rTog.): This is also a very frequently used term in Buddhist texts. It has many meanings, such as the incessant flow of thoughts; illusory conceptions; uncontrollable and wild notions; and wrong ideas. See Story 1, Note 12.

5 Treading the Path of the Cemetery: Tantric yogis are urged to practice meditation in a cemetery, such surroundings being considered extremely helpful in furthering one's progress.

6 Measureless Palace (T.T.: gShal.Yas.Khan.): the heavenly "dwelling" of the Buddha in the "Pure Land," which transcends the limitation of space, and is immeasurable.

7 This implies an eclipse. See Note 1.

8 Deva (T.T.: lHa.): In Tibetan scriptures, all Buddhas, Bodhisattvas, heavenly beings, gods, and goddesses are called "Lha," but here it is used in a figurative sense.

9 Mahāyāna Buddhism teaches that all religious practices and spiritual efforts should be dedicated to the welfare and emancipation of all sentient beings.

10 Six Realms: the Six Worlds, or Lokas, in which different kinds of sentient beings live under different conditions. Devas, men, and asuras live in the upper three Lokas; animals, hungry ghosts, and denizens of hell, in the lower three.

11 Habitual thoughts, (T.T.: Bag.Chags.; Skt.: Vāsanā): According to Mahāyāna Buddhism, especially Yogācāra, sentient beings' consciousnesses are brought into play by the force of habitual thoughts. Reason and affect are all made up of the accumulated "psychic contents" that have been well-preserved in the Ālaya or Store Consciousness.

12 Suchness (T.T.: De.bShin.Ñid; Skt.: Tathatā), is also translated as "Thatness," implying that Absolute Reality is essentially indescribable; it is *as such* all the time.

13 Heart-air: See Story 1, Note 17.

14 Dharma-clinging (T.T.: Chos.hDsin.): According to Buddhism. there are two forms of clinging: (1) The Clinging-to-Ego (see Note 28), and (2) the Clinging-to-Dharma. The Clinging-to-Dharma implies an innate tendency to hold becomings and manifestations to be real and subsistent. The very conception of "being," declares Mahāyāna Buddhism, is a product of the Clinging-to-Dharma.

15 Self-awareness (T.T.: Rañ.Rig.): the self-aware or self-witnessing faculty of the consciousness which is, according to Yogācāra, the mind per se. The function of self-awareness is to be aware of the awareness itself; it is a pure awareness without any subject-content. To cultivate this pure awareness is the pinnacle practice of Mahāmudrā.

16 Distraction and drowsiness: These two hindrances are experienced by all who practice meditation — the two major enemies of the yogi.

17 The human mind is inclined either to cling to the "View of existence-and-permanency" (T.T.: rTag.lTa.), or to the "View of annihilation-and-non-existence" (T.T.: Chad.lTa.). The former holds to the eternal existence of true being, and the latter to the ultimate annihilation of all existence. The remedy for both of these extremes or "wrong views" is the Middle Way Doctrine upheld by Buddhism.

18 Or, subjectivity and objectivity: All Saṃsāric conceptions and emotions are characterized by a subjective-objective pattern — the knower and the known, the lover and the one loved, etc. This dualistic pattern of thought is the fundamental cause of Saṃsāra. Enlightenment is but the transformation and emancipation from the *two grasping jaws of the pincers* of dualism.

19 See Story 2, Note 21.

20 Joking words: Milarepa here alludes to his remarks in praise of the demoness Draug Srin Mo, made in the beginning of the first song, as merely ridicule.

21 Buddha and the Five Demons: On the eve of His enlightenment, Guatama Buddha conquered the demons of the Five Desires who came to afflict Him.

22 The stock, or accumulation of merits (T.T.: Tshogs.bSags.): another frequently used phrase in Buddhism. This term implies a rather complicated doctrine of Buddhist ethics. In brief, all the "states of well-being," worldly or religious, material or spiritual, Saṃsāric or Nirvāṇic, are brought into being through deeds-of-merit. Buddhahood is viewed as the consummation of all merits.

23 Bedma Tutrin (T.T.: Pat.Ma.Thod.Phreñ.): This is another name of Padma Saṃbhava, the great Indian Yogi, who founded the Ningmaba School of Tibet.

24 Violating the Precepts and one's Vows: This demoness once swore before Padma Saṃbhava to protect the Dharma and to observe the Precepts.

25 Three Times: Past, present, and future.

26 Passions (Skt.: Kleśas; T.T.: Ñon.Moñs.Pa.): This word is very difficult to translate into English accurately because of its various meanings. Usually it signifies the burning passions and desires, such as lust, hate, anger, blindness, distractions, and the like. Both the innate and the acquired desires which hinder the way to Nirvāṇa, are Kleśas.

27 Five Poisonous Cravings, or Five Klesas: Lust, hate, blindness, pride, and jealousy.

28 Clinging-to-Ego (Skt.: Ātma-grāha; T.T.: bDag.hDsin.): the delusion of a permanent, unconditioned Ego, which causes the continuation of Samsāric existence. The Clinging to Ego manifests itself in two forms, (1) the Innate or Inborn Ego, the fundamental notion of "self"; and (2) the acquired Ego, which is developed through experience and education.

29 Ceaseless mental activity or constant-flow-of-thought: Men's thoughts never stop, with or without their awareness. They continue to flow on unceasingly, like a waterfall.

30 The rules of Vajrayāna: Tantric or Samaya precepts.

31 Vajra Hell: The purgatory where all violators of Tantric precepts go.

32 Dorje Semba, (Skt.: Vajrasattva): Among the five "Maṇḍala" Buddhas, this is the one who sits in the center, sometimes also called Dorje-Chang, (Skt.: Vajradhara) from whom all the teachings of Tantra originated.

33 Succession: A transmission of Tantric teachings.

34 Waves-of-Grace: The blessing power that emanates from Gurus of a Succession. This blessing power, or grace-wave, is considered to be one of the determining factors of a yogi's success in his devotion. The speed of his accomplishment is said to depend largely on the intensity and amount of the grace-waves that he is capable of receiving from his Guru.

35 Hīnayāna, meaning the Small Vehicle, denotes the original form of Buddhism that developed after Sākyamuni's death. Hīnayāna Buddhism now prevails in Ceylon, Burma, and Siam, and is therefore also known as Southern Buddhism in contrast to Mahāyāna, meaning the Great Vehicle, now prevailing in Tibet, China, Korea, and Japan.

36 For the sake of respect and reverence, Draug Srin Mo called Milarepa "Trolgu," the Incarnation, or Transformation Body of Buddha (T.T.: sPrul.sKu.). However, Milarepa himself never claimed to be an incarnation of Buddha or a gifted, superior being. He asserted that he was an ordinary man.

37 Dharmata (T.T.: Chos.Ñid.), meaning the nature or truth of being.

38 Ālaya Consciousness or Store Consciousness (T.T.: Kun.gShi.rNam.Çes.): the Eighth Consciousness. This consciousness has more than ten different names, which appear in the different Buddhist texts, each indicating one of its aspects or characteristics. The philosophy of Yogācāra puts its main stress on the study of this Consciousness. "Kun.gShi.rNam.Çes." may be translated as "Universal or Primordial Consciousness," the "All-sources Consciousness," the "Conciousness of Ripening Karma," etc. A fair study of this Consciousness is necessary for a better understanding of the teachings of Mahāyāna and of Tantric Buddhism. See Story 10, Note 1.

39 The literal translation should be "the visions of ghosts." Milarepa referred to the conjurations of Draug Srin Mo.

40 The conception of "Yes and No," affirmation and negation.

41 Lit.: Form-nature (T.T.: mTshan.Ñid.). This word originally means defi-

nition, reason, essence, nature, etc. Here Milarepa used it in a very loose sense, implying something quite different from the above ordinary usage of this term.

42 Enlightened yogis always have a good sense of humor. Being fully aware of the limitation of words and the absurdity of human conceptions, they sometimes ridicule their own words, which also cannot escape the dilemma and predicament inherent in the human way of thinking and expression.

43 Great Bliss (T.T.: bDe.Chen.) implies the great ecstasy the yogi experiences in meditation.

44 Nectar: The literal translation should be, "The Nectar of Non-outflowing" (T.T.: Zag.Med.). Using yogic Power, the yogi may increase the secretion of the salivary glands to quench his feeling of thirst.

MILAREPA IN RAGMA

Obeisance to all Gurus

W^HEN the Jetsun Milarepa decided to go to Riwo Balnbar from Linba Draug to practice meditation, he notified his patrons in Ragma. They said, "Near Riwo Balnbar there is a temple in a very delightful place. We recommend that you stay there. As to Riwo Balnbar, we do not know very much about it. Revered One, you may remain in the temple at first; meantime, we will send out people to survey the region for you."

Milarepa thought to himself, "First I shall go to the temple for awhile, then I shall proceed to Riwo Balnbar." He then said to them, "I do not need your guide; I can find the way myself." When the patrons asked, "Do you have a guide?" Milarepa replied, "Yes, I have." "Who is he? Tell us more about him."

In answer Milarepa sang:

> The glorious and accomplished Guru
> Who dispels the darkness, is the guide.
>
> Away from cold and warmth, these cotton
> clothes,[1]
> By which I renounce fur-craving, are the guide.
>
> The Invocation, Identification, and
> Transformation Yogas[2]
> Which crush the delusion of Bardo, are
> the guide.
>
> That which shows you the way in all journeys
> through all lands—
> The complete mastery of Prāṇa-Mind[3]
> is the guide.

To give up one's body as a good-offering[4] —
The teaching of Subduing-the-Ego — is the guide.

To remain in solitude and practice meditation,
Leading one to Enlightenment, is the guide.

Led by these six guides, and abiding in
     Jaung Chub Tsong,[5]
All will be well with me.

Thereupon Milarepa went to the upper part of Ragma, which from that time on was called Jaung Chub Tsong. He then absorbed himself in the Samādhi of the Flowing River.[6]

One midnight, he heard a great noise and clamor, horns roaring in the air as if an army in battle were approaching. Milarepa thought, "Is there fighting in this country?" He then absorbed himself in the Samādhi of Great Compassion. But the sound came closer and closer. Both Heaven and earth seemed bathed in red light. Milarepa wondered what was happening. He looked about and saw that the whole plain was burning, that nothing was left on earth or in Heaven. A band of the [demon] army was busily engaged in lighting fires, tossing water, and throwing down mountains. Through innumerable conjurations, the demons threatened Milarepa with many types of weapons, tearing down the rocks and the cave, and also heaping him with abuse. Milarepa became aware that demons were assembling to afflict him. He thought, "What a pity, from time immemorial until now these sinful Ah Tsa Ma Demons[7] have practiced evil deeds in the Six Realms, thus becoming hungry specters flying in the sky. With vicious thoughts and evil intentions they have harmed so many sentient beings, that with this black Karma they have no choice but to go to a hell in their future life." With great compassion, therefore, Milarepa sang:

     I pay homage to you, Marpa the Translator.
     In the immense sky of your compassion
     Are gathered from all sides the clouds of mercy
     From which fell the productive rain of grace.
     Thus the harvest of your disciples was increased.
     To immeasurable sentient beings as infinite
          as space,
     Pray grant your grace-waves for the attainment
          of Enlightenment.

You assembled Non-men and demons,
You who fly and travel in the sky
Perpetually longing for food,
You hungry specters!
Driven by the force of Full-ripening Karma,[8]
In this life you were born as hungry ghosts;
Also by the Karma of evil-doing,
Through harming others,
You shall fall into a hell in your future life.
I sing of the truths of Karma.
Think closely on these beneficent words.

I am the son of Ghagyu Gurus;
With faith arising in my heart,
I am learning the Dharma.
Knowing the Law of Cause and of Effect,
I practice austere living;
Diligent and persevering,
I see the true nature of Mind.

I realize that all forms are but illusions [Māyā].
I thus free myself from the illness of ego-clinging,
I thus cut off the Subject-Object Fetter[9]
    of Saṃsāra,
And reach the Buddha's realm, the immutable Dharmakāya.

I am a yogi who has gone beyond the [human] mind;
How can you afflict me, you troublemakers?
Your vicious deeds and mischievous intentions,
Weary you, but do me no harm.

Again, you must know that mind is the
    source of hatred.
Though from the depths of the eighteen
    hells below
To the Heaven of Brahmā above,
You collect all the forces therein to
    throw against me,
It can hardly ripple my all-embracing Wisdom,
For in my mind no fear can arise.

You assembled demons and Non-men,
With all your spells and magic weapons,

You cannot hurt me;
All you have done is useless.
What a waste and pity if you return
    without harming me!
Show your power and do your worst, you
    pitiable demons.

Whereupon Milarepa became absorbed in the Samādhi of Suchness. [Awed and overpowered by his greatness], all the demons repented before him and became faithful to him. They made obeisance and circumambulated him many times, saying: "We were indeed blind, not knowing that you are such an accomplished yogi. Pray forgive us for what we have done to you. From now on we will follow whatever instructions you may give. Pray grant us the teachings, so a relationship in Dharma may thus be established between us."

Milarepa replied, "Very well. In that case I shall give you this teaching":

Refrain from sin,
Practice virtue!

All the demons cried, "Yes, we will obey!" Then they offered him their lives and hearts, and also promised the Jetsun to obey his orders. Following this, they all went back to their own realm.

Among them was one called Seyi Lhamo, from Mang, and others were local deities from Riwo Balnbar. Milarepa felt that, since the demons of Riwo Balnbar had already been subdued, it would not be necessary to go there to meditate any more. He decided to remain at the Bodhi-Place for a few days. In a very elated mood he sang:

Here in the home of Enlightenment,
I, the Bodhi-Path [practitioner], Milarepa,
Who has mastered the Mind-of-Bodhi,
Practice the Yoga of Bodhi-Heart.
I will soon obtain the great Bodhi,
And bring the innumerable mother-like beings[10]
To the sanctuary of Perfect Enlightenment.

One day, a patron came to Milarepa's hut bringing with him a load of wood and a half-measure of flour. The visitor did not wear enough clothes and felt very cold. He said, "Ragma is the coldest region in the South and this is the coldest place in Ragma. I would like, Lama, to offer you a fur coat if you would accept it."

Milarepa asked, "My dear patron, what is your name?" and the man replied, "Labar Shawa." Milarepa then said, "You have a very good name, indeed. Although I do not need your flour and fur coat, I thank you very much. I'll take the flour, if you wish, but as to the fur coat, I really do not need it." And he sang:

> As a child who loses his way home,
> The confused mind wanders in the Six
>   delusive Realms.
> By the force of illusory Karma,
> One sees a myriad visions and feels
>   endless emotions.
>
> Sometimes I have illusory feelings of hunger,
> Therefore I prepare my food and dinner.
> Sometimes I exert myself to build a house;[11]
> At others I endure the hardship of eating
>   stones.[12]
> Sometimes I eat the food of Śūnyatā [Voidness];
> Or I change my ways and do not eat at all.[13]
>
> At times when I feel thirsty, I drink pure
>   blue water;
> At others, I rely on my own secretions.
> Frequently, I drink the flow from the
>   Fountain of Compassion;
> Quite often, I sip enchanting nectar of goddesses.
>
> Sometimes I feel cold, so I wear the clothes
>   of the Two Channels;[14]
> At others, Heat Yoga gives burning bliss
>   and warmness.
>
> Occasionally, I change my ascetic way of life;
> At times when I feel like having friends
>   around me;
> I live with the Wisdom of Awareness as my companion.
>
> I practice the white deeds of the Ten Virtues;
> I contemplate the true knowledge of Reality,
> And know for certain the self-radiant mind.
>
> Adorned with the precious gem of true knowledge,

I am the Yogi Milarepa — a lion among men.

Proficient and victorious, I am skilled in
    meditation.
On the snow mountain I practice in solitude.
I am the yogi who obtains the fruits of merit,
I am the Yogi Milarepa, a tiger among men.

I have thrice animated the Bodhi-Mind,[15]
I smile with joy at the Non-distinction of
    Means and Wisdom;[16]
I dwell in the woods of the Radiant Valley
    of Remedy;[17]
And produce the fruits of the welfare of
    sentient beings.

I am the Yogi Milarepa—an eagle among men.
I have a pair of mighty wings of the clear-
    sighted Arising Yoga;[18]
I possess two flying wings of the stable
    Perfecting Yoga.[19]
I soar to the sky of Two-in-One Suchness;[20]
I sleep in the cave of transcendental Truth;
I attain the fruits of self and others' benefit.
I am the Yogi Milarepa—a man among men.

I am the one who sees the face of form,
I am he who gives good counsel.
I am a yogi without attributes.

I am a man who cares not what may happen.
I am an almsbeggar who has no food,
A nude hermit without clothes,
A beggar without jewels.
I have no place to lay my head;
I am the one who never thinks of external
    objects—
The master of all yogic action.

Like a madman, I am happy if death comes:
I have nothing and want nought.

If one desires to acquire property,

It only leads to jealousy and anger;
It merely causes trouble to the patrons
And leads them into erring ways of life.

To a yogi, all is fine and splendid!
With a benevolent heart and accompanying blessings,
Almsgiving should ever be your practice.

I wish you all happiness and prosperity;
I wish you good health, leisure, and long life.
May you, in the next life, be born in the Pure
      Land of Buddha,
There to practice [joyfully] the Dharma.
May you then be able without ceasing
To devote yourself to the welfare of all men.

Thereupon, great faith in the Jetsun was aroused in this man. He said, "Because you are the accomplished Yogi Milarepa, you can do without these things. It is only for the sake of benefiting us sinful people that you remain here. Pray pity me and take my offerings."

Thereafter, while Milarepa stayed at the Bodhi-Place, this man always brought bountiful food and provisions to him. Imbued with great joy, Milarepa remained there for some time.

One day, some villagers from Ragma came to see the Jetsun. They asked him, "Do you like this place? Do you feel happy in remaining here?" He replied, "Yes, I am very happy indeed. I am also greatly pleased with my progress." They asked "Why do you like this place so much? Why is it that you are so happy here? Pray tell us what you think of all these things!" In answer, Milarepa sang:

Here is the Bodhi-Place, quiet and peaceful.
The snow mountain, the dwelling place of
      deities, stands high above;
Below, far from here in the village, my
      faithful patrons live;
Surrounding it are mountains nestling in
      white snow.

In the foreground stand the wish-granting trees;
In the valley lie vast meadows, blooming wild.
Around the pleasant, sweet-scented lotus,
      insects hum;
Along the banks of the stream

And in the middle of the lake,
Cranes bend their necks, enjoy the scene,
    and are content.

On the branches of the trees, the wild birds sing;
When the wind blows gently, slow dances
    the weeping willow;
In the treetops monkeys bound and leap with joy;
In the wild green pastures graze the scattered herds,
And merry shepherds, gay and free from worry,
Sing cheerful songs and play upon their reeds.
The people of the world, with burning desires
    and craving,
Distracted by affairs, become the slaves of earth.

From the top of the Resplendent Gem Rock,
I, the Yogi, see these things.
Observing them, I know that they are fleeting
    and transient;
Contemplating them, I realize that comforts
    and pleasures
Are merely mirages and water-reflections.

I see this life as a conjuration and a dream.
Great compassion rises in my heart
For those without a knowledge of this truth.

The food I eat is the Space-Void;
My meditation is Dhyāna—beyond distraction.

Myriad visions and various feelings all
    appear before me—
Strange indeed are Saṃsāric phenomena!
Truly amusing are the dharmas in the
    Three Worlds,[21]
Oh, what a wonder, what a marvel!
Void is their nature, yet everything is manifested.

The villagers were [delighted with this song], and, with their faith
also strengthened, they all returned home [in a very joyful mood].

This is the first part of the story of Milarepa's stay at Ragma.

NOTES

1 The yogi who practices Heat Yoga is supposed to wear only cotton clothing, no fur being allowed. The purpose of this rigid practice is twofold: to renounce the procurement of fur and the craving for it, and to train himself for doing without furs in an extremely cold region such as Tibet, thus stimulating the production of more inner heat.

2 The Yogas (lit.: Instructions) of Invocation, Identification, and Transformation (T.T.: bSre.hPho.sKor.gSum.): In the Bardo plane (the intermediate stage between death and rebirth) the deceased sees numerous visions and images which are actually manifestations of his own mind. But, because of habitual-thinking and the Clinging-to-Ego, the uninitiated one cannot identify these visions and see into their true nature. Tantric Yoga not only serves the purpose of enabling one to realize the innate Buddhahood in this life, but also is a preparation for the stage of Bardo. When a proficient yogi sees the various manifestations of the Bardo, he can immediately identify the sound which he hears with the Mantra (or invocation) of his patron Buddha, and the images he sees with figures of the same. Through the practice of the Yogas of Invocation, Identification, and Transformation in this lifetime, the yogi is able to dispel the fear of Bardo. These three Yogas may be described as follows:

> (1) Invocation Yoga: By praying, and reciting the Mantra of a special patron Buddha, the yogi invokes the protection of that tutelary.
> (2) Identification Yoga: In Yoga practice, the yogi identifies or unites himself with the tutelary. Thus in the stage of Bardo, when wrathful and peaceful deities appear, the yogi may identify himself with them. (See W. Y. Evans-Wentz' "Tibetan Book of the Dead," Oxford University Press, London, 1957.)
> (3) Transformation Yoga: Through the practice of this Yoga the visions of the Bardo may be transformed at will.

3 Prāna-Mind or Energy-Mind (T.T.: Rluñ. Sems.): This is an important term in Tantrism. It is said that a yogi who has mastered the Mind-energy, or Energy-mind, is capable of performing supernormal feats, one of them being to fly wherever he chooses. (See also Story 3, Note 2.)

4 A special Tibetan Yoga called "gCod," devised for destroying one's Ego-clinging. In practicing this Yoga, the yogi offers his own body to sentient beings through special visualizations.

5 Jaung Chub Tsong: The Castle of Bodhi (T.T.: Byañ.Chub.rDson.).

6 Samādhi of the Flowing River: This refers to a mental state experienced by the yogi in Mahāmudrā practice, in which he feels he is free from attachment to all phenomena. Although immersed in phenomenal existence, he is not affected by it; he encompasses the flux of things, he watches the flux of becoming flow by. Though he is aware of the identity of himself and the flux, he knows that he is the master, and enjoys a liberated spirit within the great flow. (See also Story 2, Note 4.)

7 Ah Tsa Ma demons: See Story 2, Note 5.

8 Full-ripening Karma: See Story 2, Note 6.

9 Subject-Object Fetter: The doer, and that which is done; the seer, and that which is seen; etc. This dualistic pattern of thought is considered to be the basic cause of Saṃsāra.

10 Since in every incarnation one has a mother, from beginningless time one must have had innumerable mothers. In fact, according to Mahāyāna Buddhism,

all sentient beings have had, more than once, a parental relationship between one another. This calls forth the great compassion of a Bodhisattva.

11 This refers to Milarepa's labors for his Master, Marpa, in the trial period of his discipleship. (See Milarepa's Biography, "Tibet's Great Yogi, Milarepa," 2nd ed., edited by W. Y. Evans-Wentz, Oxford University Press, London, 1951.)

12 Eating stones: To avoid involvement in the world, a technique for eating stones in place of food is provided for determined Tantric yogis.

13 Through the power of Samādhi, the yogi is able to live without eating for a long time.

14 Two Channels (T.T.: rTsa.gÑis.): the mystical right and left Channels in the human body through which yogic heat powers are engendered. See also Story 1, Note 28.

15 The meaning of this sentence is not very clear. The translator believes that "thrice animated the Bodhi-Mind" signifies the complete unfoldment of the so-called three-fold Bodhi-Mind: (1) the Bodhisattva's Vow, (2) the Transcendental Bodhi-Mind, or the Non-distinction Wisdom, and (3) the "Occult" Bodhi-Mind, that is, according to Tantrism, the essence (semen), or the source-energy of the physical body.

16 Non-distinction of Means and Wisdom, or, rendered in a different way, the Two-in-One Means-Wisdom: The Bodhisattva's activity includes two main facets, (1) the cultivation of Wisdom, i.e., the practice and realization of the Prajñāpāramitā (Perfect Wisdom); and (2) the practice of Means or Virtue, i.e., the first five Pāramitās, namely, charity, discipline, patience, diligence, and meditation. Only advanced yogis are capable of realizing the Non-distinction or Non-differentiation of these two practices.

17 "Radiant" denotes the self-radiant or self-illuminating nature of Mind; "Valley of Remedy" denotes the realization of the Self-mind as being the cure or remedy for all evils.

18 Arising Yoga (T.T.: sKyed.Rim.): In the Anuttara Tantra, the Supreme Tantra, there are two major practices: one is the Arising Yoga, the other is the Perfecting Yoga. The former is the preparation for the latter — it places emphasis on concentration and visualization exercises, and through them the Dhyāna or Samādhi state is reached. Unless the yogi has reached a stage of advanced Dhyāna or Samādhi, he is not capable of practicing the latter.

19 Perfecting Yoga (T.T.: rDsogs.Rim.): the advanced Yoga of Tibetan Tantrism. It is a practice of uniting mind and Prāṇa. (See W. Y. Evans-Wentz' "Tibetan Yoga and Secret Doctrines," 2nd ed., Oxford University Press, London, 1958.)

20 Two-in-One Suchness: This term may also be rendered as "Non-dualistic Suchness." In the realm of Saṃsāra, different views and interpretations on a thing are formed from different levels and positions. To the average person, a glass of water is merely a means of quenching thirst; to a physicist, it is a combination of elements in motion; and to a philosopher, it is a series of relationships. These different views or understandings, arising from different levels and realms of thinking, are thus the distinctive characteristic of Saṃsāric thought, whereas in the Two-in-One or Many-in-One State, these different views do not exist as such.

21 The Three Worlds, or the Three Realms (T.T.: Khams.gSum.): According to Buddhism, these are the World of Desire, the World of Form, and the World of Non-form. They are believed to include all sentient beings in the various realms of Saṃsāric existence.

MILAREPA AT JUNPAN NANKA TSANG

Obeisance to all Gurus

FROM Ragma, Milarepa went to Junpan Nanka Tsang[1] and remained there for some time.

One day a monkey came to Milarepa's hut riding on a rabbit, wearing mushroom armor and carrying a bow and arrow made from stalks. [His appearance was so ludicrous that] Milarepa could not help laughing. The demon said to the Jetsun, "You came here through fear.[2] If you are no longer afraid, you can go away." Milarepa replied, "I realize fully that manifestation is Mind itself; also, I see that Mind-Essence is identical with the Dharmakāya. You pitiable wraith! Whatever apparitions you may conjure, they are a mere laughing matter to me." Thereupon, the demon made his offering and took an oath before Milarepa. Then, like a rainbow, he disappeared into the sky. He was the demon king of Dro Tang.

One day, Milarepa's patrons from Dro Tang came to visit him. They aaked him what benefits Junpan Nanka Tsang had to offer. In reply, Milarepa sang:

> I pray to my Guru, the Holy One.
> Listen, my patrons, and I will tell you
> the merits of this place.
>
> In the goodly quiet of this Sky Castle of Junpan
> High above, dark clouds gather;
> Deep blue and far below flows the River Tsang.
>
> At my back the Red Rock of Heaven rises;
> At my feet, wild flowers bloom, vibrant
> and profuse;

At my cave's edge [wild] beasts roam, roar,
    and grunt;
In the sky vultures and eagles circle freely,
While from heaven drifts the drizzling rain.

Bees hum and buzz with their chanting;
Mares and foals gambol and gallop wildly;
The brook chatters past pebbles and rocks;
Through the trees monkeys leap and swing;
And larks carol in sweet song.

The timely sounds I hear are all my fellows.
The merits of this place are inconceivable—
I now relate them to you in this song.

Oh, good patrons,
Pray follow my Path and my example;
Abandon evil, and practice good deeds.
Spontaneously from my heart
I give you this instruction.

There was a Tantric yogi among the patrons who said to Milarepa, "We would be deeply grateful if you would graciously give us the essential instructions on the View, Meditation, and Action,[3] as a greeting or a gift of welcome."
Milarepa sang in reply:

The grace of my Guru enters my heart;
Pray help me to realize the truth of the Void!

In answer to my faithful patrons,
I sing to please the Deities and Buddhas:

Manifestation, the Void, and Non-differentiation,
These three are the quintessence of the View.

Illumination, Non-thought, and Non-distraction
Are the quintessence of the Meditation.

Non-clinging, Non-attachment, and complete
    Indifference
Are the quintessence of the Action.

No Hope, no Fear, and no Confusion
Are the quintessence of Accomplishment.

Non-attempt, Non-hiding, and Non-discrimination,
These three are the quintessence of the Precept.

Having heard Milarepa's song, the patrons all returned home. A few days later, many disciples came again to visit the Jetsun, asking after his health and welfare, and giving their best wishes. Milarepa sang in response:

I bow down at the feet of my Guru.

Deep in the forest by man untrod,
I, Milarepa, happily practice meditation.

With no attachment and no clinging,
Walking and tranquility are both pleasing.

Free from sickness and disorder, I willingly
    sustain this body of illusion;
Never sleeping, I sit in the comfort of quietude.

Abiding in the Samādhi of Non-permanence,[4]
    I taste enjoyment.
Continuance in Heat-Yoga without cold is
    indeed felicitous.

With no cowardliness or dismay,
Joyfully I follow the Tantric practice;
With no effort I perfect the cultivation;
With no distraction whatsoever,
Remaining in solitude, I am truly happy.
These are the pleasures of the body.

Happy is the path of both Wisdom and Means![5]
Happy the Yoga of Arising and Perfecting;
    the meditation of the Two-in-One.
Happy the Prajñā; the awareness of no-
    coming-and-going!
Happy the absence of talk; no friends and
    no chatting!
These are the pleasures of words.

Happy is the understanding of Non-grasping;
Happy the meditation without interruption;
Happy the accomplishment without hope or fear;
Happy the action done without defilement.
These are the pleasures of Mind.

Happy is the illumination with no thought
  and no mutation!
Happy the great bliss in the purity of
  Dharmadhātu![6]
Happy the Non-ceasing Realm of Form!

This little song of great happiness
That flows freely from my heart,
Is inspired by meditation,
By the merging of act and knowledge.
Those who aim at the fruit of Bodhi
May follow this way of yogic practice.

The disciples said to Milarepa, "Wonderful indeed are the joys of Body, Word, and Mind, as you have just said. Pray tell us, how were they brought about?" Milarepa replied, "By the *realization* of Mind." The disciples then said, "Although we shall never be able to acquire such happiness and pleasures as you have enjoyed, we hope that we can win a small portion; we beg you, therefore, to give us a clear teaching, easy to understand and simple to practice, by which we may realize the Essence of Mind." Whereupon the Jetsun sang "The Twelve Meanings of Mind":

I bow down at the feet of my Guru.

Oh good patrons! If you wish to realize
  the Essence of Mind,
You should practice the following teachings:
Faith, knowledge, and discipline,
These three are the Life-Tree[7] of Mind.
This is the tree you should plant and foster.

Non-attachment, non-clinging, and non-blindness,
These three are the shields of Mind;
They are light to wear, strong for defense,
And the shields you should seek.

Meditation, diligence, and perseverance,
These three are the horses of Mind;
They run fast and quickly flee!
If you look for horses, these are the right ones.

Self-awareness, self-illumination, and
     self-rapture,[8]
These three are the fruits of Mind;
Sow the seeds, ripen the fruit,
Refine the fluid, and the essence emerges.
If you look for fruit, these are the fruit
     you should seek.

Sprung from yogic intuition,
This song of the Twelve Meanings of Mind is sung.
Inspired by your faith, continue with your
     practice, my good patrons!

Henceforth, the patrons placed even more faith in Milarepa, and brought him excellent offerings. Milarepa then decided to go to Yolmo Snow Range.

This is the story of Milarepa at Junpan Nanka Tsang [The Sky Castle of Junpan].

NOTES

1 Junpan Nanka Tsan (T.T.: rKañ.Phan.Nam.mKhah.rDsoñ.): a place near the Himalaya Mountains, meaning "The Sky Castle of Junpan."

2 Fear: the fear of suffering in Saṃsāra, that motivates the yogi's striving for emancipation.

3 View, Meditation, and Action; or View, Practice, and Action (T.T.: lTa., sGom., sPyod.): "View" is the knowledge or principle upon which all meditations are based and religious activities conducted. "Practice" refers to the yogic exercise of the View; "Action" to a state in which the yogi is absorbed in the View while carrying out his daily activities. The following example illustrates these terms: In the case of the Mahāmudrā teaching, the View is the understanding of the void nature of Mind; the Practice is the contemplation on this understanding; and the Action is the mindfulness of this View in daily activities, meaning that the yogi is able to remember his meditation experience even during all the vicissitudes of his daily existence.

4 Non-permanence: The realization of higher Samādhis should transcend both transitoriness and permanence.

5 Wisdom and Means (Skt.: Prajñā [and] Upāya; T.T.: Thabs. [and] Çes. Rab.): Wisdom is the understanding, or the View, or the "eye" of the yogi, while Means are the methods, the techniques, or the "legs."

6 Dharmadhātu (T.T.: Chos.dWyin.): This term has several different meanings. Here it means the Universal, Infinity, Totality, and the like.

7 Life-Tree (T.T.: Srog.Çiñ.): a symbolic term used to denote the life force upon which the existence of one's life depends. It also refers to the spine. Sometimes it denotes the center pillar in Buddhist stūpas.

8 Self-awareness, self-illumination, self-rapture (T.T.: Rañ.Ri., Rañ.gSal., Rañ bDe.): Despite the fact that the nature of Mind is indescribable, it can be apprehended through an illustration of its three main characteristics, i.e., self-awareness, self-illumination, and self-rapture, of which, though existing all the time, the uninitiated are not aware. Being conscious of consciousness (or self-awareness) is to approach the threshold of Enlightenment; the self-illuminating and self-rapturous aspects of mind were claimed by Buddhist sages, who found, in their mystical experiences, that the mind was itself illuminating and blissful.

THE SONG
OF A YOGI'S JOY

Obeisance to all Gurus

THE Master of Yoga, the Jetsun Milarepa, in obedience to his Guru's orders, went from Junpan to Yolmo Snow Range, where he dwelt at the Tiger Cave of Senge Tson[1] in the woods of Singalin. The local goddess of Yolmo appeared in a gracious form, obeying the Jetsun's orders and rendering her best service to him. Milarepa remained there for some time in a deeply inspired mood.

One day, five young nuns came from Mon to visit him. They addressed him thus: "It is said that this place is full of terror, and an ideal place in which to attain great improvement in meditation. Can this be true? Have you found it so?" Milarepa then sang in praise of the place:

> Obeisance to you, my Guru!
> I met you through having accumulated great merits,
> And now stay at the place you prophesied.[2]
>
> This is a delightful place, a place of hills
>   and forests.
> In the mountain-meadows, flowers bloom;
> In the woods dance the swaying trees!
> For monkeys it is a playground.
> Birds sing tunefully,
> Bees fly and buzz,
> And from day until night the rainbows come and go.
> In summer and winter falls the sweet rain,
> And mist and fog roll up in fall and spring.
> At such a pleasant place, in solitude,

I, Milarepa, happily abide,
Meditating upon the void-illuminating Mind.

Oh, happy are the myriad manifestations!
The more ups-and-downs, the more joy I feel.
Happy is the body with no sinful Karma,
Happy indeed are the countless confusions!
The greater the fear, the greater the
      happiness I feel.[3]
Oh, happy is the death of sensations and passions!

The greater the distress and passions,
The more can one be blithe and gay!
What happiness to feel no ailment or illness;
What happiness to feel that joy and suffering
      are one;
What happiness to play in bodily movement
With the power aroused by Yoga.
To jump and run, to dance and leap, is
      more joyful still.

What happiness to sing the victorious song,
What happiness to chant and hum,
More joyful still to talk and loudly sing!
Happy is the mind, powerful and confident,
Steeped in the realm of Totality.

The most extreme happiness
Is the self-emanation of self-power;
Happy are the myriad forms, the myriad revelations.
As a welcoming gift to my faithful pupils,
I sing of yogic happiness.

Thereupon, Milarepa initiated the five young nun-novices and gave them the verbal instructions. After practicing these teachings for some time, the light of inner Realization was born within them. Milarepa was overjoyed and sang the "Nectar of Instruction":

Oh, my Guru, he who shows
The unmistakable path to Liberation,
The Perfect Savior, the great Compassionate One,
Pray, never leave me, ever remain
Above my head[4] as my crest-jewel!

Hearken, followers of the Dharma,
Ye meditators seated here,
Though the teachings of Buddha are most numerous,
He who can practice this Profound Path[5]
Is gifted indeed!

If you wish to become a Buddha in one lifetime,
You should not crave the things of this life,
Nor intensify your self-longing,
Else you will be entangled between good and evil,
And you may fall into the realm of misery.

When you give service to your Guru,
Refrain from thinking, "I am the one who works,
He is the one who enjoys."
Should you have this kind of feeling,
Quarrel and discord will surely follow,
And your wish can never be fulfilled.

When you observe the Tantric Precepts,
Cease association with the vicious,
Else you will be contaminated by evil influences,
And you may risk breaking the Precepts.

When you engage in study and learning,
Do not attach yourself to words with pride,
Else the dormant fire of the Five
    Poisonous Passions[6] will blaze,
And virtuous thoughts and deeds will be consumed.

When you meditate with friends in retreat,
Do not attempt too many things,
Else your virtuous deeds will cease,
And your devotion will be distracted.

When you practice the Path with Form[7]
    of the Whispered Transmission,[8]
Do not exorcise demons, nor curse ghosts for others,
Lest demons rise within your mind
And a longing for worldly aims will blaze.

When you have acquired Experience and
    Realization,[9]

Do not display your miraculous powers, nor prophesy,
Lest the secret words and symbols slip away
And merits and spiritual insight will diminish.

Beware of these pitfalls and avoid them.
Commit not evil deeds. Eat not beguiling food.
Take not the burden of the corpse.[10]
Utter not sweet words to please others.
Be humble and modest, and you will find your way.

The nuns then asked Milarepa how they might find their own way, beseeching him for further instruction. In reply, Milarepa sang:

I pay homage to my Guru, the gracious one.
I pray you to vouchsafe me your grace-waves.
Pray help me, the mendicant, happily to meditate.

Though you children of the new generation
Dwell in towns infested with deceitful Karma,
The link of Dharma still remains.
Because you have heard the Buddha's teaching
You now come to me,
And thus avoid going astray.

By constant practice of the Accumulation-
    of-Merits[11]
You will foster an aptitude for devotion.
The grace-waves will then enter you,
While the corresponding and actual
    Realization[12] will grow.

But even if you do all this, it will help
    but little
If you cannot reach full mastery.
Having pity on you, I now give you this instruction.
Listen closely, my young friends!

When you remain in solitude,
Think not of the amusements in the town,
Else the evil one will rise up in your heart;
Turn inward your mind,
And you will find your way.

When you meditate with perseverance and
    determination,
You should think upon the evils of Saṃsāra
And the uncertainty of death.
Shun the craving for worldly pleasures;
Courage and patience then will grow in you,
And you will find your way.

When you solicit the deep teachings of
    the Practice,
Do not long for learning, nor to become a scholar,
Else worldly actions and desires will dominate;
Then this very life will be thrown away.
Be humble and modest,
And you will find your way.

When the various experiences come to you
    in meditation,
Do not be proud and anxious to tell people,
Else you will disturb the Goddesses and Mothers.[13]
Meditate without distractions,
And you will find your way.

When you accompany your Guru,
Do not look upon his merits or demerits,
Else you will find mountains of faults.
Only with faith and loyalty
Will you find your way.

When you attend holy meetings
With brothers and sisters in the Dharma,
Do not think of heading the row,
Else you will arouse both hate and craving,
And offend against the Precepts.
Adjust yourselves, understand each other,
And you will find your way.

When you beg for alms in the village,
Do not use the Dharma for deceit and exploitation,
Else you will force yourself down to the lower Path.
Be honest and sincere,
And you will find your way.

Beyond all else remember, at all times and places,
Never be overweening, nor of yourself be proud,
Else you will be overbearing in your self-esteem
And overloaded with hypocrisy.
If you abandon deceit and pretense,
You will find your way.

The person who has found the way
Can pass on the gracious teachings to others;
Thus he aids himself and helps the others, too.
To give is then the only thought
Remaining in his heart.

The disciples were all greatly inspired with the determination to practice diligently and to renounce the world. An unalterable faith in the Jetsun was established in them. They said, "We want to offer you a golden Maṇḍala.[14] Pray accept it, and give us the practical teaching of the View, Practice, and Action."

Milarepa replied, "I do not need the gold; you may use it to maintain your meditation. As for the teaching of the View, Practice, and Action, I shall tell you. Pray hearken to my song":

Oh, my Guru! The Exemplar of the View,
     Practice, and Action,
Pray vouchsafe me your grace, and enable me
To be absorbed in the realm of Self-nature!

For the View, Practice, Action, and Accomplishment
There are three Key-points you should know:

All the manifestation, the Universe itself,
     is contained in the mind;
The nature of Mind is the realm of illumination
Which can neither be conceived nor touched.
These are the Key-points of the View.

Errant thoughts are liberated in the Dharmakāya;
The awareness, the illumination, is always
     blissful;
Meditate in a manner of non-doing and non-effort.
These are the Key-points of Practice.

In the action of naturalness

The Ten Virtues spontaneously grow;
All the Ten Vices are thus purified.
By corrections or remedies
The Illuminating Void is ne'er disturbed.[15]
These are the Key-points of Action.

There is no Nirvāṇa to attain beyond;
There is no Saṃsāra here to renounce;
Truly to know the Self-mind
It is to be the Buddha Himself.
These are the Key-points of Accomplishment.

Reduce inwardly the Three Key-points to One.
This One is the Void Nature of Being,
Which only a wondrous Guru
Can clearly illustrate.

Much activity is of no avail;
If one sees the Simultaneously Born[16] Wisdom,
He reaches his goal.

For all practitioners of Dharma
This preaching is a precious gem;
It is my direct experience from yogic meditation.
Think carefully and bear it in your minds,
Oh, my children and disciples.

The disciples then asked Milarepa, "As we understood you, the un-mistakable guide along the Path of Practice is to pray to one's Guru with great earnestness. Is there anything else beyond this?" Milarepa smiled and answered, "The Tree of Guidance has also many branches."
In explaining this to them, he sang:

The Guru, the disciple, and the secret teachings;
Endurance, perseverance, and the faith;
Wisdom, compassion, and the human form;
All these are ever guides upon the Path.

Solitude with no commotion and disturbance
Is the guide protecting meditation.
The accomplished Guru, the Jetsun,
Is the guide dispelling ignorance and darkness.
Faith without sorrow and weariness

Is the guide which leads you safely to happiness.

The sensations of the five organs
Are the guides which lead you to freedom
   from "contact."[17]
The verbal teachings of the Lineage Gurus
Are the guides which illustrate the Three
   Bodies of Buddha.
The protectors, the Three Precious Ones,
Are the guides with no faults or mistakes.
Led by these six guides,
One will reach the happy plane of Yoga—
Abiding in the realm of Non-differentiation
In which all views and sophisms[18] are no more.

Remaining in the realm of self-knowledge
   and self-liberation
Is indeed happy and joyful;
Abiding in the valley where no men dwell,
With confidence and knowledge, one lives
   in his own way.
With a thundering voice,
He sings the happy song of Yoga.
Falling in the Ten Directions is the rain of fame;
Brought to blooming are the flowers and
   leaves of Compassion.
The enterprise of Bodhi encompasses the Universe;
The pure fruit of the Bodhi-Heart thus
   attains perfection.

The disciples thought, "It makes no difference now to the Jetsun where he stays. We will invite him to our village." Thereupon they said to Milarepa, "Revered One, since your mind no longer changes, there is no need for you to practice meditation. Therefore, for the sake of sentient beings please come to our village and preach the Dharma for us." Milarepa replied, "Practicing meditation in solitude is, in itself, a service to the people. Although my mind no longer changes, it is still a good tradition for a great yogi to remain in solitude." He then sang:

Through the practice [of meditation] I
   show gratitude to my Guru.
Pray grant me your grace, ripen and liberate me.

You, gifted disciples, the followers of Dharma,
Heed carefully, with all attention
While I sing of the profound Essential Teaching.

The great lioness in the upper snow mountain
Poses proudly on the summit of the peak;
She is not afraid—
Proudly dwelling on the mountain
Is the snow lion's way.

The queen vulture on Red Rock
Stretches her wings in the wide sky;
She is not afraid of falling—
Flying through the sky is the vulture's way.

In the depths of the great ocean
Darts the Queen of fish, glittering;
She is not afraid—
Swimming is the fish's way.

On the branches of the oak trees,
Agile monkeys swing and leap;
They are not afraid of falling—
Such is the wild monkey's way.

Under the leafy canopy of the dense wood,
The striped tiger roams and swiftly runs,
Not because of fear or worry—
This shows her haughty pride,
And is the mighty tiger's way.

In the wood on Singa Mountain,
I, Milarepa, meditate on Voidness,
Not because I fear to lose my understanding—
Constant meditation is the yogi's way.

Without distraction, the yogi meditates absorbed
Upon the pure Maṇḍala of Dharmadhātu,
Not because he fears to go astray—
But to hold to Self-quintessence is the yogi's way.

When he works on the Nādis, Prāṇa, and Bindu[19]
He avoids hindrances and errors,

Not that the teaching has faults in itself —
But it is a good way to improve true Realization.

With natural and spontaneous behavior
One surely meets with countless ups-and-downs,[20]
Not because there is discrimination and
    dualistic thought —
But because to manifest all, is causation's nature.

When he develops other beings by
    demonstrating the power of Karma,
Though seemingly he sees as real both good and evil,
It is not because he has gone astray in his
    practice,[21]
But because, to explain the truth to different
    people,
He must use appropriate illustrations.

Those great yogis who have mastered the Practice,
Never desire anything in this world.
It is not because they want fame that
    they remain in solitude;
It is the natural sign springing from their hearts—
The true feeling of non-attachment and renunciation.

Yogis who practice the teaching of the
    Path Profound,
Dwell always in caves and mountains;
Not that they are cynical or pompous,
But to concentrate on meditation is their
    self-willing.

I, the cotton-clad,[22] have sung many songs,
Not to amuse myself by singing sophistries,
But for your sake, faithful followers who
    assemble here,
From my heart I have spoken words helpful
    and profound.

The disciples then said to Milarepa, "One may live alone in solitude, but it is necessary to have food and a suitable dwelling in which
he can meditate properly." The Jetsun replied, "I have my own food
and dwelling which I will illustrate to you."

I bow down at the feet of the wish-fulfilling Guru.
Pray vouchsafe me your grace in bestowing
     beneficial food,
Pray make me realize my own body as the
     house of Buddha,
Pray grant me this sure knowledge.

I built the house[23] through fear,
The house of Sūnyatā, the void nature of being;
Now I have no fear of its collapsing.
I, the Yogi with the wish-fulfilling gem,
Feel happiness and joy where'er I stay.

Because of the fear of cold, I sought for clothes;
The clothing I found is the Ah Shea Vital Heat.[24]
Now I have no fear of coldness.

Because of the fear of poverty, I sought for riches;
The riches I found are the inexhaustible
     Seven Holy Jewels.[25]
Now I have no fear of poverty.

Because of the fear of hunger, I sought for food;
The food I found is the Samādhi of Suchness.
Now I have no fear of hunger.

Because of the fear of thirst, I sought for drink;
The heavenly drink I found is the wine
     of mindfulness.[26]
Now I have no fear of thirst.

Because of the fear of loneliness, I searched
     for a friend;
The friend I found is the bliss of
     perpetual Sūnyatā.[27]
Now I have no fear of loneliness.

Because of the fear of going astray,
I sought for the right path to follow.
The wide path I found is the Path of
     Two-in-One.[28]
Now I do not fear to lose my way.

I am a yogi with all desirable possessions,
A man always happy where'er he stays.

Here at Yolmo Tagpu Senge Tson,
The tigress howling with a pathetic, trembling cry,
Reminds me that her helpless cubs are
    innocently playing.
I cannot help but feel a great compassion for them,
I cannot help but practice more diligently,
I cannot help but augment thus my Bodhi-Mind.

The touching cry of the monkey,
So impressive and so moving,
Cannot help but raise in me deep pity.
The little monkey's chattering is amusing
    and pathetic;
As I hear it, I cannot but think of it with
    compassion.

The voice of the cuckoo is so moving,
And so tuneful is the lark's sweet singing,
That when I hear them I cannot help but listen—
When I listen to them,
I cannot help but shed my tears.

The varied cries and cawing of the crow,
Are a good and helpful friend unto the yogi.
Even without a single friend,
To remain here is a pleasure.
With joy flowing from my heart, I sing this happy song;
May the dark shadow of all men's sorrows
Be dispelled by my joyful singing.

The disciples were all deeply moved, and a feeling of weariness with Saṃsāra overwhelmed them. They swore to Milarepa that they would never leave the mountain. Afterwards, through the practice of meditation, they all reached the state of perfection.

One day, Milarepa's patron Buddha[29] told him the time had come for him to go to Tibet proper and there meditate in solitude to help sentient beings. The patron Buddha also prophesied the success of his career in helping people and in spreading the Dharma. Hence, about this time, Milarepa decided to go to Tibet.

This is the story of Yolmo Snow Mountain.

NOTES

1 T.T.: sTag.Pug.Sen.Ge.rDson. — the Tiger Cave at Lion Place.

2 Marpa, Milarepa's Guru, admonished Milarepa to remain in solitude for most of his life. He also prophesied as to those places wherein Milarepa should practice meditation.

3 The one who practices Mahāmudrā should know that, from the ultimate viewpoint, Saṃsāra is Nirvāna, evil is good, Kleśas are Bodhi. The up-and-down feelings, or the vicissitudinous emotions occurring in meditation, do not in their ultimate sense differ from Mind-Essence. To an advanced yogi, the greater the Kleśas that arise in his mind, the brighter, deeper, and better his illumination as to Reality.

4 According to Tantrism the Guru is even more important than Buddha. To be blessed by one's Guru is of the utmost importance. According to Tibetan tradition, in the beginning of any type of meditation, the yogi always visualizes the Guru sitting above his head, and prays to him.

5 Here Milarepa implies the teaching of advanced Tantrism.

6 The Five Poisonous Passions or Desires (the Five Kleśas) are lust, hate, blindness, pride, and jealousy.

7 Path with Form: the Arising Yoga and the Perfecting Yoga of Tantrism (see the translator's comments in the Appendix, and Story 5, Notes 18 and 19).

8 Whispered Transmission (T.T.: sÑan.brGyud.): (1) We are told that in olden days the hidden teachings of Tantra were given to the disciples in a most secret manner, i.e., through whispering; (2) this term is used as another name for the Ghagyuba School, the School of Marpa and Milarepa.

9 Experience (T.T.: Ñams.) and Realization (T.T.: rTogs.): These two words, Ñams. and rTogs., are difficult to translate into adequate English. Ñams is the indirect, incomplete, imperfect, and "half-opaque" experience and understanding that the yogi attains in meditation; while rTogs (Realization) is the direct, complete, clear, and perfect experience. The former is *similar* to Enlightenment, while the latter is the *real Enlightenment*. Ñams is like the experience of a traveler approaching a city who sees the city as a whole, but has not yet reached it: nevertheless, he gets an over-all picture and impression. However, Realization (rTogs.) of the city comes when he is *in* the city and knows what it really is at first hand.

10 This means, "Do not unscrupulously take the offerings of the relatives of a deceased person."

11 "Accumulation of Merits" (T.T.: Tshogs.bSags.) is a frequently used Buddhist term that can be explained in a variety of ways. Generally it means all the virtuous and spiritual practices. Specifically, in Mahāyāna Buddhism, it denotes the first five Pāramitās of the Bodhisattva, i.e., charity, discipline, patience, diligence, and meditation. See Story 9, Note 8.

12 Corresponding and actual Realization (T.T.: Ñams.rTogs.): Realization or Englightenment brought about in meditation usually follows a sequence: the corresponding, or resembling Realization comes first; the actual Realization follows: See Note 9.

13 Mothers: Here this term seems to imply the Mother-Divinities such as Tārā, Dorje Paumo, Lhamo, and others.

14 Maṇḍala, in this case, signifies a Tantric utensil for sacramental offerings.

The original meaning of the word "Maṇḍala" is "circle" or "center"; it is a complex design of a picture that symbolizes the phenomenal world of Tantric Buddhas.

15 "Corrections and remedies" here imply all the conscious efforts toward preventing or remedying "wrong-doings," which are, in reality, not against the Illuminating Void, but rather identical with it. Illumination and Voidness are the two immanent characteristics of Mind for which no corrections or remedies are needed.

16 Simultaneously Born Wisdom (T.T.: Lhan.Cig.sKyes.Pahi.Ye.Çes.): When one is born the Wisdom of Buddhahood is also born with him, implying that the Buddha-nature is innate and exists all the time. See Story 3, Note 18.

17 "Contact": All the sensations and perceptions are produced through contact of the consciousness with objects.

18 Lit.: Beyond empty words or sophisms, away-from-playwords, or away-from-nonsense (T.T.: sPros.Bral.). All ideas, such as monism, dualism, being or non-being, existence or non-existence, etc. — all these conceptual notions — are equal to empty words, playwords, or nonsense to enlightened beings.

19 Nāḍis, Prāna, and Bindu (T.T.: rTsa.rLuñ. [and] Thig.Le.): The Path-with-Form of Tantrism emphasizes the physical practice as well as the mental practice. In order to build up a favorable condition in which the realization of transcendental Truth may easily be achieved, Tantrism provides exercises to purify the nervous, breathing, and excretory systems.

20 "Ups-and-downs" here signifies the fluctuating actions and emotions in daily activity.

21 To those who have not reached the state of the Perfect Mutual-containing, or the Non-discriminating Whole, the antithetical aspect of being, which originates from dualistic ideas, becomes the paramount obstacle that debars them from realizing the non-differentiated Totality. Also, it produces a belief in the incompatibility of opposites, i.e., of being and non-being, existence and non-existence, etc. — in this case, Voidness and moral values. In certain aspects, the yogi who realizes the teaching of Voidness should not even see the existence of good and evil in his practice.

22 Cotton-clad (T.T.: Ras.Pa.): The yogi who is able to produce bodily heat through Yoga, thus wearing only cotton clothes in severe cold weather, is called Repa (Ras.Pa.).

23 This house is, of course, symbolic; but Milarepa did build many houses for Marpa before he was accepted by him.

24 Ah Shea (T.T.: Ā.Çad.) Vital Heat: the heat produced in Tantric meditation. See "The Six Yogas of Nāropa," in "Tibetan Yoga and Secret Doctrines," edited by W. Y. Evans-Wentz.

25 The Seven Holy Jewels are: gold, silver, crystal, ruby, coral, agate, and carnelian. Here Milarepa spoke of them in a figurative sense.

26 The text is not clear here. The translator presumes that it implies the voluntary springing forth of secretion through self-suggestion, by the yogic power.

27 Perpetual Sūnyatā: the eternal Voidness.

28 Path of Two-in-One (T.T.: Lam.Zuñ.hJug.): A very widely used phrase in Tibetan Buddhism. It means the unification of antitheses, the joining of opposing forces, the merging of differentiations, and the like.

29 Patron Buddha (T.T.: Yi.Dam.): Every Tantric yogi has a chosen patron Buddha, who is his protector, to whom he prays, and upon whom he relies.

8

MILAREPA
AND THE PIGEON

Obeisance to all Gurus

IN ACCORDANCE with the prophecy [of his Patron Buddha], Milrepa went to Tibet proper from Yolmo. He arrived at Gu Tang and lived in a cave, absorbing himself in the Meditation of the Great Illumination.

One day a pigeon wearing golden ornaments came to Milarepa. The bird nodded, bowed, and circled him many times. Then it flew away in the direction of the Immaculate Rock. Milarepa understood that this must be a spell of the Non-men to make him welcome. So he followed the pigeon and went up to the hill, where he found a heap of white rice. The bird pecked the rice with its bill and brought some to Milarepa as if showing him hospitality and welcome. Milarepa, [surprised and delighted], broke into song:

> Oh! My gracious Guru, Marpa Lho Draug Wa,
> From the depth of my heart I think of you.
> In deepest earnestness I meditate on you.
> That I never be separated from you, is my prayer.
>
> Merging the Self-mind with the Guru is indeed
>   a happy thing.
> Manifestation itself is the essence of Reality.
> Through the realization of this unborn Dharmakāya,
> I merge myself in the Realm of Non-effort.[1]
> To both the high and low Views[2] am I indifferent.
> In the mind of Non-effort I feel happiness and joy.
>
> The nature of Mind is the Light and the Void.

By realizing the awareness of Light-Void,
I merge myself in the original state of Non-effort.
To good and bad experiences am I indifferent.
With a mind of Non-effort, I feel happiness and joy.

The Six Senses and Sense Objects³ of themselves
        dissolve [into the Dharmadhātu].
Where the Non-differentiation of subject
        and object is realized.
I merge happiness and sorrow into one;
I enter the original state of Non-effort.
To right and wrong actions, am I indifferent.
Happy indeed is the Non-effort mind.

The very nature of the Dharmakāya
Is identified through its myriad forms;
The myriad forms are the Nirmāṇakāya of Buddha.
With this understanding in mind,
Whatever circumstance I may encounter,
I am free in the happy realm of Liberation!
To return to the home of Buddha
I have no longing!
Happy indeed is this mind of Non-effort.

Whereupon the pigeon, with seven companions, came nearer to Milarepa. They all bowed to him and circled him many times, as the first bird had done before. Milarepa thought, "These pigeons must be Non-men. I shall ask them and see whether they will tell the truth." So he said, "Who are you, and why do you come here?" The pigeons then broke the spell and displayed their real forms as female Devas. Their leader said, "We are the angel-maidens of Heaven. Because we have great faith in you, we come here to learn the Dharma from you. We beseech you to give us the instructions."

In response, Milarepa sang:

Oh! The wondrous Transformation Body of my Guru!
Pray, kindly grant me your grace-wave.

You eight charming maidens of Heaven,
Who appeared just now in pigeon form,
Your spell was fine, and in conformity
        with the Dharma!
If you, the eight beautiful maidens of Heaven,

Wish to practice the white Dharma of Buddha,
Pray remember the meaning of this song.

Though worldly happiness and pleasure
Seem delightful and pleasing,
They soon will pass away.

Though high-ranking ladies are proud and exultant
In their lofty dignity,
What refuge and shelter do they have?

To dwell in the fiery home of Saṃsāra
Sometimes seems pleasant, but is mostly misery.

If a well-endowed and well-loved son
Has no self-respect and makes no self-effort,
His father will meet nothing but distress.

If a disciple commits evil deeds,
He must fall into Saṃsāra,
No matter how superb his Guru may be.

You maidens of Heaven, the conjurers of
    the pigeons!
It is easy for you to ask for Dharma,
But hard to have deep faith in it.
You should remind yourselves
Of the inevitable misfortunes
Connected with worldly joys.
The pains and miseries of this life,
You should regard as friends leading
    you toward Nirvāṇa.
As for me, I am very grateful for
The misfortunes I have met.
Oh, my friends, bear this in mind, and do the same!

The Devas smiled at Milarepa and said, "We shall do so." Then
they made obeisance and circumambulated him many times. The Jetsun then asked the angels, "Why did you come here in pigeon form?"
They replied, "You are a yogi who has not the slightest attachment
to yourself, nor any desire for this worldly life. It is only for the
sake of Bodhi and the welfare of sentient beings that you have remained in solitude and meditated without distraction. With our heav-

enly eyes, we have been able to see you; and with respect and faith
we now come to you for Dharma. But in order to [conceal our real
form from] sinful beings, we have transformed ourselves into pigeons.
We pray that your Reverence will now be kind enough to go up into
Heaven with us to preach the righteous Dharma for us." But Milarepa
replied, "As long as life lasts, I shall remain in this world to benefit
sentient beings here. You must know that *Heaven is far from de-*
pendable; it is not eternal, and one should not rely on it. To be born
in Heaven is not necessarily a wonderful thing. You should pay heed
and follow these instructions":

> I bow down at the feet of Marpa Lho Draug.
> Oh, Father Guru! Pray grant me your
> > grace-wave and accomplishment.

> You, eight beauties of the Deva-realm,
> Have offered me white rice, the wondrous
> > fruit of Dhyāna.
> Eating it my body is strengthened, and my
> > mind enlivened.
> As a token of my gratitude, I sing this
> > song of Dharma to you.
> Now, lift up your ears, and listen to me carefully.

> Even though one reaches the highest Heaven
> > of the White Devas,[4]
> It has no permanent value and meaning!
> Lovable and touching are those flowers of
> > youth in Heaven.
> But however pleasant it may seem to be,
> In the end comes separation.

> Although the bliss in Heaven seems to be very great,
> It is merely a deceitful mirage, a
> > bewildering hallucination;
> In fact, it is the very cause of the
> > return to suffering!

> Thinking of the miseries of the Six Realms in Saṃsāra,
> I cannot help but have a feeling of disgust
> > and aversion —
> A feeling of anguish and distressed emotion!

Should you intend to practice the teaching of Buddha,
You must take refuge in the Three Precious
        Ones and pray to them.

Sentient beings in the Six Realms
You should consider as your parents.

Give to the poor, and offer to the Guru!
For the benefit of all, dedicate your merits.
Always remember that death may come at any moment.

Identify your body with Buddha's body!
Identify your own voice with Buddha's Mantra.
Contemplate the Śūnyatā of self-awakening Wisdom,
And always try to be master of your mind!

The Devas of Heaven said, "In ignorant beings like us, the Kleśas always follow the mind. Pray give us a teaching with which we can correct this fault, so we may depend upon it and practice it frequently."

In response to their request, Milarepa sang:

Obeisance to Marpa, the gracious one!
Pray grant me the blessing of virtuous remedy.

Should you, oh faithful lady Devas, intend
        to practice the Dharma often,
Inwardly you should practice concentration
        and contemplation.
The renunciation of external affairs is
        your adornment.

Oh, bear in mind this remedy for external
        involvement!
With self-composure and mindfulness, you
        should remain serene.
Glory is the equainimity of mind and speech!
Glory is the resignation from many actions!

Should you meet disagreeable conditions,
Disturbing to your mind,
Keep watch upon yourself and be alert;
Keep warning yourself:

"The danger of anger is on its way."
When you meet with enticing wealth,
Keep watch upon yourself and be alert;
Keep a check upon yourself:
"The danger of craving is on its way."

Should hurtful, insulting words come to your ears,
Keep watch upon yourself and be alert,
And so remind yourself:
"Hurtful sounds are but delusions of the ear."

When you associate with your friends,
Watch carefully and warn yourself:
"Let not jealousy in my heart arise."

When you are plied with services and offerings,
Be alert and warn yourself:
"Let me beware, lest pride should spring up
    in my heart."

At all times, in every way, keep watch upon
    yourself.
At all times try to conquer the evil thoughts
    within you!
Whatever you may meet in your daily doings,[5]
You should contemplate its void and
    illusory nature.

Were even one hundred saints and scholars
    gathered here,
More than this they could not say.
May you all be happy and prosperous!
May you all, with joyful hearts,
Devote yourselves to the practice of the Dharma!

The maidens of Heaven were all very happy, and in their delight and satisfaction they again turned their bodies into pigeons, and flew up toward Heaven. Milarepa then ate the offered rice, and set out for the Gray Rock Vajra Enclosure.

This is the story of the angel-maidens [in pigeon form] and their offerings.

All the preceding stories have dealt with the accounts of Milarepa's subjugation and conversion of demons.

NOTES

1 Non-effort (T.T.: rTsol.Med.), or no action, no disturbance, no doing, and the like: The Non-effort or Non-doing technique of meditation is the most important teaching of Mahāmudrā.

2 The high and low Views: Since the different Schools hold different views on Buddhist doctrine, they classify Buddhism into different groups of teaching — the high, the low, the expedient, the Ultimate, and so forth. For instance. the Yogācāra School holds that the "Mind-only" doctrine is the high view and the "Void" doctrine of the Middle Way (Mādhymika) School is the low view; the Middle Way School says just the opposite. This dissension also exists in other Buddhist Schools and Sects.

3 Six Senses and Sense Objects (T.T.: Tsogs.Drug.): Literally, this term should be translated as the Six Groups; e.g., eyes and form comprise one group, ears and sound another, and so on.

4 The Heaven of the White Devas: According to Buddhism, there are many different levels of heavens, some with form and some without. The Devas in the "highest" Heaven are supposedly without form or desires. However, Buddhism claims that even these heavenly beings are still in Saṃsāra.

5 Lit.: four kinds of daily activity — walking, standing, sitting, and lying down.

PART TWO

MILAREPA AND HIS HUMAN DISCIPLES

9

THE GRAY ROCK
VAJRA ENCLOSURE

Obeisance to all Gurus

THE Jetsun Milarepa, having arrived at the Gray Rock Vajra Enclosure, stayed in a state of inspiration at the Saddle Cave.

Now there was a Tantric yogi at Gu Tang who had heard the
preaching of the Jetsun, and became imbued with a deep faith in him.
[Coming] to Milarepa, he said, "Revered One, although I have practiced meditation for some time, I have not had the experiences or
earned the merits [that should have resulted]. This is probably due
to my ignorance of the proper way to practice. Pray, be kind enough
to grant me the appropriate teachings!" Milarepa replied, "In that
case, it is necessary that you should know all the essential points."
Therefore he sang for him a song, "The Six Essentials":

> The manifestations of mind outnumber the
>   myriads of dust-motes
> In the infinite rays of sunlight;
> The lord-like Yogi knows
> The self-nature of these manifestations.
>
> The reality of the true nature of beings
> Is neither produced by cause nor by conditions;
> The lord-like Yogi knows
> The sole truth precisely and positively.
>
> Even when he is faced with the threat
>   of a hundred spears,
> His thorough-knowing View will not be shaken;
> Thus the lord-like Yogi naturally subdues
>   all attachments.

The ever-moving mind is hard to tame
Even when shut up in an iron box;
The lord-like Yogi knows
That all these emanations are illusions.

The disciple then asked, "Are experiences such as you have just mentioned brought about gradually, or instantaneously?" Milarepa replied, "Well-endowed people will attain Enlightenment instantaneously; average and inferior people will gradually attain their Realizations. I shall describe to you the signs of real Enlightenment, and also the signs of those experiences *resembling* Enlightenment, but which are wrongly considered by some people to be the real ones."

Thereupon he sang the following song to explain the different experiences, both real and false, of the four stages of Mahāmudrā,[1]

I bow down at the feet of the supreme Guru.

To cling to the actuality of mind is the
        cause of Saṃsāra;
To realize that non-clinging and illuminating
        Self-awareness
Is unborn and immanent,
Is the consummation sign of the
        Stage of One-Pointedness.

If one talks about the Two-In-One
But still meditates on form,
If one acknowledges the truth of Karma
But still commits wrong-doing,
He is actually meditating with blindness
        and passion!
Things, as such, are never found
In the true Stage of One-Pointedness.

In realizing that the non-clinging and
        illuminating mind,
Is embodied in bliss and transcends all playwords,[2]
One sees his mind's nature as clearly as
        great Space.
This is the sign of the consummation
Of the Stage of Away-from-Playwords.

Though one talks about the Stage of

Away-from-Playwords,
Still he is declaring this and that;
In spite of illustrating what is beyond
    all words,
Still he is but piling words on words.
He then, is the ignorant one,
Who with self-clinging meditates.
In the Stage of Away-from-Playwords,
There is no such thing as this.

The non-differentiation of manifestation
    and Voidness
Is the Dharmakāya,
In which Saṃsāra and Nirvāṇa are felt to be the same.
It is a complete merging of Buddha and
    sentient beings.
These are the signs of the Stage of One-Taste,
As many have declared.

He who says that "all is one,"
Is still discriminating;
In the Stage of One-Taste,
There is no such blindness.

A wandering thought is itself the essence
    of Wisdom—
Immanent and intrinsic.
Cause and effect are both the same.
This is a realization of Buddha's Three Bodies[3]
Existing within oneself.
These are the consummation signs
Of the Stage of Non-Practice.

When one talks about Non-Practice,
His mind is still active;
He talks about illumination,
But in fact is blind.
In the Stage of Non-Practice,
There is no such thing!

The disciple cried, "These instructions are indeed extraordinary! To help ignorant men like us, pray now, instruct us on the practice of the Six Pāramitās." Milarepa sang in reply:

I bow down at the feet of the perfect Jetsun Gurus.

Property and wealth are like dew on grass;
Knowing this, gladly should one give them away.

It is most precious to be born a worthy and
    leisured human being;[4]
Knowing this, one should with care observe
    the precepts
As if protecting his own eyes.

Anger is the cause of falling to the Realms Below;
Knowing this, one should refrain from wrath,
Even at the risk of life.

Benefit to oneself and to others
Can never be achieved through sloth;
Strive, therefore, to do good deeds.

A perturbed, wandering mind never sees the
    truth of Mahāyāna;
Practice, therefore, concentration.

Buddha cannot be found through searching;
So contemplate your own mind.[5]

Until the autumn mists dissolve into the sky,
Strive on with faith and determination.

Having heard this song, a great admiration and faith toward the
Jetsun arose in the heart of the disciple, and he returned home. Several days later, he and many other patrons came to entertain Milarepa,
and brought copious offerings. They had all heard the Jetsun's life
story, and with great faith, they came this time to learn the Dharma.
They asked Milarepa how he had managed to undergo the trials of
probationship[6] and had exerted himself in ascetic practice, and to re-
count the way through which he had finally obtained his Enlightenment. Milarepa answered with "The Six Resolutions":

When one has lost interest in this world,
His faith and longing for the Dharma is confirmed.

To relinquish one's home ties is very hard;

Only by leaving one's native land
Can one be immune from anger.

It is hard to conquer burning passions
Toward relatives and close friends;
The best way to quench them
Is to break all associations.

One never feels that he is rich enough;
Contented, he should wear humble, cotton clothes.
He may thus conquer much desire and craving.

It is hard to avoid worldly attractions;
By adhering to humbleness,
Longing for vainglory is subdued.

It is hard to conquer pride and egotism;
So, like the animals, live in the mountains!

My dear and faithful patrons!
Such is the real understanding
That stems from perseverance.
I wish you all to practice deeds that
        are meaningful,[7]
And amass all merits![8]

Like space, the Dharmakāya pervades
        all sentient beings,
Yet [Karmic] blindness drives them into Saṃsāra.

Easy it is to glimpse the Dharmakāya,
But hard to stabilize its realization.
Hence, one is still beset by the Five Poisons.[9]

If the realization [of Sūnyatā] is stable,
The organs and senses[10] move freely but do not cling.
One then forever merges with the Trikāya.
This is the conviction of Enlightenment.

The Main and the Ensuing Samādhis[11]
Are two states only for beginners.
In stabilized minds they are as one.

In the Yoga of Non-wandering,[12]
The Six non-attached Senses e'er arise,
Yet I remain steadfast in the inseparable Trikāya.
Unattached, I walk with power;
Free from clinging, I gain
The wish-fulfilling merits.[13]

A wise man knows how to practice
The space-like meditation.
In all he does by day
He attaches himself to nothing.
With a liberated spirit,
He desires nor wealth nor beauty.

One should see that all appearance
Is like mist and fog;
Though one has vowed to liberate all
     sentient beings,
He should know that all manifestations
Are like reflections of the moon in water.

Without attachment, he knows
That the human body is but a magic spell.
So from all bindings he gains freedom.
Like the immaculate lotus growing out of mud,
He attains the conviction of Practice.

The mind is omnipresent like space;
It illumines all manifestations as the Dharmakāya;
It knows all and lightens all.
I see it clearly like a crystal
In my palm!

In the beginning, nothing comes;
In the middle, nothing stays;
At the end, nothing goes.
Of the mind there is no arising and extinction!
Thus, one remains in the Equality of past,
     present, and future.

Immanent, the mind, like the sky, is pure.
The red and white clouds[14] vanish of themselves;
No trace of the Four Elements[15] can be found.

The omnipresent mind resembles Space:
It never separates from the Realm of the Unborn,
It cuts the path of the Three Worlds of Saṃsāra.
This is the conviction of Enlightenment.

If a yogi realizes this,
When he leaves his mortal body
And enters into the [momentous] Bardo,[16]
He may then perfect all merits.

With an understanding of the profound instruction.
One makes the Mother and Son Minds[17] meet;
If he then fails to unite them,
Through the teaching of the Simultaneously Born
He can still transform the phantom Bardo form
Into the Pure Body of Bliss!

If he knows that even the Sambhogakāya is
        unreal, like a shadow,
How can he ever go astray?
This is infallibly my own—
The yogi's sure conviction about Bardo!

The people of Gu Tang were all strongly confirmed in their faith, and thereafter often brought offerings to Milarepa.

One day, in the very early morning, Milarepa, in a state of Illumination, saw the Vajra Ḍākinī appear before him. She prophesied: "Milarepa! You will have one sun-like, one moon-like, twenty-three star-like, and twenty-five accomplished human disciples; one hundred enlightened beings who never fall back; one hundred and eight great men who will attain the initial Realization of the Path;[18] and one thousand male and female yogis who will enter the Path. Those who, with you, have the affinity of Dharma and thus forever escape the lower path of Saṃsāra, are beyond number. In the upper part of Gung Tang there is a destined man, who will be your moon-like disciple. Go there for his sake." And so Milarepa set his mind upon going to the Upper Gung Tang.

This is the first of the series of stories of the Gray Rock Vajra Enclosure.[19]

NOTES

1 The four stages of Mahāmudrā are:
   (1) The stage of One-Pointedness (T.T.: rTse.gCig.),
   (2) The stage of Away-from-Playwords (T.T.: sProd.Bral.),
   (3) The stage of One-Taste (T.T.: Ro.gCig.),
   (4) The stage of Non-Practice (T.T.: sGom.Med.).
In the *first* stage the meditator experiences the tranquility of Mind-Essence. However, he still has not eradicated the dualistic view, nor has he actually realized in full the uncreated voidness of the mind.

In the *second* stage the meditator sees clearly the "original state of mind." In virtue of this direct experience with Mind-Essence, he rids himself once and for all of Saṃsāric views — the views of "playwords," such as "one and many," "good and bad," "yes and no," "finite and infinite," etc. This stage is considered by Tibetan sages to be that of initial Enlightenment.

In the *third* stage the meditator is completely free from all obstacles or hindrances. It is therefore called the Stage of One-Taste (the Realm of Universal Totality, or the Realm of the Identity of Saṃsāra and Nirvāṇa). However, this experience should by no means be regarded as a realization of any form of monism — a major "false view," that has been refuted by many Buddhist scholars, notably those of the Mādhyamika School. (See Story 18, Note 9.)

In the *fourth* stage the meditator has already reached the Ultimate Realm. He has nothing more to look for or to learn: he has reached the State of Buddhahood.

These four stages represent the complete process through which a Buddhist yogi proceeds to Ultimate Enlightenment.

2 Playwords: All Saṃsāric conceptions and ideas which have to be expressed through words and symbols are meaningless sophistries from the viewpoint of an enlightened being. The term "Playwords" (T.T.: sPros.Pa.) also implies that all Saṃsāric conceptualizations and verbalizations are on a par with children's prattle — little more than nonsense. Realization of this is considered the initial stage of Enlightenment.

3 Three Bodies: the Trikāya, or Three Bodies of Buddha, i.e., the Dharmakāya, the Sambhogakāya, and the Nirmāṇakāya.

4 The human body is considered to be a precious possession, without which no spiritual development is possible.

5 This sentence is extremely important as representing the essence of the teaching of Mahāmudrā. In general Buddhism one is taught to search for Enlightenment and to attain Buddhahood, while in Mahāmudrā the Guru points out to the disciple that one's own mind is Buddha Himself, and therefore, to search for anything, even Buddhahood, is a waste of time.

6 This refers to the trials imposed on Milarepa by his Guru, Marpa, before he was accepted for initiation. (See Milarepa's Biography, edited by W. Y. Evans-Wentz.)

7 Meaningful deeds: the virtuous deeds that lead one to Enlightenment.

8 "Amass merits": This phrase is often used by Buddhists to denote all virtuous deeds. (See Story 4, Note 22; and Story 7, Note 11.)

9 Five Poisons: the Five Kleśas, the basic causes of all miseries of Saṃsāra. They are lust, hate, blindness, pride, and envy.

10 Lit.: Six Groups: a general term denoting the six outer objects, six organs, and six senses.

11 Main Samādhi and Ensuing Samādhi (T.T.: mÑam.bShag. [and] rJes.Tob.): mÑam.bShag. may be otherwise translated as the "Actual-Meditation-State," and rJes.Tob. as the "After-Meditation-State."

12 Yoga of Non-wandering: The state of concentration in which the mind is fixed and does not wander.

13 If the yogi can free himself from all clinging, he will gain all the miraculous powers, which in turn will enable him to grant all sentient beings' wishes.

14 "Red-and-White" denotes the positive and negative elements in the body.

15 The text is very obscure here and the meaning is not certain.

16 The Bardo stage, or the stage between death and rebirth, is a critical stage wherein one can either attain liberation easily, or fall back into Saṃsāric existence. (See Story 3, Note 4).

17 The Mother and Son Minds: The Mother Mind, or more correctly, Mother Light (T.T.: Mahi.Ḥod.Zer.) exists all the time, but is not yet unfolded. The Son Mind (T.T.: Buhi.Ḥod.Zer.), or Son Light, is the enlightened mind, or the Enlightenment of the Path.

18 Initial Realization of the Path: This is the first stage of Enlightenment. (See Note 1.)

19 This is a literal translation of the original text. The latter part of the series seems to be missing.

MILAREPA'S FIRST MEETING
WITH RECHUNGPA

Obeisance to all Gurus

As PROPHESIED by [Marpa], Milarepa went to the upper part of
Gung Tang. When he arrived at the Castle there, he found that
many people were building a house and asked them for some food.
They replied, "We are working on this building. You can see that
we are very busy and have no time for that sort of thing. It looks
as though you have plenty of time to spare, so why don't you join us
in the work?"

Milarepa said, "Yes, I now have plenty of leisure, but I have earned
it by finishing the construction of my 'house' in my own way. Even if
you do not give me any food, I will never work on a worldly building, which I would most certainly abandon." The men asked him, "How
did you build your house, and why do you spurn our work so
strongly?"

Milarepa sang in reply:

> Faith is the firm foundation of my house,
> Diligence forms the high walls,
> Meditation makes the huge bricks,
> And Wisdom is the great cornerstone.
> With these four things I built my castle,
> And it will last as long as the Truth eternal!
> Your worldly houses are delusions,
> Mere prisons for the demons,
> And so I would abandon and desert them.

The workers said, "What you have sung is most enlightening. Please
also tell us whether, in your way of life, you have anything like our

farms, properties, relatives, companions, wives, and children? It seems to us that these things are worth more than you have suggested. Please tell us what possessions you have that are so much better than ours? Why do you look upon our way of life as worthless?"

Milarepa answered:

> The Alaya Consciousness[1] is the good earth,
> The inner teaching is the seed that is sowed,
> Achievement in meditation is the sprout,
> And the Three Bodies of Buddha are the
>   ripened crop.
> These are the four lasting mainstays of
>   heavenly farming.
> Your worldly farming, delusive and deceiving,
> Is merely the slave-labor of the hungry;
> Without hesitation I discard it!
>
> The fine warehouse of Śūnyatā,
> The Supramundane Jewels,[2]
> The service and action of the Ten Virtues,
> And the great happiness of Non-outflow[3] —
> These four jewels are the lasting proper-
>   ties of Heaven.
> Your worldly jewels and possessions are
>   deceiving and delusive;
> Like deceptive magic spells, they lead you astray.
> Without any hesitation, I discard them.
>
> The Father and Mother Buddha are my parents,
> The immaculate Dharma is my face,
> The assembly of Saṅgha are my cousins and nephews,
> And the guardians of Dharma are my friends.
> These four are my lasting, heavenly kinsmen.
> Your worldly kinsmen are deceitful and delusive;
> Without hesitation I throw all ephemeral
>   associates away!
>
> The Blissful Passing[4] is like my father,
> The Blissful Illumination in well-done
>   work is [my background],
> The Two-in-One is my glossy, lustrous skin,
> The Experiences and Realization[5] are my
>   glorious clothing.

These four are my heavenly and lasting wives.
Delusive and deceiving are your worldly companions,
They are but temporary friends, inclined to quarrel;
Without hesitation, I throw them all away.

Mind-Awareness is my new-born babe,
Experience of Meditation is my infant,
Understanding-and-Realization is my child,
And the grown youth who can keep the
      Doctrine is my young companion.
These four are my lasting, heavenly sons.
Your worldly offspring are delusive and deceitful;
Without hesitation I throw them all away.

I wish sincerely that I and you, the good
      folk of Gung Tang,
Through the Karma-affinity of this conversation,
May meet once more in the Pure Land of Oujen.[6]

The villagers, strongly moved with faith, then made obeisance and offerings to Milarepa. Later, they all became his sincere disciples.

After this, Milarepa went to the upper part of Goat Hill (Ra La) where he found Silk Cave (Zhaoo Pug). Now, there was at Goat Hill a youth, who in his early infancy had lost his father. He was a fine, intelligent boy, whom his mother and uncle jointly supported. Having an excellent memory, he could recite a great many stories and sermons from the Buddhist Sūtras. Thus he always received many gifts from the people.[7] One day, while herding oxen on his donkey in the upper part of the valley, he came upon the cave where Milarepa was meditating. Thinking that he heard someone singing, he got off the donkey, left the oxen, and approached the cave. As soon as he saw Milarepa, an ineffable experience of Samādhi arose within him, and for a moment he stood transfixed in ecstasy. (Afterwards, he became a Heart-Son of Milarepa—the renowned Rechung Dorje Dragpa.)

Awakened thus from Karma, an immutable faith toward the Jetsun arose within the boy. He offered Milarepa all the gifts that he had acquired for his services. Then he stayed with him to learn the Dharma, completely forgetting his mother and uncle. Because of this, he naturally received no income, and his mother and uncle thought, "what has happened? [Where is he?] Have people stopped paying him?" With misgivings they began asking the patrons whether they had duly paid Rechungpa. Everybody said that he had been paid. It then dawned upon the uncle and mother [where the boy must be, and] that all the gifts must have been offered to Milarepa. They tried in every way to stop Rechungpa from continuing in this course, but to no avail. The young lad remained with Milarepa and learned the Dharma from him. Before long, the Experience and Realization of meditation grew within him. By virtue of mastering the art of Heat Yoga he was able to wear merely a single piece of cotton clothing, and thus earned the name of Rechungpa.[8]

Meanwhile, Rechungpa's mother and uncle became very angry. They sent him a pot on which a curse had been placed.[9] As a result, Rechungpa contracted leprosy.[10] Hoping to be cured, he confined himself [in the hermitage] for meditation.

One day, five Indian yogis arrived, to whom Rechungpa offered some roasted barley which had been sent by his mother and uncle. While the Indians were eating they exclaimed, "What a deadly disease! What a deadly disease!" They knew that Rechungpa had caught leprosy. Rechungpa then asked them whether there was any cure. One of the yogis said, "You are indeed a pitiful person deserving of sympathy, and I feel for you. I have a Guru called Wala Tsandra who may be able to relieve you. As he will not be coming to Tibet, you will have to go to India." And so Rechungpa asked the Jetsun for permission to go. Milarepa agreed and sang as a parting gift:

> I pray my Guru to whom I owe immense gratitude,
> I pray you to protect and bless my son, Rechungpa.
>
> Son, you should renounce the world,
> And work hard at the Dharma.
> To the Guru, Patron Buddha,[11] and the Three
>   Precious Ones,
> You should pray with sincere heart and not
>   just words.
> Bear this in mind when you travel in India.
>
> By taking the food of Perseverance in Samādhi,
> By wearing the clothes of Ah Tung,[12]
> And by riding the horse of the magic
>   Prāṇa-Mind,[13]
> Thus, my son, should you travel in India.
>
> You should always keep the non-defiled mind clean;
> You should always remember the silver-bright
>   mirror of the Tantric Precept,

And observe it without vexation.
Bear this in mind, my son, as you travel in India.

If you are followed and captured by bandits,
You should remind yourself how worthless
    are the Eight Worldly Claims.[14]
Conceal your powers and merits.
With a humble and merry mind travel in India.

My son, with my sincere prayer and blessing,
May you recover from your illness and enjoy long life.

Milarepa then resumed his meditation in the cave. Rechungpa
closed the cave's mouth with clay, and set out for India with the
yogis. [Upon arriving] there, he met Lama Wala Tsandra, who [con-
sented to give] him the complete teachings of the Wrathful Thunderbolt-Holder with Eagle Wings.[15] By practicing this for some time
Rechungpa was cured.

When he returned to Tibet and reached Happy Valley, he inquired
of the whereabouts of the Jetsun from a native of that valley who
said, "Some time ago, I heard that there was a yogi called Mila, but
I have heard nothing about him recently." Hearing this, Rechungpa
became very disturbed. He thought, "Is my Guru dead?", and in great
distress he proceeded to Silk Cave. He saw that the clay wall with
which he had blocked the entrance was still there. Thinking, "I wonder if the Jetsun is dead inside," he tore down the wall and entered.
Seeing Milarepa sitting upright in meditation, he felt extremely happy
and relieved. He asked the Jetsun about his health and welfare. In
answer Milarepa [arose from meditation and] sang:

I bow down at the feet of Marpa, the Gracious One.

Because I have left my kinsmen, I am happy;
Because I have abandoned attachment to my
    country, I am happy;
Since I disregard this place, I am happy;
As I do not wear the lofty garb of priesthood,
    I am happy;
Because I cling not to house and family, I am happy;
I need not this or that, so I am happy.
Because I possess the great wealth of Dharma,
    I am happy;

Because I worry not about property,
    I am happy;
Because I have no fear of losing anything,
    I am happy;
Since I never dread exhaustion, I am happy;
Having fully realized Mind-Essence,
    I am happy;
As I need not force myself to please my patrons,
    I am happy;
Having no fatigue nor weariness, I am happy;
As I need prepare for nothing, I am happy;
Since all I do complies with Dharma,
    I am happy;
Never desiring to move, I am happy.
As the thought of death brings me no fear,
    I am happy;
Bandits, thieves, and robbers ne'er molest me,
So at all times I am happy!
Having won the best conditions for Dharma
    practice, I am happy;
Having ceased from evil deeds and left off
    sinning, I am happy;
Treading the Path of Merits, I am happy;
Divorced from hate and injury, I am happy;
Having lost all pride and jealousy,
    I am happy;
Understanding the wrongness of the Eight
    Worldly Winds,[16] I am happy;
Absorbed in quiet and evenmindedness, I am happy;
Using the mind to watch the mind, I am happy;
Without hope or fear, I am ever happy.
In the sphere of non-clinging Illumination,
    I am happy;
The Non-distinguishing Wisdom of Dharmadhātu
    itself is happy;
Poised in the natural realm of Immanence,
    I am happy;
In letting the Six Groups of Consciousness go by
To return to their original nature,
    I am happy.
The five radiant gates of sense all make me happy;
To stop a mind that comes and goes is happy;
Oh, I have so much of happiness and joy!

This is a song of gaiety I sing,
This is a song of gratitude to my Guru and
    the Three Precious Ones—
I want no other happiness.

Through the grace of Buddhas and the Gurus,
Food and clothes are provided by my patrons.
With no bad deeds and sins, I shall be
    joyful when I die;
With all good deeds and virtues, I am happy
    while alive.
Enjoying Yoga, I am indeed most happy.
But how are you Rechungpa? Is your wish
    fulfilled?

Rechungpa said to Milarepa, "I am well again. I have obtained
what I wanted. From now on I would like to remain in solitude and
stay near you. Please be so kind as to grant me further inner teachings." Milarepa then imparted to Rechungpa additional instructions,
and stayed with him in the Silk Cave. Through the continued practice
of meditation Rechungpa attained the perfect Experiences and Realization.

This is the story of Milarepa meeting his Heart-Son Rechungpa in
the Cave of Zhaoo.

NOTES

1 Ālaya means store or reservoir. The main function of this consciousness
is to preserve the "seeds" of mental impressions. Without it, memory and learning
would become impossible. Ālaya consciousness is also called the primordial consciousness, or the "Fruit-bearing Consciousness." In some aspects, it is quite
similar to Jung's "Collective Unconscious."

2 Supramundane Jewels: a symbolic term which denotes the transcendental
merits and virtues of Buddha.

3 Non-outflow (T.T.: Zag.Med.) means non-desire. The term usually denotes
the realm of transcendency.

4 The Blissful Passing: This may be otherwise rendered as "The Blissful Manifestation or Becoming." When one reaches a higher level of consciousness, even the
contacts with outer manifestations become blissful.

5 See Story 7, Notes 9 and 12.

6 Oujen (T.T.: Ao.rGyan.): the name of the Pure Land of Padma Saṃbhava.

7 Tibetans are very generous in offering Lamas and story-tellers gifts for their services in reciting Buddhist Sūtras and relating Buddhist legends.

8 Rechungpa: the chief and closest disciple of Milarepa, who served and lived with Milarepa for most of his life. Since he was the youngest disciple, he was called Rechungpa, meaning the little Repa.

9 A pot cursed by a malignant spell.

10 Lit.: the disease of the Earth Lord, or the disease of the Dragon. Tibetans believe that leprosy is a disease caused by malignant, metamorphic dragons.

11 Yidham (T.T.: Yi.Dam.): See Story 7, Note 29.

12 Ah Tung (T.T.: A.Thuñ.): the small seed-syllable "Ah" which is visualized at the navel center in the Heat-Yoga practice. See "The Six Yogas of Nāropa," in Evans-Wentz' "Tibetan Yoga and Secret Doctrines," and the translator's "Teachings of Tibetan Yoga."

13 Prāṇa-Mind: See Story 3, Note 2.

14 Eight Worldly Claims, or Eight Worldly Winds or Desires: See Story 1, Note 13.

15 The Wrathful Thunderbolt-Holder with Eagle Wings (T.T.: Phyag.rDor. gTum.Po.Khyuñ.gÇog.Can.).

16 See Note 14.

11

ADMONISHMENT ON THE "RARE OPPORTUNITY OF PRACTICING DHARMA"

Obeisance to all Gurus

FROM Zhaoo, the Jetsun Milarepa went to the Light Cave of Runpu and remained there for some time. One day, some young men from his native country came to visit him. They said, "In the past you destroyed all your enemies for revenge, and now you are practicing the Dharma in such an outstanding way. This is indeed marvelous and extraordinary! When we are near you we cannot help but feel like devoting ourselves to religion; but when we return home, we again become preoccupied with worldly affairs. How can we correct this?" Milarepa replied, "If one is really determined to free himself from the sufferings of Saṃsāra, such as birth, old age, illness, death, and so on, he will have peace of mind all the time and will not need to make any effort. Otherwise he should bear in mind that the sufferings in a future life could be much more durable and long-lasting than those in this life; and the burden could also be much heavier. It is therefore of paramount importance to take ·steps to prepare for the next life.

"Please hearken, and I will sing a song for you."

> We sentient beings moving in the world
> Float down the flowing stream
> Of the Four sufferings.[1]
> Compared to this, how much more formidable
> Are the unceasing future lives in Saṃsāra.
> Why not, then, prepare a boat for the "crossing"?

The state of our future lives is far more fearful
And deserving of far more concern
Than are the dreadful demons, ghosts, and Yama.
So why not prepare for yourself a guide?

Even the dread passions—craving, hatred and blindness—
Are not so fearful as the state of our
      [unknown] future,
So why not prepare for yourself an antidote?

Great is the kingdom of the Three Realms
      of Saṃsāra,
But greater is the endless road of birth-and-death,
So why not prepare for yourself provisions?
It will be better that you practice Dharma
If you have no assurance in yourselves.

The young men said, "Your admonishment is very helpful. We will come and practice the Dharma with you. However, as it makes no sense to punish oneself by practicing the extreme ascetic way of living, we beg you, for the sake of protecting the resources of your patrons and disciples, to keep for yourself a tiny share of belongings as a token. Also, we do not quite understand what you have just said in your song. Please make it clearer."
In reply Milarepa sang:

Reliance on a qualified Guru is the
      guide to Saṃsāra and Nirvāṇa;
Unsparing charity provides for the journey;
As the rising moon shines brightly in the darkness,
The real experiences in meditation
      [enlighten one's mind].
This is the companionship
One should search for as a guide.

To give accumulated wealth for the cause of Dharma
Prepares one's boat for Saṃsāra's stream.
Holding the View without sectarian bigotry,
One can meditate without distraction.
If action accords with Buddhist teaching
Precept is clear, and the Guru pleased.
The reward is to die without regret.

Kinsmen, patrons, and disciples
Mean nought to me, the Yogi;
Only you worldly beings need them.

Fame, grandeur, and honor
Mean nought to me, the Yogi.
Pursuers of the Eight Desires need them.

Property, goods, and social life
Mean nought to me, the Yogi.
Pursuers of fame require them.

Tidiness, washing, and sanitation,
Mean nought to me, the Yogi.
Never do I want them.
They are what you young men need.
These twelve things do not concern me.

[I know well] that it is not everyone
Who can practice all these things;
But you young men assembled here,
Remember the "boastful talk" of this old man!
If you want happiness in life
Practice, then, the Dharma,
Renounce distractions, and remain in solitude.
Cling to the hermitage with perseverance.
Yearn for Buddhahood and your fortitude will grow.
You will then vanquish the Four Demons.

Among the youths was a well-gifted, most intelligent, hard-working, and compassionate young man. He said to Milarepa, "My Guru, it is solely because we have been attached to the affairs of this life that we have neglected to look after our destiny in future lives. Please accept us as your servants. We shall renounce this life and devote ourselves to the preparation for our future lives. [In this light] please be kind enough to give us some further instructions."

"A human body, free and opportune, is as precious as a jewel," replied Milarepa, "and to have a chance to practice the Dharma is likewise very rare. Also, to find one serious Buddhist in a hundred is difficult! Considering the difficulties of meeting the right Gurus, and other necessary favorable conditions for practicing Buddhism, you should deem yourselves very fortunate that you have now met all these requirements. Do not, therefore, [waste them], but practice the Dharma."

Milarepa then sang:

To escape from the Eight Non-Freedoms[2] is hard,
As it is to gain the human form, free and opportune.

To realize the sorrows of Saṃsāra
And to seek Nirvāṇa is difficult!

Out of one hundred seekers of Bodhi, it is
hard to find
One who may attain the pure and favorable conditions!

To renounce the pleasures of this life is hard,
As it is to make full use of the gem-like human body.

Slight is the chance to meet a compassionate Guru
Who knows the traditional and expedient[3]
inner Teachings.

A sincere and faithful disciple
With ability to practice Dharma, is most rare.

To find a temple without fear
And commotion is most hard.

To find a congenial companion, whose Views
Practice, and School agree with you, is rare.

To attain a body without pain and sickness,
Able to endure hard practice, is difficult!

Even when you have fulfilled all these conditions,
It is still hard to concentrate on meditation!

These are the nine hard conditions;
However formidable and exacting they may be,
With determination and practice one can
conquer them.

Having heard this admonishment, the young man could not but develop a very strong faith in the Jetsun. He devoted himself to serve

Milarepa, who gave him the Initations and Instructions. Later he became a well-accomplished yogi and attained Liberation. He was known as Milarepa's intimate son-disciple, Tsapu Repa.

This is the story of Tsapu Repa meeting Milarepa in the Great Light Cave.

NOTES

1 Four Sufferings: those of birth, of age, of sickness, and of death.

2 The Eight Non-Freedoms (T.T.: Mi.Khom.brGyad.) are the eight conditions in which it is difficult to receive and practice Dharma: in the hells; as hungry ghosts or animals; in Uttarakuru (the legendary "Northern Continent" where all is pleasant); in the heavens (where life is long and easy); as deaf, blind, and dumb; as a worldly philosopher; and in the intermediate period between a Buddha and his successor.

3 A qualified Guru should be able to give not only the traditional teachings of the Dharma, but also the appropriate or expedient teachings for the individual disciple. But literally, this line should be translated as: "Who knows the essential instructions of Sūtra and of Reasoning" (T.T.: Luṅ. [and] Rig.Pa.).

12

THE SHEPHERD'S SEARCH FOR MIND

Obeisance to all Gurus

O NE day, Jetsun Milarepa descended from the Great Light Cave to the Happy Village of Mang Yul for food and alms. Seeing many people in the center of the village, he said to them, "Dear patrons, please give me some food this morning." They asked, "Are you the much-talked-about yogi who formerly resided at Ragma?" He replied, "Yes, I am." Then a great respect for him arose within them and they cried, "Oh, here comes the wonderful yogi!"

Among them was a married couple who had no children. Inviting Milarepa to their house, they served him and said, "Dear Lama, where are your home and relatives?" Milarepa replied, "I am a poor beggar who has disavowed his relatives and native land and has also been forsaken by them." Then the couple cried, "In that case we would like to adopt you into our family! We have a good strip of land which we can give you; you can then marry an attractive woman, and soon you will have relatives." Milarepa replied, "I have no need of these things, and will tell you why":

> Home and land at first seem pleasant;
> But they are like a rasp filing away one's
> body, word, and mind!
> How toilsome ploughing and digging can become!
> And when the seeds you planted never
> sprout, you have worked for nought!
> In the end it becomes a land of misery—
> desolate and unprotected—
> A place of Hungry Spirits, and of haunting ghosts!
> When I think of the warehouse
> For storing sinful deeds,

It gnaws at my heart;
In such a prison of transciency I will not stay,
I have no wish to join your family!

The married couple said, "Please do not talk like that! We will find you a fine girl from a prominent family, who is fit to be your bride and who will suit your taste. Please consider this." Milarepa sang:

At first, the lady is like a heavenly angel;
The more you look at her, the more you want to gaze.
Middle-aged, she becomes a demon with a
      corpse's eyes;
You say one word to her and she shouts back two.
She pulls your hair and hits your knee,
You strike her with your staff, but back
      she throws a ladle.
At life's end, she becomes an old cow with
      no teeth.
Her angry eyes burn with a devilish fire
Penetrating deep into your heart!
I keep away from women to avoid fights and
      quarrels.
For the young bride you mentioned, I have
      no appetite.

The husband then said, "Dear Lama, it is true that when one grows old and close to death he has not the same capacity for enjoying life or for being pleasant as when he was young. But if I have no son, my grief and disappointment will be unbearable. How about you? Don't you need a son at all?" Milarepa sang in reply:

In youth, a son is like the Prince of Heaven;
You love him so much that the passion is
      hard to bear.
In middle age, he becomes a ruthless creditor
To whom you give all, but he still wants more.
Driven from the house are his own parents,
Invited in is his beloved, charming lady.
His father calls, but he will not answer;
His mother cries out, but he will not listen.
Then the neighbors take advantage, spreading
      lies and rumors.

Thus I learned that one's child oft becomes
    one's enemy.
Bearing this in mind, I renounce the
    fetters of Saṃsāra.
For sons and nephews I have no appetite.

Both husband and wife agreed with him, replying, "What you have said is indeed true. Sometimes one's own son becomes an enemy. Perhaps it would be better to have a daughter. What do you think?"
In answer Milarepa sang:

In youth, a daughter is like a smiling,
    heavenly angel;
She is more attractive and precious than are jewels.
In middle age, she is good for nothing.
Before her father, she openly carries things away;
She pilfers secretly behind her mother's back.
If her parents do not praise her and satisfy
    her wants,
They will suffer from her bitterness and temper.
In the end, she becomes red-faced and wields
    a sword.
At her best, she may serve and devote herself
    to others;
At her worst, she will bring mishaps and disaster.
Woman is always a trouble-maker;
Bearing this in mind, one should avoid
    irretrievable misfortunes.
For women, the primary source of suffering,
    I have no appetite.

The husband and wife then said, "One may not need sons and daughters, but without relatives, life would be too miserable and help-less. Is that not so?"
Milarepa again sang:

At first, when a man greets his relatives,
He is happy and joyful; with enthusiasm
He serves, entertains, and talks to them.
Later, they share his meat and wine.
He offers something to them once, they may
    reciprocate.

In the end, they cause anger, craving, and
    bitterness;
They are a fountain of regret and unhappiness.
With this in mind, I renounce pleasant and
    sociable friends;
For kinsmen and neighbors, I have no appetite.

The couple then said, "Indeed, you may not need kinsmen. However, since we own a great deal of property, would you like to have
and take care of it?" Milarepa replied, "As the sun and moon never
stop to brighten one small place, so I devote myself to the welfare of
all sentient beings. I cannot, therefore, become a member of your
family. By merely beholding me, both of you will be benefited in this
and future lives. I will also make a wish that we may meet in the
Pure Land of Oujen."
    Milarepa then burst into another song:

Wealth, at first, leads to self-enjoyment,
Making other people envious.
However much one has, one never feels it is enough,
Until one is bound by the miser's demon;
It is then hard to spend it on virtuous deeds.

Wealth provokes enemies and stirs up ghosts.
One works hard to gather riches which others
    will spend;
In the end, one struggles for life and death.
To amass wealth and money invites enemies;
So I renounce the delusions of Saṃsāra.
To become the victim of deceitful devils,
I have no appetite.

These songs gave the couple unshakable faith in Milarepa and they
gave away all their possessions for the sake of the Dharma. They began to practice the Jetsun's teachings and were forever released from
falling into the three lower Realms. When they died, they entered
the Path [of Bodhi] and step by step approached Buddhahood.
    After this, the Jetsun returned to the Bodhi Cave of Ragma. His
former patrons gave their services and offerings to him, and he remained there in an inspired mood.
    One day, two young shepherds came to him. The younger one asked,
"Dear Lama, have you a companion?"
    Milarepa replied, "Yes, I have."

"Who is he?"

"His name is 'Friend Bodhi-Heart'."

"Where is he now?"

"In the House of the Universal Seed Consciousness."[1]

"What do you mean by that?"

"My own body."

The elder boy then said, "Lama, we had better go, as you cannot guide us." But the younger one said, "Do you mean this Consciousness is mind itself, and that the physical body is the house of the mind?"

"Yes, that is correct."

The boy continued, "We know that although a house usually belongs only to one person, many people can enter it, so we always find a number of people living in one house. In the same way, is there only one mind in the body, or are there many? If there are many, how do they live together?"

"Well, as to whether there is only one mind in the body or many, you had better find that out by yourself."

"Revered One, I will try."

At this point, the boys took their leave and went home. Next morning, the younger boy returned and said to Milarepa, "Dear Lama, last night I tried to find out what my mind is and how it works. I observed it carefully and found that I have only one mind. Even though one wants to, one cannot kill this mind. However much one wishes to dismiss it, it will not go away. If one tries to catch it, it cannot be grasped; nor can it be held by pressing it. If you want it to remain, it will not stay; if you release it, it will not go. You try to gather it; it cannot be picked up. You try to see it; it cannot be seen. You try to understand it; it cannot be known. If you think it is an existing entity and cast it off, it will not leave you. If you think that it is non-existent, you feel it running on. It is something illuminating, aware, wide-awake, yet incomprehensible. In short, it is hard to say what the mind really is. Please be kind enough to explain the meaning of the mind."

In response, Milarepa sang:

> Listen to me, dear shepherd, the protector
>   [of sheep]!
> By merely hearing about sugar's taste,
> Sweetness cannot be experienced;
> Though one's mind may understand
> What sweetness is,
> It cannot experience directly;
> Only the tongue can know it.

In the same way one cannot see in full
    the nature of mind,
Though he may have a glimpse of it
If it has been pointed out by others.[2]
If one relies not on this one glimpse,
But continues searching for the nature of mind,
He will see it fully in the end.
Dear shepherd, in this way you should observe
    your mind.

The boy then said, "In that case, please give me the Pointing-out-Instruction,[3] and this evening I will look into it. I shall return tomorrow and tell you the result." Milarepa replied, "Very well. When you get home, try to find out the color of the mind. Is it white, red, or what? What is its shape? Is it oblong, round, or what? Also, try to locate where in your body it dwells."

The next morning when the sun rose, the shepherd drove the sheep before him, and came to Milarepa, who asked, "Did you try last night to find out what the mind is like?" The boy replied, "Yes, I did."

"What does it look like?"

"Well, it is limpid, lucid, moving, unpredictable, and ungraspable; it has no color or shape. When it associates with the eyes, it sees; when with the ear, it hears; when with the nose, it smells; when with the tongue, it tastes and talks; and when with the feet it walks. If the body is agitated, the mind, too, is stirred. Normally the mind directs the body; when the body is in good condition, the mind can command it at will, but when the body becomes old, decayed, or bereft, the mind will leave it behind without a thought as one throws away a stone after cleaning oneself. The mind is very realistic and adaptable. On the other hand, the body does not remain quiet or submissive, but frequently gives trouble to the mind. It causes suffering and pain until the mind loses its self-control. At night in the state of sleep the mind goes away; it is indeed very busy and hard-working. It is clear to me that all my sufferings are caused by it [the mind]."

The Jetsun then sang:

Listen to me, young shepherd.
The body is between the conscious and
    unconscious state,
While the mind is the crucial and decisive factor!
He who feels sufferings in the lower Realms,
Is the prisoner of Saṃsāra,
Yet it is the mind that can free you from Saṃsāra.

Surely you want to reach the other shore?
Surely you long for the City of Well-Being
    and Liberation?
If you desire to go, dear child, I can show
The way to you and give you the instructions.

The shepherd replied, "Certainly, dear Lama, I have made up my mind to seek it." Milarepa then asked, "What is your name?"

"Sangje Jhap."

"How old are you?"

"Sixteen."

Thereupon the Jetsun gave him the teaching of "Taking Refuge,"[4] explaining briefly its benefits and significance. He then said, "When you get back home this evening, do not stop reciting the Prayer; and in the meantime try to find out which takes refuge, the mind or the body. Tell me the result tomorrow."

The next morning the shepherd came and said to Milarepa. "Dear Lama, last night I tried to find out which of these two takes refuge, the body or the mind. I found that it is neither of them. [I observed the body first.] Each part, from the head down to the toes, has a name. I asked myself, 'Is it the body as a whole which takes refuge?' It cannot be so, for when the mind leaves the body, the latter no longer exists. People then call it a 'corpse,' and certainly it cannot be called a 'refuge-seeker.' Furthermore, when it disintegrates, it ceases to be a corpse; therefore, it cannot be the body which takes refuge in Buddha. I then asked myself, 'Is it the mind that takes refuge?' But the refuge-seeker cannot be the mind, as the latter is only the mind and nothing else. If one says that the present mind is the [real] mind, and the succeeding one is the one which takes refuge, there will be two minds; and names for both, such as the 'present mind,' and the 'future mind' should then be given them. Besides, when the act of 'Refuge-seeking' takes place, both the present and succeeding minds have passed away! If one says both take refuge, then the mind will [become something immutable] which never [grows] or ceases to be. If that is so, then in all the lives of the past and future in the Six Realms of Saṃsāra, we need nothing but this 'Refuge-seeker.' But I cannot remember anything in my past life; nor do I know what will take place in my future one. The mind of last year and yesterday are gone; that of tomorrow has not yet come; the present flowing one does not stay. Pray, my teacher, please give me an explanation! I submit everything to you; you know everything, you know what I need!"

In answer to his request, Milarepa sang:

I sincerely pray to my Guru
Who realized the truth of Non-ego,
I pray with body, words, and mind;
I pray with great faith and sincerity.
Pray bless me and my disciples,
Enable us to realize the Truth of Non-ego!
Pity us and deliver us from the plight of
    ego-clinging!

Listen carefully, dear shepherd.
Clinging to the notion of ego is
    characteristic of this consciousness.
If one looks into this consciousness itself,
He sees no ego; of it nothing is seen!

If one can practice the teaching of Mahāmudrā
And knows how to see nothing, something will
    be seen.

To practice the teaching of Mahāmudrā
One needs great faith, humility, and zeal
    as the Foundation.[5]
One should understand the truth of Karma
    and Causation as the Path.[6]
In order to achieve the Accomplishment,[7]
    one should depend upon a Guru
For the Initiation, Instruction, and Inner Teaching.

It requires a disciple possessing merit[8]
    to receive the teaching;
It requires a man who disregards discomfort
    and suffering;
It requires the courage of fearlessness,
    the defiance of death!
Dear shepherd, can you do these things?
If so, you are well-destined;
If not, it is better not to talk about the subject.
This ask yourself, and think carefully.

When you sought the "I" [last night] you
    could not find it.
This is the practice of Non-ego of Personality.
If you want to practice the Non-ego of Existence,[9]

Follow my example and for twelve years meditate.
Then you will understand the nature of Mind.
Think well on this, dear boy!

The shepherd said, "I offer you my body and my head. Please make me understand my own mind definitely and clearly." The Jetsun thought, "I shall see whether this child can really practice," and then he said, "First pray to the Three Precious Ones, then visualize an image of Buddha in front of your nose." Thus Milarepa gave the shepherd the instruction of concentration and sent him away.

There was no sign of the boy for seven days. On the seventh day, his father came to Milarepa, saying, "Dear Lama, my son has not come home for a week. This is very unusual. Wondering whether he was lost, I inquired of the other shepherds who had been with him. They all said that he had come to you for the Dharma, and thought he had then gone home. But where is he?" "He was here," replied Milarepa, "but has not come back now for seven days."

The father was deeply grieved and wept bitterly as he left Milarepa. Many people were then sent out to search for the boy. Finally, they found him in a clay pit sitting upright with his eyes wide open staring straight in front. They asked him, "What are you doing here?" He replied, "I am practicing the meditation my Guru taught me." "Then why have you not returned home for seven days?" "I have only been meditating a little while, you must be joking!" As he said this, he looked at the sun and found that it was earlier than the time he had started to meditate. In his bewilderment he asked, "What has happened?"

From that day on, the boy's family had great difficulty with him, because he had almost completely lost the notion of time. What appeared to him to have been only one day, was the passing of four or five days to others. Many times his parents sent people out to search for him. Thus both he and his family began to feel miserable. At this juncture they asked him whether he wanted to live with Milarepa for good. He said that he would like nothing better. So they provided him with food and sent him to the Teacher.

Milarepa first gave him the Precepts of Five Virtues,[10] preached the doctrine of Dharma, and then granted him the teaching of the Innate-born Wisdom.[11] Through practice, the boy gradually attained good meditation experience and Milarepa was very pleased. [In order, however, to clarify the boy's misapprehension on the nature of true Realization], he sang:

I bow down at the feet of Marpa,
He who received grace from Nāropa and Medripa.

Those who practice the Dharma with their mouths
Talk much and seem to know much teaching,
But when the time comes for the perceiver to
    leave the deadened body,
The mouth-bound preacher into space is thrown.

When the Clear Light[12] shines, it is cloaked
    by blindness;
The chance to see the Dharmakāya at the time
    of death
Is lost through fear and confusion.

Even though one spends his life in studying
    the Canon,
It helps not at the moment of the mind's departure.

*Alas! Those proficient yogis who long
    have practiced meditation
Mistake the psychic experience of illumination
For Transcendental Wisdom,*
And are happy with this form of self-deception.[13]
Therefore when at death the Transcendental
    Wisdom of the Dharmakāya shines,
These yogis cannot unify the Light of
    Mother-and-Son.[14]
Since meditation cannot help them as they die,
They are still in danger of rebirth in
    lower Realms.[15]

My dear son, best of laymen, listen to me carefully!

*When your body is rightly posed, and your
    mind absorbed deep in meditation,
You may feel that thought and mind both disappear;
Yet this is but the surface experience of Dhyāna.
By constant practice and mindfulness thereon,
One feels radiant Self-awareness shining like
    a brilliant lamp.
It is pure and bright as a flower,
It is like the feeling of staring
Into the vast and empty sky.
The Awareness of Voidness is limpid and
    transparent, yet vivid.*

*This Non-thought, this radiant and transparent
      experience
Is but the feeling of Dhyāna.
With this good foundation
One should further pray to the Three Precious Ones,
And penetrate to Reality by deep thinking
      and contemplation.*[16]
*He thus can tie the Non-ego Wisdom
With the beneficial life-rope of deep Dhyāna.*
With the power of kindness and compassion,
And with the altruistic vow of the Bodhi-Heart,
He can see direct and clear
The truth of the Enlightened Path,
Of which nothing can be seen, yet all is
      clearly visioned.
He sees how wrong were the fears and hopes
      of his own mind.
Without arrival, he reaches the place of Buddha;
Without seeing, he visions the Dharmakāya;
Without effort, he does all things naturally.
Dear son, the Virtue-seeker, bear this in-
      struction in your mind.

Milarepa then gave the boy the complete Initiation and verbal instructions. After practicing them, the boy attained superlative Experience and Realization. He was known as one of the "Heart-Sons" of the Jetsun, Repa Sangje Jhap.

This is the story of Milarepa's second visit to Ragma, and of his meeting with Repa Sangje Jhap.

NOTES

1 This is another name for the Ālaya Consciousness. See Story 4, Note 38.

2 Lit.: "Through the 'Pointing-out-Instruction' one may glimpse it." The Pointing-out-Instruction (T.T.: Ño.sProd.) is an essential practice of Mahāmudrā. The main concern of Mahāmudrā is the unfoldment of the essence of one's mind. To accomplish this, the disciple is given by his Guru the "Pointing-out" demonstration. This can be done in different ways with different gestures — a smile, a blow, a push, a remark, etc. This is strikingly similar to the tradition of Zen, though the style and process appear somewhat different.

3 See Note 2.

4 "Taking Refuge" (T.T.: sKyabs.hGro.): This is the basic and universal prayer of all Buddhists. It reads: "I take refuge in the Buddha, I take refuge in the Dharma, I take refuge in the Sangha."

5, 6, 7 Foundation, Path, and Accomplishment (T.T.: gShi, Lam, hBres.Bu.): These three terms are frequently used in Buddhist Tantric texts. They have various meanings and uses. Generally speaking, the "Foundation" (gShi.) implies the basic principles of Buddhism; the "Path" (Lam.) is the practice, or way of action which is in conformity with the principles of the "Foundation"; and the "Accomplishment" (hBres.Bu.), otherwise translated as "Fruit," is the full realization of the principles of the Foundation. For example, the Foundation of the teaching of Mahāmudrā is the view that the innate Buddha-nature is within all sentient beings, without which no sentient being could possibly become Buddha regardless of how hard he attempted to practice the Dharma. "Foundation" is, therefore, the cause, the seed, the potentiality, or the original innate Suchness that exists in all beings at all times. The Path of Mahāmudrā is the practice that one follows within the framework of the basic Mahāmudrā Doctrine. The Accomplishment of Mahāmudrā is the full realization of the original, endowed Buddha-nature — the Foundation — within oneself. These three terms, in addition to their special and specific connotations, are used here, as well as in many other places throughout the book, in a very general sense to denote religious faith, practice, and achievement.

8 A merit-possessor is a good vessel for Dharma, a well-destined person. According to Buddhism, a person becomes a good vessel for Dharma in this life partly because he has performed meritorious deeds in his past lives.

9 Non-ego of existence (T.T.: Chos.Kyi.bDag.Med.): the truth of Non-being or Voidness.

10 The Precepts of Five Virtues: These are the basic precepts for all Buddhists, including monks and laymen. They are: One should not (1) kill, (2) steal, (3) commit adultery, (4) lie, or (5) take intoxicants.

11 Innate-born Wisdom: From the Tantric viewpoint, the realization of this inborn and ubiquitous Wisdom is the realization of Buddhahood itself, and so is the core of Tantric teachings.

12 At the time of death, the Clear Light of the Dharmakāya will shine for a short while, but because of ignorance and habitual clinging men cannot recognize it, thus they miss the chance of Liberation. See "The Tibetan Book of the Dead," edited by W. Y. Evans-Wentz, Oxford University Press, 1957.

13 Milarepa gave this very important warning to yogis, pointing out that there are many different *kinds and degrees* of illumination. Some are mundane, some are transcendental, some are psychic phenomena, and some are the real illuminations of Transcendental Wisdom.

14 Mother-and-Son Light: See Story 9, Note 17.

15 Buddhism claims that faith and meditation alone cannot liberate one from Saṃsāra. Without the complete destruction of ego-clinging, or the absolute annihilation of the habitual-thinking seeds in the Store Consciousness (Ālaya-vijñāna), a real Liberation is impossible. Various teachings are given by different Buddhist Schools to attain this Liberation, such as the Prajñāpāramitā of Mādhyamika; the Contemplation-on-Away-from-Subjective-Objective-Ideas of Yogācāra; the Sameness of Saṃsāra and Nirvāṇa of general Tantrism; and the Unification of the Mother-and-Son Light of Mahāmudrā.

16 Faith, good will, compassion, and Samādhi cannot bring one to Enlightenment without the Prajñā insight. Deep contemplation on Śūnyatā, or Voidness, is therefore absolutely necessary.

13

THE SONG OF
REALIZATION

Obeisance to all Gurus

THE Jetsun Milarepa returned to Nya Non from the Happy Town of Mang Yul. His former patrons were all delighted [to see him again] and begged him to stay in Nya Non permanently. At the foot of a huge tree stood a belly-shaped rock, beneath which there was a cave, and Milarepa took up his abode there. Then the Venerable Shaja Guna and a number of patrons of Nya Non came and asked him what progress and Realization he had attained during his sojourn in other places. In answer he sang:

I make obeisance to Marpa, the Translator.

During my stay elsewhere
I realized that nothing is;
I freed myself from the duality of
    past and future;
I apprehended that the Six Realms do not exist.
I was delivered once and for all from
    life and death,
And understood that all things are equal.
I shall cling no more to happiness or sorrow.
I realized as illusion all that I perceive,
And was freed from taking and from leaving.
I realized the truth of Non-difference,
And was freed from both Saṃsāra and Nirvāṇa.
I also realized as illusions the Practice,
    Steps, and Stages.
My mind is thus devoid of hope and fear.

The patrons again asked Milarepa, "What else did you understand?" Milarepa replied, "Well, to please you, I will sing an appropriate, helpful song":

> One's parents provide the outer cause
> and conditions;
> One's Universal Seed Consciousness[1]
> is within;
> The acquired pure human body is between these two.
> With these three endowments one stands apart
> From the Three Miserable Realms.
> By observing the wearisome process of
> birth in the outer world,
> The longing for renunciation and the
> faith for Dharma will grow from within.
> In addition, one should e'er remember the
> teaching of Buddha;
> Thus will one be freed from worldly kinsmen
> and enemies.
>
> The Father-Guru provides help from without;
> Self-discrimination arises from the effort within;
> Between these two grows confidence and conviction.
> Thus is one freed from all doubt and confusion.
>
> One thinks of sentient beings in the Six
> Realms without,
> While unbounded love shines from the mind within.
> Between the two come the experiences of
> meditation.
> Thus one is freed from all partial compassion.[2]
>
> Outwardly, the Three Kingdoms are self-liberated;
> Inwardly, self-present Wisdom[3] brightly shines;
> Between the two, faith in Realization stands firm.
> Thus fade anxiety and fear.
>
> The Five Desires manifest without;
> Non-clinging Wisdom shines within;
> A feeling of [the two] tasting as one[4]
> Is experienced in between.
> Thus one is freed from the distinction of
> weal and woe.
>
> The absence of act and deed appears without,
> The departure of fear and hope is seen within;

Between the two, and from you apart,
Is the sickness that comes from effort.
Thus one is freed from choosing
     between good and evil.

The Venerable Shaja Guna said to Milarepa, "My dear Jetsun, your mind has long been absorbed in Purity, yet though I was with you before, I never received a definitive and convincing teaching from you. Now, please give me the Initiations and instructions." The Jetsun complied with his request, and made him start practicing.

After some time, Shaja Guna had an experience, and came to Milarepa, saying, "If Saṃsāra and manifestations do not exist, there is no need to practice Dharma; if the mind is non-existent, there is no need for the Guru; but if there is no Guru, how can one learn the practice? Please explain the nature of these things and enlighten me upon the Essence of Mind."

Milarepa then sang:

Manifestation is not [something] coming
     into being;
If one sees something happen, it is merely clinging.
The nature of Saṃsāra is the absence of substance;
If one sees substance therein, it is merely
     an illusion.

The nature of mind is two-in-one;
If one discriminates or sees opposites,
It is one's attachment and affection.

The qualified Guru is the Lineage-possessor;
It is then folly to create one's own Guru.

The Essence of Mind is like the sky;
Sometimes it is shadowed by the clouds
     of Thought-flow.
Then the wind of the Guru's inner teaching
Blows away the drifting clouds;
Yet the Thought-flow itself is the illumination.
The Experience is as natural as sun- and moon-light;
Yet it is beyond both space and time.

It is beyond all words and description.
But assurance grows in one's heart, like
     many stars a'shining;
Whenever it so shines, great ecstasy arises.

Beyond all playwords lies the nature of
    the Dharmakāya;
Of the action of the Six Groups, it is
    utterly devoid.
It is transcendant, effortless, and natural,
Beyond the grasp of self and non-self.
Dwelling forever in it is the Wisdom of
    Non-clinging.
Wondrous is the Trikāya, Three in One.

He then told Shaja Guna not to become attached to pleasure, fame,
and the world, but to devote himself to the practice of the Dharma
all his life and urge others to do likewise.

Then Milarepa sang:

Hear me, you well-gifted man!
Is not this life uncertain and delusive?
Are not its pleasures and enjoyments like a mirage?
Is there any peace here in Saṃsāra?
Is not its false felicity as unreal as a dream?
Are not both praise and blame empty as an echo?
Are not all forms the same as the Mind-nature?
Are not Self-mind and the Buddha identical?
Is not the Buddha the same as the Dharmakāya?
Is not the Dharmakāya identical with Truth?

The enlightened one knows that all things are mental;
Therefore one should observe one's mind by
    day and night.
If you watch it, you can still see nothing.
Fix then your mind in this non-seeing state.

There is no self-entity in Milarepa's mind;
I, myself, am the Mahāmudrā;
Because there is no difference between Static
    and Active Meditation,
I have no need for the different stages in the Path.
Whatever they may manifest, their essence
    is Voidness;
There is neither mindfulness nor non-
    mindfulness in my contemplation.

I have tasted the flavor of Non-existence;

Compared to other teachings, this is the highest.
The Yoga-practice of the Nāḍīs, Prāṇa, and Bindu,[5]
The teaching of Karma Mudrā[6] and of Mantra Yoga,
The practice of visualizing Buddha and the
    Four Pure Positions,
These are only the first steps in Mahāyāna.
To practice them uproots not lust and hate.

Bear what I now sing firmly in your minds;
All things are of the Self-mind, which is void.
He who ne'er departs from the Experience and
    Realization [of the Void],
Without effort has accomplished all practices
    of worship and discipline.
In this are found all merits and marvels!

Thus Milarepa sang, and the teacher, Shaja Guna, devoted himself to practicing meditation. He attained an extraordinary understanding and became one of the intimate Son-Disciples of the Jetsun.

This is the story of Milarepa's ripening the priest, Shaja Guna of Nya Non, in the Belly Cave.

NOTES

1 Universal Seed Consciousness: Store Consciousness (Ālaya-vijñāna). See Story 4, Note 38.

2 Partial compassion: An enlightened being should have an unlimited and indiscriminative compassion in contrast to the limitative and favoring love of ordinary men. This ever-present infinite compassion is brought about by the Mahāmudrā Practice. It is said an infinite compassion will flow naturally from the Inborn-Buddha-Mind when one reaches the advanced stage of Mahāmudrā.

3 Self-present Wisdom: An enlightened being never feels that he *attains* the Wisdom of Buddha, he merely *discovers* it — the ever-present Wisdom.

4 Tasting as one, or One-taste (T.T.: Ro.gCig.): When one is freed from discriminitive thoughts, he then reaches the realm of "One-taste," whence he sees the non-differentiation of beings and becomes one with the "Universal Harmony" and the "Interpenetrating Totality." (See the "Avataṁsaka Sūtra"; and D. T. Suzuki's "The Essence of Buddhism," The Buddhist Society, London, 1957.)

5 Nāḍīs, Prāṇa, and Bindu: See Story 7, Note 19.

6 Karma Mudrā: an advanced Perfecting Yoga through which the sexual energy is sublimated.

14

A WOMAN'S ROLE IN
THE DHARMA

Obeisance to all Gurus

O NCE Jetsun Milarepa intended to go to North Horse Gate snow mountain to practice meditation. [On the way], he came to Gebha Lesum in the district of Jung. It was autumn, and the villagers were busy harvesting. In a large field a very beautiful girl, about fifteen years of age, was leading a group of laborers. She seemed to have all the qualifications of an Angel of Wisdom (Ḍākinī). Milarepa approached her and said, "Dear Patroness, please give me alms." "Dear Yogi, please go to my house," the girl replied, "It is over there. Wait for me at the door. I will come directly."

Accordingly, Milarepa went to her home, pushed the door open with his staff, and entered. Immediately, an ugly old woman with a handful of ashes rushed at him, shouting, "You miserable yogi-beggars! I never see you in one place! In the summer you all show up begging for milk and butter! In the winter you all come for grain! I'll wager you wanted to sneak in to steal my daughter's and daughter-in-law's jewelry!" Grumbling and trembling with rage, she was about to throw the ashes at Milarepa, when he said, "Wait a minute, Grandmother! Please listen to me!" He then sang a song with nine meanings:

> Above is the auspicious Heaven,
> Below are the Three Paths of misery,
> In between, are those who are not free to
>   choose their birth.[1]
> These three all converge on you.
> Grandmother, you are an angry woman,
> And dislike the Dharma!

Question your own thoughts and your mind examine.
You should practice the Buddha's teaching,
You need a qualified and dependable Guru.
Think carefully, dear lady;
When you were first sent here,
Did you dream you would become an old nanny-goat?

In the morning you get up from bed,
In the evening you go to sleep,
In between, you do the endless housework;
You are engrossed in these three things.
Grandmother, you are the unpaid maid.
Question your own thought and your mind examine.
You should practice Buddha's teaching,
You need a qualified and dependable Guru,
And then things may be different for you.

The head of the family is the most important one,
Income and earnings are the next most longed-for
        things,
Then sons and nephews are wanted most.
By these three you are bound.
Grandmother, for yourself you have no share.
Question your own thought and your mind examine.
You should practice Buddha's teaching,
You need a qualified and dependable Guru,
And then things may be different for you.

Attaining what you want even though you steal,
Getting what you desire even though you rob,
Fighting your foe without regard for death
        and wounds,
To these three things you are subjected.
Grandmother, you are burned up with fury
When you come upon your foe.
Question your own thought and your mind examine.
You should practice Buddha's teaching,
You need a qualified and dependable Guru,
And then things may be different for you.

Gossip about other women and their manners
Is what interests you;
To the affairs of your own son and nephew

You pay attention;
To talk of widows and relatives is your delight.
These three things enchant you.
Grandmother, are you so gentle when you gossip?
Question your own thought and your mind examine.
You should practice Buddha's teaching,
You need a qualified and dependable Guru,
And then things may be different for you.

To lift you from a chair is like pulling out a peg;
With feeble legs
You waddle like a thieving goose;
Earth and stone seem to shatter
When you drop into a seat;
Senile and clumsy is your body.
Grandmother, you have no choice but to obey.
Question your own thought and your mind examine.
You should practice the Buddha's teaching,
What you require is a qualified and dependable Guru,
And from that you may find out how you have changed.

Your skin is creased with wrinkles;
Your bones stand out sharply from your shrunken flesh;
You are deaf, dumb, imbecile, eccentric, and
        tottering;
You are thrice deformed.
Grandmother, your ugly face is wrapped in wrinkles.
Question your own thought and your mind examine.
You should practice Buddha's teaching,
You need a qualified and dependable Guru,
And then things may be different for you.

Your food and drink are cold and foul,
Your coat is heavy and in rags,
Your bed so rough it tears the skin;[2]
These three are your constant companions.
Grandmother, you are now a wretch,
        half woman and half bitch!
Question your own thought and your mind examine!
You should practice Buddha's teaching,
What you need is a qualified and dependable Guru,
And then things may be different for you.

To attain a higher birth and Liberation
Is harder than to see a star in daytime;
To fall into Saṃsāra's wretched path
Is easy and happens often.
Now, with fear and grief at heart,
You watch the time of death draw nigh.
Grandmother, can you face death with confidence?
Question your own thought and your mind examine!
What you need is to practice the teaching of Buddha,
What you need is a qualified and dependable Guru.

Upon hearing this profound, yet melodious song, the old woman was so moved that she could not but develop a deep faith in the Jetsun. Unconsciously her fists loosened, and the ashes slipped through her fingers to the floor. She regretted what she had done to the Jetsun, and touched by his compassion and words, she could not help shedding tears.

Meantime the girl in the field [whose name was Bardarbom] was just entering the house. Seeing the old woman in tears she turned to Milarepa and cried, "What is the matter? Did you, a follower of Buddha, strike a poor old woman?" The grandmother quickly intervened, "No, no, please do not wrongly accuse him! He never said anything unkind to me. It was I who treated him wrongly. He gave me such a proper and much-needed lesson that it moved me very deeply. It also awakened me to my neglect of religion. I was touched with such great remorse that it compelled me to shed tears. Oh, you are young and different from me; you have faith as well as wealth, and it is very fortunate for you to meet such a teacher as Milarepa. You should give him offerings and service, and ask him to bestow upon you the teachings and instructions."

The girl replied, "Both of you are very wonderful! Are you the great Yogi, Milarepa? By merely meeting you I shall have accumulated a great deal of merit. If you would kindly tell us your Lineage, it will inspire us and also your other disciples. It will certainly change our hearts. So, please do relate it for me."

Milarepa thought, "This is a well-gifted woman; she will become a good disciple of mine." And so he sang:

The omnipresent Dharmakāya is Buddha
    Samantabhadra;
The majestic Sambhogakāya is Buddha
    the Thunderbolt-Holder;

The Savior of sentient beings, the
    Nirmāṇakāya, is Gautama Buddha.
One may find [the teachings] of all
    three Buddhas in my Lineage.
Such is the Lineage of this yogi; will you
    entrust yourself to it?

"Your Lineage is indeed superb," said Bardarbom, "it is what the
snow mountain is to rivers—the original source of all [merits]. I have
heard people say that you, the followers of Dharma, have a so-called
'Outer Pointing Guru'; and that by relying on him, one will be able
to observe and see inwardly the so-called Uncreated Dharmakāya.
What kind of Guru do you have? Who is your primary Guru?"
    Milarepa replied, "I will sing a short song to explain the qualifica-
tions of a genuine Guru."

The Guru who indicates the true knowledge
    from without,
Is your Outer Guru;
The Guru who elucidates the Awareness of
    Mind within,
Is your Inner Guru;
The Guru who illuminates the nature of your mind,
Is your real Guru.
I am a yogi who has all three Gurus,
Is there a disciple here who wishes to
    be faithful to them?"

"These Gurus are extraordinary!" exclaimed the girl, "It is just like
a string of gems on a golden chain. But before we beseech the
teachings from them, what kind of Initiations are required?" Milarepa
then sang:

The Vase placed on your head
Is the Outer Initiation;
The proof of the identity of self-body
    and the Body of Buddha
Is the Inner Initiation;
The Illumination of the self-recognition
    of Mind-Essence
Is the real Initiation.
I am a yogi who has attained all three.
Is there a disciple here who wishes to attain them?

Bardarbom cried out, "These Initiations are indeed profound! It is just like the majesty of the lion, which overawes all other animals. I have also heard that after the Initiation there is an absolute teaching called 'Leading Awareness into the Path.' What is that? Please be kind enough to explain it to me."

In answer to her question, Milarepa sang:

> The Outer Teaching is hearing, thinking,
>   and practicing;
> The Inner Teaching is the clearest
>   elucidation of Awareness;
> The Absolute Teaching is the non-gathering
>   or separation of Experience and Realization.[3]
> I am a yogi who has all three Teachings.
> Is there a disciple here who wishes to attain them?

Bardarbom declared, "These teachings are indeed like a rustless mirror, which reflects images flawlessly." Milarepa replied, "Having attained these teachings, one should go to a hermitage and practice." The girl then asked, "Will you tell me about these practices?" Milarepa sang in answer:

> Living in a rugged, deserted, and solitary hut
> Is the Outer Practice;
> Complete disregard of the self-body
> Is the Inner Practice;
> Knowing the sole Absolute, through and through,
> Is the Absolute Practice.
> I am a yogi who knows all three.
> Is there a disciple here who wishes to learn them?

After hearing this, the girl said, "The Practice you have mentioned is like a great eagle flying in the sky. Its splendor overshadows all other birds!" She continued, "I have heard people say that some yogis know a teaching called 'Pai Practice,'[4] which is very helpful in improving meditation. Could you tell me about it?" Milarepa then sang:

> By applying the Outer "*Pai* Teaching" to
>   the distracted thought-flow,
> The mind is collected;
> By applying the Inner "*Pai* Teaching" to awareness,
> The mind is awakened from drowsiness.
> To rest [the mind] on the innate nature,

Is the Absolute "*Pai* Teaching."
I am the Yogi who knows all three.
Is there a disciple here who wishes to know them?

"This *Pai* Teaching of yours is indeed wonderful!" exclaimed Bardarbom, "It is just like the order or summons of the Emperor; it quickens and intensifies one's accomplishments. But if one practices it, what experiences will one have?" Milarepa sang in reply:

> One will experience the great and
>   omnipresent Non-effort Root;
> One will experience the Non-effort
>   Path, the great transparency;
> One will experience the Non-effort
>   Fruit,[5] great Mahāmudrā.
> I am a yogi who has experienced them all.
> Is there a disciple here who wishes to do likewise?

Bardarbom then said, "These three experiences are like the bright sun shining from a cloudless sky, outlining everything on the earth clearly and distinctly. They are indeed wonderful! But what assurance have you gained through them?" Milarepa sang again:

> No Heaven and no Hell, is the assurance
>   of Knowledge,[6]
> No meditation and no distraction is the
>   assurance of Practice,
> No hope and no fear is the assurance of Accomplishment.
> I am a yogi with these three assurances.
> Is there a disciple here who wishes to attain them?

Thereupon, the girl became very faithful to the Jetsun. She bowed down at his feet, and with great veneration she invited him to the inner [chamber], and gave him perfect service and offerings. Then she said "Dear Guru, so far, I have been hindered by ignorance, and so have not been able to think of the real Teachings. Now, through your great compassion, please take me as your servant and disciple." Thus the girl fully realized her past faults of self-conceit. She then sang:

> Oh! You peerless Teacher!
> You most perfect of men, the incarnation of Buddha!
> How stupid, blind, and ignorant am I.

How wrong and sinful is this world!
The heat of summer was so great that it
    scattered the cool clouds,
And I found no shelter in the shade.
The cold of winter was so severe
That though flowers still grew, I
    never found them.
The influence of my evil habitual-thinking
    was so strong
That I never saw you as an accomplished being.

Let me tell you my story:
Because of my sinful Karma I was given
    this inferior [female] body.
Through the evil-hindrance of this world,
I never realized the identity of self and Buddha.
Lacking the necessary diligence,
I seldom thought of Buddha's teaching.
Though I desired the Dharma,
Lazy and inert, I frittered time away.

To a woman, a prosperous birth means
    bondage and non-freedom.
To a woman, a wretched birth means the
    loss of companionship.
To our husbands we sometimes talk of suicide;
We set aside and leave our gracious parents;
Great is our ambition, but our perseverance small.
We are experts in slander, ingenious to blame,
The source of news and gossip.
We are those who must be kept away from the betrothed,
For though to all we give food and money,
We are ever slandered as stingy and ill-tempered.
Seldom do we think of impermanence and death.
The sinful hindrances always follow us like shadows.
Now, with deep sincerity, I look forward to
    the Dharma.
Pray, give me a teaching easy to practice
    and understand!

This pleased Milarepa very much and he sang in reply:

Happy and fortunate girl,

Should I praise your story or disparage it?
If I praise it, you will be proud;
If I disparage it, you will be angry;
If I tell the truth, it will expose your
    hidden faults.

Now, listen to the song of an old man:
If you sincerely wish to practice Dharma,
Wash the dirt from off your face,
And sweep away the filth from your heart.

Sincerity and earnestness are good,
But humility and modesty are better.
Even though you may give away your son and husband,
It is better to rely on a qualified Guru.
Though you may abandon worldly life,
To strive for future Enlightenment[7] is better.
Though one may renounce parsimony and avarice,
It is better still to give without sparing.
It is wise to know these things.

With high spirits,
You play and sport as shrewdly as a rat.
You may be very eloquent,
But have no Dharma in your heart.
Like a wild peahen you play—
Of coquetry you know too much,
But too little of devotion.
My dear, you are full of cunning and deceit
Like a merchant in the market-place.
It is hard for you to practice Dharma.

If you want to practice Buddha's teaching rightly,
You should follow me and my Path,
Meditating without distraction in a remote
    mountain.

Bardarbom then sang:

You are the Jetsun, the precious Yogi!
One surely will gain benefits by associating with you.
In the daytime I am busy working;
Drowsy, I go to bed at night.

A slave of household work am I.
Where can I find the time to practice Dharma?

Milarepa replied, "If you seriously want to practice the Dharma, you must learn that worldly affairs are your enemies and renounce them." And he sang a song called "The Four Renunciations":

Listen, you fortunate girl,
You who have wealth and faith!

Future lives last longer than this life—
Do you know how to make provision?
Giving with a niggardly heart
As if feeding a strange watchdog,
Only brings more harm than good—
Bringing nothing in return but a vicious bite.
Renounce parsimony, now that you know its evil.

Listen, you fortunate girl!
We know less of this life than the next one.
Have you prepared and lit your lamp?
Should it not be ready,
Meditate on the "Great Light."

If you choose to help an ungrateful foe,
You will gain not a friend, but damage.
Beware of acting blindly;
Beware of this evil and discard it.

Listen, you fortunate girl.
Future lives are worse than this life—
Have you a guide or escort for your journey?
If you have not the right companion,
Rely on the holy Dharma.
Beware of relatives and kinsmen;
They hinder and oppose [the Dharma].
They never help, but only harm one.
Did you know that your kinsmen are your foes?
If this be true, surely you should leave them.

Listen, you fortunate girl.
The journey in the future life is more
       hazardous than this one—

Have you prepared a fine horse of
 perseverance for it?
If not, you should strive hard and work
 with diligence.
The excitement of the start will soon diminish;
Beware the foe, "Inertness," which makes
 one go astray.
Of no avail are hurry and excitement, which
 only harm one.
Do you yet know that your enemies are
 laziness and caprice?
If you understand my words, you should
 cast them both away.

Bardarbom then said, "Dear Lama, I have not yet made any preparation for the next life, but will now begin to do so. Please be
kind enough to teach me the Practice." Thus with great sincerity she
besought him. Milarepa was delighted, and replied, "I am glad that
you are really earnest in devoting yourself to religion. In the tradition
of my Lineage, it is not necessary to change one's name or to cut off
one's hair.[8] One may reach Buddhahood either as a layman, or as a
monk. Without changing one's status, one may still become a good
Buddhist." Then he sang for her a song called "The Four Parables
and Five Meanings," giving the instruction of Mind-Practice:

Listen, you fortunate girl,
You who have wealth and faith!
Thinking of the magnitude of the sky,
Meditate on the Vastness with no center
 and no edge.

Thinking of the sun and moon,
Meditate upon their light
Without darkness or obscurity.

Resembling the unchanging, solid mountain
 before you,
You should meditate with steadiness and solidity.

Like the ocean, infinitely great and un-
 fathomably deep,
Absorb yourself in deepest contemplation.
Thus meditate on your Self-mind;

Thus, with no doubt and error, practice.

Then Milarepa instructed her in the physical and mental practices, and sent her to meditate. Later on the girl, having had some experiences, and in order to dispel her doubts and break down her hindrances, came and sang to him:

> Oh You, the Jetsun, the precious Guru,
> You man of consummation, the Transformation
>   Body of Buddha!
>
> It was fine, when I contemplated on the sky!
> But I felt uneasy when I thought of clouds.
> How should I meditate on them?
>
> It was good, when I contemplated on the sun and moon!
> But I felt uneasy when I thought of stars
>   and planets.
> How should I meditate on them?
>
> It was fine, when I contemplated the solid mountain!
> But I felt uneasy when I thought of trees and bushes.
> How should I meditate on them?
>
> It was good, when I contemplated the great ocean!
> But I felt uneasy when I thought of waves.
> How should I meditate on them?
>
> It was fine, when I contemplated the nature
>   of Self-mind,
> But I felt uneasy when I encountered ever-
>   flowing thoughts![9]
> How should I meditate on them?

After hearing her song, Milarepa was greatly pleased. He knew that she really had had the Experiences in meditation. Thus, in order to clear her doubts and further her understanding, he sang:

> Listen, you fortunate girl,
> You who have wealth and faith!
>
> If you felt fine in meditating on the
>   sky, so be it with the clouds.

Clouds are but manifestations of the sky;
Therefore, rest *right in the sphere of the sky!*

The stars are but reflections of the sun and moon;
If you can meditate on *them,* then why not
    on the stars?
Therefore, absorb yourself *in the light of
    the sun and moon!*

Bushes and trees are but manifestations of
    a mountain;
If you can meditate well on that, so be it with the trees!
Therefore, *abide in the steadfastness of the mountain!*

Waves are but the movement of the ocean;
If you can meditate well on that, why not
    on the waves?
Therefore, dissolve yourself *right in the ocean!*

The disturbing Thought-flow manifests the mind;
If you can meditate well on that, so be it
    with the Thought-flow!
Therefore, dissolve yourself into the very
    Essence of Mind!

From then on, Bardarbom strove to contemplate on the real nature of the mind, and eventually she achieved perfect Realization in one life. At her death she flew to the Ḍākinī's Pure Land in her human body. People all heard the sound of the small drum that she was carrying at the time.

This is the story of Milarepa meeting his woman disciple, Bardarbom, one of his four female heirs, at the place of Gebha Lesum of Jung.

NOTES

1 Driven by the force of Karma, Saṃsāric beings are not able to choose their own birth when they reincarnate.

2 This is a free translation.

3 Experience and Realization: See Story 7, Notes 9 and 12.

4 *"Pai* Practice," or the Teaching of *Pai* (T.T.: Phat): The Tibetan word "Phat," pronounced "Pai," is common in Tantric incantations. It is used as a means of cutting distracting thoughts and to arouse the consciousness from drowsiness occurring in meditation. In applying the *Pai* teaching, the yogi first concentrates on the thought-flow, drowsiness, apparitions, or whatever hindrances appear, and then suddenly shouts "Pai!" with all his strength. By doing this the hindrances are eventually eliminated.

5 The Non-effort Root, Path, and Fruit: "Root" means the basic principle, the nature of Buddhahood. "Path" refers to the practice of this basic principle. "Fruit" is the resulting accomplishment or realization of the basic principle. (See Story 12, Notes 5, 6, and 7.)

6 Knowldege, (T.T.: lTa.Wa.), or the "View" of the absolute non-existence of being

7 Lit.: "to strive for the Great Affair."

8 To cut off the hair: This refers to the shaving of a monk's head during the ceremony of ordination.

9 Ever-flowing thoughts: Only through actual meditation practice can one experience the ungovernable and ever-running errant thoughts that constantly arise in one's own mind.

15

THE SONG AT THE INN

Obeisance to all Gurus

Having meditated at Jundhagho [North Horse Gate], the Jetsun Milarepa went to Shri Ri to meditate; on his way, he lodged in an inn at Yei Ru Jang. A scholar named Yaugru Tangbha, with many monk disciples, and a merchant called Dhawa Norbu [the Moon Jewel], with a great retinue, were also stopping there. Milarepa begged alms from the merchant, who said, "You yogis are accustomed to taking the belongings of others to enjoy yourselves; why don't you try to earn your own living? It would be much better to be self-supporting!" Milarepa replied, "It is true that by following your way one may have more immediate happiness and enjoyment, but this very enjoyment will cause more suffering in the future. This is the important point you have neglected. Now listen to my song, 'The Eight Reminders' ":

> Castles and crowded cities are the places
> Where now you love to stay;
> But remember that they will fall in ruins
> After you have departed from this earth.
>
> Pride and vainglory are the lure
> Which now you love to follow;
> But remember, when you are about to die
> They offer you no shelter and no refuge!
>
> Kinsmen and relatives are the people
> With whom now you love to live!
> But remember that you must leave them all behind
> When from this world you pass away!
>
> Servants, wealth, and children

Are things that you love to hold;
But remember, at the moment of your death
Your empty hands can take nothing with you!

Vigor and health are dearest to you now;
But remember that at the moment of your death
Your corpse will be bundled up[1] and borne away!

Now your organs are clear, your blood and
    flesh are strong and vigorous;
But remember, at the moment of your death
They will no longer be at your disposal!

Sweet and delicious foods are things
That now you love to eat;
But remember, at the moment of your death
Your mouth will let the spittle flow!

When of all this I think, I cannot help
But seek the Buddha's teachings!
The enjoyments and pleasures of this world,
For me have no attraction.

I, Milarepa, sing of the Eight Reminders,
At the Guest House of Garakhache of Tsang.
With these clear words I give this helpful warning;
I urge you to observe and practice them!

Thus he sang, and his song roused in the merchant, Dhawa Norbu, such a deep faith that he exclaimed, "Dear Lama, what you have sung is indeed very true and clear and has made me think of the Dharma. Pray, instruct me how to practice the teaching of Buddha." In answer, Milarepa sang:

The rugged hermitage is the place of virtue,
The Guru with knowledge and practice is the
    precious jewel
To whom one should pray with sincerity and reverence.
Without errors the teachings should be practiced.

He who feels his mind run wild,
Should apply his View[2] [of Voidness] for the cure.
The attachments of his mind are thus freed.

How wonderful this is!

He whose mind feels sick,
Should beg the alms of Non-discrimination.[3]
He will then experience the self-liberation
    of the places to which [he travels].
How wonderful this is!

He who dislikes his meditation experiences,
Should compare and discuss them with
    proficient Gurus.
To talk and live with these experienced yogis,
Surely will help his mind!

If sometimes doubts arise, and skepticism,
One should read the holy sayings of the Buddha.
With conviction in the true words of the Dharma,
Confidence and faith in one's heart will grow!

He who feels uneasy and unwell,
Should pray to his Father Guru
With all earnestness;
Thus will he be blessed and his mind made tranquil.

Again, one should think of those faithless men
Who lay their bodies down on Saṃsāra's bed,
Who lay their heads upon the pillows of the Five Poisons
And fling the dung of their passions to the Ten
    Directions.
One should search for [the physician who
    can] cure them.
With the devotion of the Three Gates[4]
    one should make the diagnosis;
Through the Six Merits of the Guru-Doctor
    one should give the medicine.
Thus one is assured that the Three Bodies
    will be attained,
And the Five Poisonous Passions cured!

In order to beg pardon and forgiveness
One should give offerings sincerely.

Upon hearing this song the merchant was confirmed with the deepest faith toward the Jetsun. From that time on, as a layman, he followed the Jetsun's instruction in Dharma practice and became a very good yogi.

At the same time in the inn, while Milarepa was appearing as an ascetic, the scholar-doctor, Yaugru Tangbha was preaching the Dharma. His monk-disciples busily recited prayers in the evening, and sat in a crouching posture practicing Samādhi in the daytime. They even held religious ceremonies and started their sermons before daybreak.

One day, Milarepa went to the congregation during the midday meal to beg a little food.[5] Several monks said, "What a pitiful sight this man is! He acts and dresses like a yogi, but does not practice or learn any teaching of the Dharma; without any knowledge or desire for meditation, he fails even to recite a single prayer; and he even asks alms from the priests! What a pity! What a pity!" And they all felt great pity and sorrow for him. Milarepa then said to them, "My mind is always at ease and happy, because I can practice simultaneously the various devotions, such as reciting Mantras and visualizing Devas' bodies, while learning and carrying out the teachings of the Buddha. Please listen to my song":

> The Three Precious Ones, supporting all
> In the realm of Non-doing Awareness —
> I realize them all!
> Why then should I pray to them?
> Happy is the practice of Yoga
> Without Mantra and muttering!
>
> The bestower of the two Siddhis[6] is
>   the protecting Buddha.
> In the realm of Great Illumination,
> I have completely realized the Buddha
>   of Non-existence,
> And so I need not practice the Arising Yoga!
> Happy is the experience
> Of identifying the Self-body with the Buddha!
>
> The Ḍākinīs sweep all obstacles away and
>   destroy misfortunes;
> In the realm of Self-essence, the plane of origin,
> I have completely realized them.
> And so I have no need to make the ritual offering!
> Happy is the Yoga

In which the six sense-organs relax at ease!

Apprehensions are the source of hindrances.
In the realm of Dharma-Essence,
I identify demon-seeing with the Perfection;
Therefore, I need do no exorcising.
Happy is the Yoga
In which I identify the Dharmakāya with apprehensions!

The words and writing, the dogmas
And the logic I absorb
In the Realm of Illuminating Consciousness.
For me, there is no need of learning.
Happy is the experience of Yoga,
The source of all the Sūtras.

Whereupon the Doctor, Yaugru, said to Milarepa, "Dear Yogi, your experience and understanding are indeed marvelous. However, according to the principles of Buddhism, an object or teaching must be given from which beginners may learn; also it is desirable and helpful to encourage people to follow the Yellow-robed [monks] in the practice of virtuous deeds. Is that not so?" Milarepa replied, "This may be the teaching of your School, and you may do what you like. But my teaching is a little different. In it, if one feels he has nothing to be ashamed of, that will be sufficient! From what I can see, your way of devotion is like this—judge for yourself and see whether what I am going to say is true":

I take refuge in the Three Precious Ones;
May my compassionate Guru ever protect and bless me.

You scholar-doctor of the Eight Worldly Engagements,
How can you clear away ignorance and distraction
for others,
When you cannot conquer your own mind?

Under the white canopy, stands a lovely peacock;
But he vanishes as quickly as the lightning!
Think, my dear Doctor! Is that not true?

The kitchen of the monastery behind the village
Is a symbol of misery and cheating;
Think, my dear Doctor! Is that not so?

Attending a boisterous public meeting
Is like being driven round in a circle of fierce foes!
Think, my dear Doctor! Is that not true?

Accumulating horses, sheep, and jewels
Is like dew upon the grass
Under the warm breath of the wind.
Think, my dear Doctor! Are they not alike?

The illusory human body with its mass of passions
Is like a corpse that has been gilded!
Think, my dear Doctor! Are they not alike?

Leading women practicers, without inner experience,
Is a travesty of dignity, and a disgrace.
Think, my dear Doctor! Is that not so?

The food and offerings in the sacrificial circle
Are like the tax collections of an arrogant inspector.
Think, my dear Doctor! Are they not alike?

Divination, Astrology, and Bon[7] rituals —
These three Dharmas-of-the-town are like
      swindler's tricks.
Think, my dear Doctor! Are they not alike?

The tuneful hymns which enchant disciples
Are like the malicious invocation of the Dragon Demon.
Think, my dear Doctor! Are they not alike?

Country, home, and fields are not true possessions
But delusive, and tantalizing like rainbows
      to the young!
Think, my dear Doctor! Is that not so?

To sway and dominate disciples by fraud and hypocrisy
Is like a lackey serving many masters.
Think, my dear Doctor! Is that not true?

To preach without the Essence
Is a lie and fraud!
Think, my dear Doctor! Is that not so?

If you cannot help yourself
How can you help others?

After hearing this song, Doctor Yaugru took a very reverent attitude toward the Jetsun. Rising from his seat he bowed, with his eyes
full of tears, and said, "What you say is very true. Please teach me
the Dharma and allow me to become your disciple."

Among the disciples of Doctor Yaugru there was a young monk
called Sevan Dunchon Shawa who followed the Jetsun and obtained
from him the Initiations and instructions. Having devoted himself
to meditation, he attained the highest accomplishment. He was one
of the heart-sons of the Jetsun, known as Sevan Repa from Dodra.

This is the story of how Milarepa met his disciple Sevan Repa at
the Garakhache Guest House of Yei Ru Jang in Tsang.

NOTES

1 In Tibet the corpse is usually loaded on a horse, like a folded bundle, and
so carried away to the cemetery by the relatives.

2 View: the basic understanding of the Voidness. If distracting thoughts run
wildly during meditation, the yogi should identify them with the Void. They can
thus be tranquilized and transformed.

3 Non-discrimination: Whether his patrons are rich or poor, high or low, the
yogi should beg alms without discrimination. At the same time he should remember
that the giver, the receiver, and the alms are all non-existent, or illusory.

4 Three Gates: body, mouth, and mind.

5 The food remaining from the sacrament.

6 The two Siddhis are the mundane and transcendental "accomplishments,"
or powers.

7 Bon: the pre-Buddhist, native religion of Tibet.

THE BANDIT-DISCIPLE

Obeisance to all Gurus

ONE day when the Jetsun Milarepa was meditating in Shri Ri of Deut Jal, several bandits came to his hermitage. When they could not find any food or clothes, and learned how he lived and made his devotions, they could not help but have deep faith in him. They said, "Dear Lama, this place is very bad. Because of the unfavorable conditions, it must be very hard to get food. Please come to our country, and we will supply you properly."

Milarepa replied, "It is true that conditions here may not be favorable, but I have everything I need to further my devotion. Though your place may be better, I do not want to go there. Instead, I would like you, on my behalf, to send to your country for well-endowed devotees to come here for meditation." And he sang a song called "Welcome to Meditate in Shri Ri":

> Shri Ri, that wondrous place in Jal,
> Is far to circle, but near to approach.
> Come here, you faithful and destined devotees
> And all who would renounce this world and life.
>
> Here is the wonderland, Shri Ri,
> Far indeed from towns,
> But close to meditation and accomplishment!
> Come to Shri Ri, you faithful and destined devotees
> And all who would renounce this world and life!
>
> Though the water here is scarce, the
> goddesses are many.
> Come to Shri Ri, you faithful and well-
> gifted devotees!

Come to Shri Ri of Jal, you disavowers of
    this world and life.

Here is the wonderland, Shri Ri of Jal.
It is a place of blessing, the palace of Dem Chog,
He who bestows accomplishments and Siddhis!
Come to Shri Ri, you faithful and well-gifted
        devotees,
All you who disavow this world and life!

This is the land of wonder, Shri Ri of Jal,
Where the marvelous Guardian-brothers dwell,
They who destroy your obstacles and difficulties!
Come to Shri Ri, you faithful and destined devotees,
And you who disavow this world and life.

Having heard this song, the leader of the bandits was deeply moved
with faith. He bowed down at Milarepa's feet and told him that he
would come back to see him soon. Some time later, when he returned, he brought with him a large turquoise, but could not decide
whether to offer it to Milarepa. Having a small present with him as
well, he gave this to the Jetsun first.

Milarepa smiled and said, "Do not hesitate! You may offer me
that turquoise, although I have little use for jewels. I will accept it to
perfect your merits." The bandit leader realized that Milarepa pos-
sessed the perfect miraculous power of knowing others' thoughts. He
then offered him the turquoise. After accepting it, Milarepa said, "I
now give you back this jewel, hoping that you will use it to sustain
your devotion."

The leader thought: "How wonderful! He has not the slightest desire for money!" And his faith in the Jetsun was confirmed. Milarepa
then gave him the Initiations and instructions. After practicing them,
he eventually attained superlative Experiences and Realization. Later
on, he was known as Drigom Linkawa, and became one of the heart-
sons of Milarepa.

This is the story of how Milarepa met Drigom Repa in Shri Ri of Jal.

THE MEETING
AT SILVER SPRING

Obeisance to all Gurus

ONE summer, the great Yogi, Jetsun Milarepa, was meditating at North Shri Ri. When autumn came and the harvest was ready, he went out for alms, but fell asleep in Upper Gog Tang. He dreamed that he saw a green girl with golden hair and shining eyebrows, leading a youth about twenty years old. She said, "Milarepa, you will have eight petals from [the lotus of] your heart. This is one of them. Please bless him and bring him up!" She then disappeared.

Upon awakening from his sleep, Milarepa thought over the meaning of his dream. He decided that the girl must have been a Ḍākinī and that the "eight petals" must imply that he would have eight superlative, destined, heart-like disciples. "Today, I shall probably meet a Karma-exhausted disciple, and I will try my best to help him." With this in mind, he climbed the road leading to Bong. When he reached a brook which flowed like silver, he paused for another nap. After a while, a young man riding on a black horse approached and asked, "Why, dear Yogi, do you sleep here?" Milarepa parried the question by another one: "My dear patron, where are you going?"

"I am going to cross this brook to Din Ri."

Milarepa then explained, "Because of my age, I find it very difficult to wade through water. Could you give me a ride?"

The young man replied, "As I am going to play with some youths over there, I am in a very great hurry and will not be able to take you with me. Besides, it would strain my horse too much, and he might be hurt."

After saying this he went on ahead, alone, without even looking back.

Thereupon Milarepa, with sincere concentration, entered the

Samādhi of Guru-Union.[1] Holding his breath he walked softly on the water, gliding smoothly across the stream to the other bank. He looked back and saw that the young man and the horse were floundering in midstream, making a big splash. In the meantime, the boy had noticed Milarepa walk past him on the water without sinking. Although he had seen it with his own eyes, he still could not accept it. He muttered to himself, "What's the matter with me? Am I having an hallucination? [If not,] this man must have been born to float!"

When he reached the other bank, he approached Milarepa and observed his feet carefully, discovering that not even his soles were wet; whereupon, a deep faith toward the Jetsun arose within the youth. He cried out, "I did not realize that you were an accomplished Lama. I regret very much that I did not allow you to mount my horse. Please forgive me and accept my apology." Saying this, he bowed to Milarepa many times. With great sincerity and faith, he asked, "Lama, from whence do you come? To what Order do you belong? Who is your Guru? Where is your temple? What meditation do you practice? Where did you come from this morning? Where will you stay tonight?" In answer, the Jetsun sang:

> Ah! My good young friend!
> Listen to me, young playboy!
>
> Do you know who I am? I am the Yogi Milarepa;
> Gung Tang is whence I came.
> My feet have trod all over Weu and Tsang,[2]
> While learning the orders and decrees.
>
> From the gracious Guru Ngomi to Lama Rondonlaga,
> I have studied with ten Gurus and learned the
>   Tantras five,
> The views, and the philosophies of Dharma.
>
> From my teacher, Lhaje Nu Chon, I learned
> The fierce exorcism of the Black and Red Planets.
> Though he was very expert,
> He could never clear my doubts.
>
> Then I heard people say there was a wondrous teacher
> Dwelling in the South, in the river-circled Valley.
> He was blessed by the Lords Nāropa and Medripa,
> And had experienced the mother-like Essence of Mind.
> Having mastered the control of his body,

He dwelt alongside the South River.
He, whose fame had spread afar
Was the father Guru, Marpa the Translator.

Just to hear his name caused my skin to
    tingle and my hair to rise.
Despite the hardships of the journey, I made
    my way to him.
Just by glancing at his face, my heart was changed.
In my life, he is the only Guru,
The peerless one, the gracious Lho Draug Wa.[3]

No money or wealth had I to offer him,
So I reduced my body to powder in his service.
From him, I learned the profound Hevajra Tantra
And the teachings of Nāropa's Skillful Path.[4]
I took the vows and won the Four Initiations
    of the blessed Dem Chog.

When I realized the essence of Mahāmudrā,
I saw plainly the real nature of the mind;
I realized in full the ultimate "Beyond-all-Playwords."

In the Four River-like Teachings[5] of the
    Whispered Succession
I practiced the profound doctrine of the
    Nine Essentials.
Having practiced the art of manipulating
    the Nāḍīs, Prāṇa, and Bindu,
I completely mastered both the mind and Prāṇa.[6]

I am a yogi [who can] dwell in the sky;
Having united the Four Elements,
I have no fear of water.

For your information,
My temple is at Shri Ri.
This morning I came from Upper Gog Tang;
Where I shall go this evening, I am not certain,
For mine is the yogi's way of life.

Have you heard what I have sung,
My happy boy who seeks nought but pleasure?

After hearing this song, an unalterable faith in the Jetsun was established in the young man. His tears fell incessantly. He then handed the reins of his black horse to Milarepa, and sang:

You are the Sage unrecognized, a man of
    the beyond!
You are the Buddha whom one meets so rarely.
Your instructions are the preaching of Nirmāṇakāya.

It seems that I have heard your name before,
But yet I am not sure.
It seems that I may have seen you before,
But again, I am not sure.

Whether the obeisance that I made you
Was sincere enough, I do not know.
If my questions were improper, my mien irreverent,
I beg for your forgiveness, for I did not know you.

This black horse of mine runs like the wind.
On his neck hangs a wondrous bell;
On his back of well-known pedigree
Is a saddle cloth, most warm and smooth;
On it rests a strong wooden saddle.
The girth is fashioned of steel from Mon.
A dainty knot adorns his reddish crupper;
Close to the headstall of reddish-gray
His forelock curls like a tiger's smile,
Shining brightly like a mirrored star.

Whip in hand, give your command;
Shake the rein, he will obey and run.
When he sees the flag before him
He will win the race!
When you cry "Run fast!" he'll gallop
    at full speed.
To a man of the world, a good horse is his pride.
I give you this fine horse as an offering,
Praying that you may keep me from the hell
Into which I else would fall.

Having ended his song, the young man offered Milarepa his horse, but the Jetsun would not accept it, and told him that he had another, even better one. And he sang:

> Listen to me, dear patron!
> A horse of Prāṇa-Mind have I;
> I adorn him with the silk scarf of Dhyāna.
> His skin is the magic Ensuing Dhyāna Stage,[7]
> His saddle, illuminating Self-Awareness.
> My spurs are the Three Visualizations,[8]
> His crupper the secret teaching of the Two Gates.[9]
>
> His headstall is the Prāṇa of Vital-force;[10]
> His forelock curl is Three-pointed Time.[11]
> Tranquillity within is his adornment,
> Bodily movement is his rein,
> And ever-flowing inspiration is his bridle.
>
> He gallops wildly along the Spine's Central Path.
> He is a yogi's horse, this steed of mine.
> By riding him, one escapes Saṃsāra's mud,
> By following him one reaches the safe land of Bodhi.
>
> My dear patron, I have no need of your black horse.
> Go your way, young man, and look for pleasure!

The youth thought, "Though he does not want my horse, his feet are bare. He must need a pair of shoes!" So thinking, he offered his own to Milarepa, singing:

> Revered Yogi, jewel-like accomplished Saint,
> Because there is no attachment in your heart,
> You wander aimless from place to place.
> Sometimes you meet dogs with sharp teeth;
> At others, you walk through brambles and defiles;
> And so your bare feet may be hurt.
>
> Walking without shoes is painful;
> These blue boots shall be your faithful servants.
> With brass spurs on their heels
> And silk-embroidered, they are costly;
> A skillful craftsman made them
> With the skins of elk, wild yak, and crocodile.

These boots are my mark, the mark of the young man,
Which I now offer you.
Pray, grant me your compassionate blessing.

Thus he sang; but the Jetsun would not accept the gift. He told the boy that he had a better pair of boots, singing:

Listen, you faithful young man.
This land of darkness and blind views
Is part of the Three Kingdoms of Saṃsāra.

Full of mud is Craving Meadow,
Full of thorns is Jealous Swamp.
Savage and malignant is the furious dog of Hate,
Dangerous and steep the hill of Pride.

But I have crossed the Rivers Four[12]
And reached the shore of the Pure Land.
I cut my boots from the hide of the
        renunciation of Saṃsāra
And with the leather of awakening from
        transciency and delusion.
I made my boots with the craftsmanship
        of deep faith in Karma,
With the dye of Non-clinging to the Myriad Forms,
And with the thread and rope of Devotion;
While the clasps are the Teachings of
        the Three Bindings.[13]

These are my boots, the boots of a yogi;
I have no desire for yours.
My dear patron, you may now leave for home.

Then the young man said, "Revered One, though you will not take my boots, I still would like to offer you my reddish-green jacket which is good to sleep in, for I see you have only a thin cloth with which to cover your body. You must feel cold all the time. *Please* accept this jacket!" In pleading with Milarepa to take it, the young man sang:

Precious and accomplished Guru,
Freed from Ego-clinging,
You wander with no bourne in mind.

Sometimes you climb the summit of a mountain;
Sometimes you sleep soundly in a city street.
To wear a thin cloth sheet is the same as starving;
It must be still worse unclad to suffer cold.

This is my best tailored jacket
Made of the reddish-green Mandari cloth.
The front is silk,
The lining of best quality.
It is trimmed with lynx fur.
A collar of otter-skin matches the hem,
The shoulder pads are well embroidered.
It is light to wear and grand to see.
In it one does not fear a biting wind,
For it is a noble's jacket.
Please accept it, Reverend Father;
Please bless me, and grant your grace.

But Milarepa would not take the coat, and replied, "I have a jacket which excels even yours!" He then sang:

Listen, you eloquent youth!
O'er the cities of the Six Realms in Saṃsāra,
With fury blows the evil, Karmic wind.
Driven by the senses and deprived of freedom,
One wanders between life and death, roving in Bardo!

Sometimes one climbs the summit of the mountain
In the dream-like state between life and death.
Sometimes one sleeps in the street
In the Bardo city of Saṃsāra.

For my part, I aspire to the Realm of Reality,
And adorn the cloth of pure mind and heart
With the embroidery of immaculate discipline.

Mindfulness is the tailor cutting
My clothes into the shape of the Three Yogas.
My coat lining is the art
Of uniting the Three Key Points.[14]
I brighten the shoulder padding
With the Great Light [which shines at the
    time] of death.

I cut the hem of Bardo Enlightenment
To the "measurement" of pure Magic-Bodies.[15]

This is my coat, the coat of a yogi;
I have no wish for yours.
Go then, young patron, and be cheerful!

Said the young man, "Revered One, since you will not accept my
jacket though your clothes are still too thin, please, then, take this
short coat." And he sang in persuasion:

Precious Guru, supreme being,
In the summer, in bright sunshine
When the cuckoo's song is heard,
One may go naked and not feel the cold.
But in the winter, when the cold moon brightly shines
And the blinding storm rages [in the hills],
Cotton clothes than silk are thinner,
And the piercing cold stings like an arrow!

Father Jetsun, this ordeal
Is too much for you.
Here is a gray-green woolen coat
With maroon fur hemmed
And gay in colored silk of five colors;
The cloth is of fine quality.
I now offer it to you.
Please accept it and grant me your blessing.

But Milarepa would not take it, saying that he had a better coat
still. And he sang:

Gracious patron, listen closely to me.
With blindness as a guide
I wandered down perilous paths;
Buffeted by Passionate Winds,[16] now hot, now cold,
I was drenched in the rain of Retribution-Karma.
Worn out by these ordeals,
I longed for Freedom City.

With the cloth of Ah Shea Vital Heat[17]
Is the lapel of Four Cakras[18] made.
My tailor is the inner Prāṇa-Mind

Who warms Tig Le[19] and makes it flow;
The merged Bliss-Void experience
Is the needle used for sewing;
The cloth is Inborn Vital Heat.
Now summer and winter are for me the same!

Though your woolen clothes are pretty,
My cotton shirt is lighter and gives more comfort.
Dear patron, I do not want your clothes;
You should now go home.

The young man replied, "Although you will not accept my coat, you must be wearied by your long practice of meditation. Please be kind enough to accept my turban, which you can trade for some meat to sustain and nourish your body." And he sang:

Precious Yogi, supreme one,
Disgusted with Saṃsāra, you look forward
To liberation from the wheel of life-and-death.
You meditate at length
And practice your devotions.

Thus you must sometimes feel the cold.
My magnificent headgear
Is the wonder of India!
Its frame of precious metal was made by
    a skilled craftsman.
'Tis covered with the skin of crocodile and vulture,
And decked with the feathers of lovely birds.
Its price equals the cost of a big Yak.
I now offer it to you—the Nirmāṇakāya Buddha.
You can trade it for much meat
For your health and nourishment.
In summer and in winter,
I will follow and pay homage to you!

But Milarepa did not accept this offer either. Instead, he sang:

My dear young man,
Do not lose your head!
I follow the Great Nāropa's Lineage,
He who has completely mastered the art of
    cosmic causations.

The master of deep practice,
I fear not the element of air within,
Nor do I depend on falcon's flesh.
I feel gay and joyous in a biting wind.

On the crown of my head[20]
Is a jewel splendid as the sun and moon,
On which sits my Guru, Marpa the Translator,
Adorned with ornaments of human bone.
He is the Wish-Fulfilling Gem, Buddha's
     Transformation Body.
If you see him with the eye of veneration,
You will find he is the Buddha Dorje-Chang!
He will forever guard you like a son.
This rare turban is my secret adornment.

The sublime Guru on my head is very beautiful.
Dear boy, I do not want a turban.
Ride off with cheerful heart!

The young man thought, "This revered Lama does not accept anything I have offered him. Perhaps he considers my gifts too small."
And so he untied the string of his neck-jewel, which was a very fine
piece of jade, and sang:

Precious Guru, supreme being,
You strive for devotion with no attachment
     in your heart.
To you, all material things are but delusions!
You have no wish for goods or wealth.
A deep faith in you has risen of itself in me.

'Tis shameful to begrudge one's father's hoardings;
People would despise one from their hearts:
One might well become a miser-ghost.
Therefore, I pray your Reverence,
Do not refuse this jade.
This white translucent six-edged jade
Gleams brightly like a sparkling light.
The supple deer skin, and red poppy,
Make the setting yet more graceful.
With this jade you never can be poor.
I offer it as a neck-ornament.

Pray, grant me your grace
And bestow the Buddha's teaching.

The boy then offered the jade to the Jetsun, but Milarepa still
would not take it, saying, "I do not need your jade; I have a jewel
which is far more precious. Listen to my song":

Listen, my dear patron,
You with a good father.
In all countries, far and wide,
I, the Yogi, roam.
In streets, at doors, I beg for food.
I am not greedy for good meals,
I long not for possessions.

There is no end to human greed.
Even with hoarded wealth head-high,
One cannot reach contentment.
I do not envy you your wealth and goods.

The greatest treasure is contentment in my heart;
The teaching of the Whispered Lineage is
    my wealth;
My devotion to the Dharma is my ornament.
I deck myself with Retaining Mindfulness;[21]
The Yogas of Four Periods are my entertainment;
The great and small Mind-Awarenesses are my
    adorations.
I have no need for your neck-jade.
Dear boy, be of good cheer and go your way.

The young man thought, "Is it because I am too great a sinner
that His Reverence will not be gracious to me?" He said to Milarepa,
"It is natural for a supreme being like you not to want these illusory possessions. I now offer you my Three Companions.[22] From
now on I will never carry a weapon or kill sentient beings. I beg you
to grant me the Ordination. I pray you to protect me with your compassionate grace!" Saying this, he untied his carrying pouch[23] and sang:

Oh supreme and compassionate Lama,
I have always seen an enemy as such,
And never lost sight of my foes.

From the right, I untie my wooden quiver;
From the left, I take my ornate bow,
And the sharp sword at my waist
Which disillusioned all my foes!

With these three things at my side,
I was like a ruthless bandit.
When I appeared before my enemies
Their hearts trembled and their bodies quivered.
Like frightened yaks, they fled away!

Thinking of them and my misdeeds
I feel regret and sorrow.
Today I offer you my Three Companions.
I will observe the precepts strictly
And follow you where'er you go.

But Milarepa was still adamant. He said, "I do not think that
you can keep your oath. Nor do I need your Three Companions,
because mine are better. Now, hearken to my song":

Listen to me, dauntless fighter.
The Five Hostile Poisons[24] run wild
In the land of evil thoughts.
He who does not renounce the "all-important" combat,
Will be imprisoned and lose his chance for freedom!
Battles and armies are not for the yogi.

The world without is my quiver,
The Non-clinging Self-Illumination within
Is my sheath of leopard skin,
My weapon is the sword of Great Wisdom.

The Two-in-One Path is my rope,
My thumb-guard is the merit of meditation.
These are my hidden inner meanings.

Upon the bow-string of Ultimate Unborn Voidness
I set steady the notch of Bodhi-Heart;
I shoot the arrow of the Four Infinities[25]
At the army of the Five Poisons.
There is no doubt that I shall win the battle;
I will destroy the hostile enemies of desire.

That is *my* way, the yogi's way of conquering.
I have no interest in your gifts.
Young patron, be of good cheer and go.

The young man said, "Revered Sir! Though you do not accept my offer of the Three Companions, I must receive your Blessing. Please, therefore, accept my belt[26] and knife." And he sang:

> You Yogi, who are the living Buddha,
> Although many know the Dharma,
> Few can practice it.
> One in hundreds is hard to find
> Who can give proof of his accomplishment.
> I would not ask the teaching from another,
> E'en though he knew a world of Dharma;
> Only from you, the living Buddha, the Father Repa.
> Your teachings spring from much hard work,
> And so I dare not ask without paying first.
>
> In the center of Nepal, an angry river flows,
> With clouds like pillars standing round.
> At the lion-head of this raging torrent
> Was made this sheath with silver ornaments,
> Slung on my belt with gold and silver cord.
> When I wear it, my whole body brightens!
> I now offer you this knife and belt.
> Later, I will ask you for the Teachings.

The youth then gave his belt and knife to Milarepa. The Jetsun said, "At present, I cannot give you the Teachings and instruction; neither do I want your offerings. I have a better belt than yours. Listen to my song":

> Listen to me, ingenuous young man!
> From my hut's roof in the snow mountain
> Flows the quintessence of milk and nectar.
> Though it is not made of gold or jewels,
> I would not pour it into earthenware.
>
> Around this waist of mine, the poor man
>   of strong will,
> Is tied to a cotton belt of fanatic devotion!
> The absence of pretence and hypocrisy

Is the pattern of my belt.
Bright wisdom is my knife,
Its sheath, the confidence of the Three
        Measurements.[27]
Faith and diligence in Dharma is my gold-and-
        silver cord.
The beauty of the Dharma is the glory over all.

Lest goddesses punish me,
I have never asked for wealth or money
When teaching in the past,
Nor shall I do so now.
Dear boy, you may go home;
I do not want your gifts.

The young man again said to Milarepa, "Revered Sir! Indeed you have not the slightest desire for wealth or goods. Therefore, I think that you may not object to my offering you a temple in a quiet place wherein you may dwell." Saying this he sang:

You are a real yogi, an ascetic worker,
Disgusted with mundane things
And indifferent to the world.
You renounced your native land and went away!
Without a bourne in mind, you wandered everywhere.

Although one thing to you is as another,
A permanent home may help your inspiration.

Let us find a good place in the hills to
        build a temple,
Let us make the pillars immaculate and tall!

Hanging above the pillars, the sun and moon
        will shine.
On the broad floor of the temple
We will draw a Mandal[28] with stone-made colors.
We will plant flowers all about
And dig a deep ditch round.
The Ka Be ornaments[29] will be of wood,
And a pagoda with eight adornments will
        make the place more beautiful.

There will be a shrine for worship and
    great reverence.
Pray, accept it as your dwelling.
Then at ease, you may stay in comfort there!

But Milarepa still would not accept this offer. He said, "I will not
stay in any temple and make it my home. Nor do I know anything
about how to please people. Now, listen":

My confused young lad!
Do you not know that this world is transient
    and unreal?
When you come before the King of the Dead
Your rich man's money is of no avail.
There your wealth can never buy you off;
There you will find no place to swing a
    strong man's sword,
No place to dance or strut about the stage.
Your flesh will be as dust.

Because I fear these things may happen to me,
I bind myself in a place of strict austerity.

The temple wherein I dwell in the inner unborn Mind;
The Ka Be ornament is unwavering Prāṇa;
I erect the pillars of the Real
On the foundation of immutability.
The sun and moon are the Arising and Perfecting Yoga.

On the ground of the Dhyānic Warmth[30]
I draw a Mandal of Clear Observation.[31]
The experiences of Bliss, Illumination, and
    Non-thought
Are the lovely flowers in my garden!
Encircling the pagoda of Ten Virtues
Is my strong ditch of Voidness.

This is mine, the Yogi's temple;
I have no need of yours.
My young patron, be of good cheer and go!

The young man said to Milarepa, "Revered Sir, though you do
not want the temple, this feeble human body is liable to sickness.

I have a very capable sister, who has great faith in the Dharma. I would like to offer her to you as a Jomo[32] servant. Pray do not disdain, but please accept this offer." And he sang:

> Revered Yogi, who clings to the hermitage,
> Though you have fully realized the faults of women,
> And have no lustful wish,
> This fragile human body is liable to sickness
> And so one always needs a solicitous companion.
>
> I offer you my only sister,
> Dearly beloved of her three brothers.
> She is sprung from an outstanding line—
> Her father and mother are of noble stock;
> She is heiress to a royal tradition.
> Do not mistakenly regard her as of common stock;
> She is the heart-taker among the crowds,
> Radiant as a rainbow, she is more beautiful
>   than angels.
> Cotton clothes on her,
> Look lovelier than silk.
> Jewelry and gold adorn her head;
> Sparkling jewels and pearl necklaces
> Cannot match her radiant beauty;
> Her grace and charm are hard to paint.
> Her suitors have been many,
> But to none have we given our consent.
> Today, I offer her to you, the Nirmāṇakāya of Buddha.
> Pray do not disdain my offer.

But Milarepa still would not accept it. He said "Do not talk like a fool. I have already renounced family ties. I am not interested in an ego-clinging woman. The so-called faith of the common people is most unstable and liable to change. I am an old beggar with no family and no relatives. People will laugh at you, if you give her to me. Afterwards, you will regret what you have done. I have no desire to become your brother-in-law. I have a consort who is much better than your sister. Listen":

> On the whole, young lord,
> Women are the cause of lust and attachment.
> A qualified Illumination-Woman[33] is indeed
>   most rare.

To have angelic company on the Bodhi-Path
Is a wonder and a marvel;
Yet you a little have exaggerated.
This is why the Mudrā Practice[34] is so very hard.

My wonder woman is the lust-free Sūnyatā.
There is compassion on her face,
And kindness in her smile.
The Red and White Elements[35] are her clothing,
The Two-in-One Unity, her silk ornaments.
Indiscriminating action is her girdle
And the Four Blisses[36] her adornments.
Her necklace makes all things Taste-as-One.
She is such a charming witch—
The realization of Truth is her origin!
This is my wife, the yogi's mate.
I have no interest in your Saṃsāric women.
Young patron, it is time for you to go!

Knowing that Milarepa would not accept this offer, the young man said, "Although to your enlightened mind, there is no such thing as shame or disgrace, to be human and to prevent possible scandal among the people, I now sincerely offer you a pair of trousers. *Please* accept them." And he sang:

You Yogi, you who have nothing left to hide,
But follow the Tantric path,
Living naked in the mountains—
Your jewel-like penis, exposed so openly,
Can be seen by all at any time.

Though you are free from all ideas of disgrace
        and shame,
We worldly men are shamed by indecent exposure.
Even the perfect Buddha, the fully enlightened
        Being,
Discreetly follows worldly customs.

This pair of trousers are for my own wear;
They are made of the finest wool
Which my mother and sister spun.
My noble wife wove it into woolen cloth,
A neighbor's daughter dyed it for me;

And my kind uncle tailored it.

With such clothes we cover the shameful part.
To you, this pair of trousers I now offer.
Please say not again, "I need it not!"

Milarepa replied, "Dear boy, it seems that you know nothing about shame! My organ hangs there very naturally. There is nothing funny about it, so why do you laugh? In the beginning, I came from my mother's belly stark naked. When death comes, I shall leave the body without any covering. And so I shall do nothing about it now. Nor do I care to know about this self-made "shame" of yours, as you call it. Now listen":

Why, my good lad, do you take
Things without shame to be shameful?
That is merely the nature-born male organ;
I cannot understand this so-called "shame" of yours.
Of the really shameful things, you are most ignorant.

Look at sinful, evil, and meaningless deeds;
You are *not* ashamed of them.
Let me tell you how I keep my self-respect:

My fine wool is the Heart-for-Bodhi
With which I spin the thread of Four Initiations;[37]
The cloth I weave is the liberation Path of Samādhi;
The dye I use is made of virtues and good-wishes;
My tailor uncle is the sense of con-
    scientious discretion
By whom the trousers of self-respect are made.

These are my dignified and altruistic trousers,
And so of yours I have no need!
Dear patron, you may now go home!

The youth thought, "This great man will not accept anything I offer. I had better find out where he lives and where he is going. I will try by all possible means to persuade him to visit my country." So he said: "Though you have not accepted anything I have offered you, please come to my country; also, please tell me where you are going now. There must be a destination in your mind, or you would not choose this particular road. Pray do not conceal your intention, but please tell me the truth."

Milarepa replied, "Son, I have nothing to hide from you. In the harvest I go to Din Ri to beg for alms. When the crops are threshed, I go to Nya Non. In the winter I remain at some remote place where only birds and marmots dwell." The young man thought, "After a few days, I shall invite him to my house to preach for us. I wonder if he will accept." And he sang:

> Peerless Guru, the Transformation Body of Buddha,
> You said that you are going to Din Ri to beg
>   for alms.
> But that is a place of the damned, and has no merit.
> Though vast sky hangs above,
> The virtue of the people there
> Is as small as mustard-seed;
> Their hands are tighter than the barred
>   doors of the congregation hall![38]
> The flour costs more than gold.
> A hundred pleas for alms are wasted time;
> Poverty and famine stalk the place.
>
> The land of Nya Non is full of fear,
> A paradise for bandits and murderers.
> Lepers are there in crowds,
> While burial grounds and cemeteries abound.
> So fearful is that country, one dares
> Not travel without a hundred friends,
> Or take three steps without a guide.
> That cursed place, Nya Non, is of the worst repute.
>
> The Nepalese-Tibetan border is cold and high—
> A land of snow where blizzards rage.
> Its people are as dumb as mules!
> Its rivers flow south to Nepal,
> Where the lower valleys steam with heat
> And dangerous rope bridges sway high above
>   the rocks.
> In Nepal heat and disease endanger life,
> While people in the South speak a different tongue,
> And the trees are stiff like corpses.
> With all my heart, I wish you would not go there,
> So please postpone your journey.

Although you would not take my gifts,
I beg that you will grant my boon
And visit my country for a fortnight.

Milarepa replied, "On the whole, I cannot tolerate arrogant patrons. I am not interested in going to your country. As for Nya Non and Din Ri, I know them better than you. Hearken to my song":

You arrogant young man with strong desires,
Listen to my song with faith.
It is hard to meet an immaculate man of merit,
Hard to find a place where men of virtue live,
For times have changed.

I am a yogi who thinks and says whate'er he likes,
But I have never caused malicious gossip.

Though the flour be very dear in Din Ri,
It is not hard for me to get it.
Yet I prefer the taste of the Five Nectars,
And never gorge myself with tasty morsels.

I am an abandoned yogi, who eats for food
The inner Samādhi of Non-discernment.
Thus the desire for tasty meals has no appeal.
Cheerful and comfortable am I in times of famine.

Though the paths are perilous and dreadful,
My prayer to the Gracious One will never fail me.
The Three Precious Ones are my safest shelter
        and refuge;
The goddesses in the Three Places will always
        be my guides.
My inseparable companion is the Bodhi-Mind;
My protectors are the Guards of the Eight Divisions.

Since I have no possessions, I have no enemy.
Cheerful and at ease I meet the bandits.
Though Nya Non may be of bad repute,
The people there are candid and ingenuous.

As in days of old, they are straightforward
        and outspoken.

Easy-going and carefree,
They eat and drink without pretension;
They keep things as they are,
And groves and forests flourish.

As for me, I take no interest in worldly wealth,
Nor am I attached to food and drink.
Contented, I care not for loitering and amusement.
When, therefore, I meditate, my Samādhi deepens.

This is why I go to Nya Non.
Having mastered the art of Dumo's Fire,[39]
I have no fear of cold or heat;
Cheerful and in comfort I meet the falling snow.

Today I see no reason to delay my journey,
But I shall not go to your country;
Proud and haughty patrons are distasteful to me.
How can I ingratiate myself with those I do not know?
Mount your horse, as it is growing late.
My dear, contented youth, it is time for you to go.
May your health be good and your life long.

Upon hearing this song of rejection, the young man was overcome with dejection and disappointment. He said, "Revered Sir, whatever I have offered you, you would not accept. Whatever instruction I have applied for, you would not grant. I realize that I am too sinful. I now swear that I will not go anywhere, but will kill myself here in your sight." So saying, he drew his razor-sharp knife, and, pressing the point against his heart, sang:

Listen to me, Revered Yogi,
On this auspicious morning, while riding on my way,
I saw a naked man, lying beside a silver spring.

I said, "Is he a mad yogi,
Or just a foolish joker?
Exposing his naked body without shame,
He must be a fool out of his mind!"

And so, not faith, but contempt arose within me.
I rejected any thought of your companionship
        and went on alone.

Of this, you, Revered One, were clearly well aware.
As if wounded badly, I now repent in pain.

When you were crossing the blue river
To reach the seat of the other shore,
I saw you fly over the water
Like an eagle in the sky.
Soaring like wind in space,
I saw you flying.
Displaying your miraculous powers,
I saw you glide over the Tsang River
And reach the other shore.

I was bewildered and overjoyed
To see such an accomplished being.
Proud and happy as I was, conceit arose
        within me;
I thought that I was a well-gifted person,
Who had few hindrances and habit-forming thoughts.
I thought that I must be a good vessel
        for the Dharma;
I thought that I must be a virtuous and
        destined person,
Who had great merits and pure wishes.[40]

Since the day that I was born,
I have never been so happy as today.
In the wealth, property, and comfort that I offered
You have not the slightest interest.
I have never heard of a yogi like you in Tibet;
I have never met such a perfect Buddhist,
One so marvelous and unusual.

On this auspicious day in my pilgrimage,
I made offerings and besought you in all ways!
Marvelous and unusual as you are,
You have paid no heed to what I said.
I feel that I am most ignorant and pitiful.
I realize that I am stupid and lack merit;
I am utterly confused and most disheartened.
With a feeling of frustration, I have lost my way.
I am beginning to believe I have no capacity
        for Dharma!

What then would be the use and meaning
Should one chance to meet a Buddha,
If from Him one does not receive a discourse?
How can one face, and what can one tell one's
    countrymen?
Rather than return in shame
I will end my life before you!
All are bound to die in time;
'Tis better for me now to die,
To die before such an accomplished saint,
When my heart is full of Dharma.
Oh, all-compassionate, revered Jetsun!
After hearing such a sorry tale from this poor lad,
With your omniscient mind, you know what
    should be said.

Having heard his sincere prayer, Milarepa thought: "He has indeed
great earnestness and sincerity. There must be a mutual vow[41] between us. The prophecy given by the goddess in my dream seems
to point to him. I must, therefore, accept him." And so he sang:

Listen to me, dear young patron!
You have a zealous aspiration for virtuous deeds.
You must be a man with little sin or evil Karma.

Since you have intense longing to solicit
    Dharma [from me]
Your pride and self-conceit must be small indeed!

Diligent and enthusiastic,
You cannot be lazy.

Since you made generous offerings,
You cannot be close or greedy.

Your intelligence and sympathy are good,
So you have little ignorance or hate.

Since you pay respect and homage to me,
You must have been closely associated
With Dharma in your previous lives!

On this auspicious morning, I, the
    vagabond from Gung Tang,

And you, the young man from lower Jhal Khrum
Met on this blue river bank.
It seems our hopes in bygone lives arranged
    the meeting;
It was our destiny to meet before the Silver Spring.
You must be one whose Karma is unstained,
Who has awakened from the habitual-thought
    of the Store-Consciousness.

Young patron, I sing this auspicious song for you.
Since you have heard authentic teaching,
Will you now be keen to practice Dharma?

If faith has risen from your heart,
If you take no heed of worldly gain,
If you really want to follow me,
Know that kinsmen are the devil-planned
    hindrances of Dharma;
Think not of them as real, but quench your
    craving for them.

Money and dainties are the devil's envoys;
Association with them is pernicious.
Renounce them and all other things that bind you.

Delight in pleasures is the devil's rope;
Think, then, of death to conquer your desires.
Young companions are the tempting devil's snare;
Knowing they are delusive, watch them carefully.

One's native land is the dungeon of the devil;
Imprisoned therein 'tis hard
To win liberation.
Try then to escape at once;
Put all aside and strive for Dharma.
Only by instant action can you succeed!

In time your body of illusion will decay.
'Tis better to associate with Dharma now.

The darting bird of mind will fly up anyway;
'Tis better now to wing your way to Heaven!

If you believe and follow what I have said,
You will be a worthy vessel for the Dharma.
You will be given benediction and instruction;
The profound teachings of the Whispered Lineage
Will also be imparted.

My son! This is the start of your journey
　　on the Bodhi-Path.
Even I, the Yogi, rejoice at your success.
You too, young man, should be glad and joyful!

The youth was indescribably happy when he heard this song. With great exhilaration, he bowed down at the Jetsun's feet, made many obeisances, and circumambulated him many times. Then he made a vow [to return], and departed.

Four months later, when Milarepa was staying at Manlun Chubar of Drin, the young man came with his nephew to visit him. The uncle offered a piece of immaculate white jade, and the nephew half an ounce of gold, but the Jetsun would not accept the gifts.

At that time, the Translator Bhari was building a stūpa of the Tsudor Namjhal Buddha at Drin, so Milarepa said to them, "It is not necessary for me to take your offerings; you may offer them to Bhari, the Translator, and ask him to initiate you. As for the Pith-Instructions,[42] I shall give them to you myself."

Accordingly, they went to Bhari, the Translator, and asked him to impart to them the complete initiation of Dem Chog. Whereupon, Bhari bestowed upon them the Outer Teachings of Tsudor Namjhal, the Me Ru Sinha practice for prolonging life, and the teachings of the Buddha of Performance. He also gave them the Inner Teachings of Dem Chog, that is, the Practice of Seven Words, the instructions of the Guru Symbol Goddess, and the meditation practice of the Goddess Kurukullā. After that they accompanied him to Sajya Monastery.[43]

Then the lad returned to Milarepa and lived with him for five years. From the Jetsun, he obtained the teaching of the renowned Six Yogas of Nāropa, and the teaching of the Mahāmudrā transmitted from the Great Master Medripa. Because he practiced these teachings diligently, Milarepa also imparted to him all the Pith-Instructions. Formerly, the young man had been called Dharma Wonshu;[44] later, Milarepa gave him another name, Repa Shiwa Aui [the Cotton-clad Light of Peace]. Before turning to religion, he was a great sensualist; afterwards, for the sake of his devotion, he utterly renounced the world. He took an oath before Milarepa that for the rest of his life, he would never wear leather shoes, or more than one piece of cotton clothing, and that he would not return to his native land, or secure provisions for more than two days' consumption. With the greatest diligence he absorbed himself in his devotions and eventually attained good experiences. Milarepa was delighted with his improvement and sang:

> I bow down to all Gurus. Great is the blessing
> From the compassionate Gurus of the
>   Practice Lineage;[45]
> Great and powerful are the Key-Instructions
>   of Marpa and Mila!
> You, Shiwa Aui, are industrious and hard-working.
> Through the grace of the Ḍākinīs you have
>   attained good understanding.

> Dear son, if you want to consummate your meditation,
> Restrain yourself from bigotry and empty talk;
> Think not of the noble glories of the past;
> Stay in the valley to which no men come;
> Keep from bad companions, and yourself examine;
> Yearn not to become a Guru;
> Be humble and practice diligently;
> Never hope quickly to attain Enlightenment,
> But meditate until you die.
> Forgetting words and studies,
> Practice the Key-Instructions.
> If you would benefit yourself,
> Renounce talk and words;
> Concentrate on your devotions.

Shiwa Aui replied, "You have just said that he who learns a great deal without actual practice is liable to go astray. Please elaborate this a little."

Milarepa answered, "By that, I mean there is a danger of clinging to the worldly affairs of this life without completely renouncing them. Another danger is that this person is liable to miss the key-point of the practice. In the teaching of Marpa's Line, we do not have such errors or dangers, for we never pay attention to words and talk. What we emphasize is the actual practice. Hearken to my 'Song of Dangers and Fallacies' ":

Obeisance to the holy Gurus.

Listen to those high-flown words, and pompous talk;
Look at those charlatans, madly engaged
        in fervent argument.

In talk they seem intent to frighten you;
In sleep, they slumber, pompous men;
They walk like haughty Mongols.
Dangers and obstacles encompass them.

The Three Kingdoms and Six Realms are jeopardized
By desires forever leading sentient beings
        into danger.

There are seven dangers you should watch:
Falling into the blissful Hīnayāna peace;[46]
Using your Buddhist knowledge to get food;
Inflating yourself with pride of priesthood;
Falling into yogic-madness;[47]
Indulging in empty speeches;
Falling into the trap of nothingness.
Thus, ignorance is the cause of fallacies and dangers.

The teaching of the Whispered Lineage
        is the Ḍākinīs' breath.
Never doubt this truth, but if you do,
Remember that this doubt occurred
Through the devil's influence.

Shiwa Aui, how can you ever go astray
Since you are near me, the great Cotton-clad One?

Lay down your doubts and meditate.
He who relies on the true Teachings will
        never go astray.

Think not, my son, of meaningless word-knowledge
But concentrate on your devotions.
Then you will soon attain the great Accomplishment.

Whereupon, Shiwa Aui abandoned his search for word-knowledge and concentrated on his devotions with never a thought for clothing and food.

One day a friend called on Shiwa Aui. Seeing his body emaciated from lack of food and clothing, the friend misunderstood, and feeling pity for him, said, "Dharma Wonshu, you were a gay spark from a rich family. But now you look old and poor, with no clothes or food. How sad! How sad!" Shiwa Aui sang in reply:

> Oh My Father Guru, the Jetsun, the real Buddha,
> The Field-of-Offering[48] for my parents!
>
> Brothers, sisters, and all [relatives] give
>   rise to Saṃsāra;
> But I have now renounced them.
> The Jetsun is my sole companion and comrade
>   in the Dharma,
> Alone he is my source for the Buddha's Teaching;
> With him, the real Buddha, I remain in solitude.
>
> A group of three or four leads but to empty talk,
> To avoid which I stay in solitude.
>
> *Books and commentaries bring one nought but*
>   *pride,*
> *But the authentic Buddha gives*
> *The one-sentence Pith-Instruction.*
> I thus renounce all books and commentaries,
> Relying on the clear-cut Pith-Instruction.
>
> The hermit-temple is a place near Buddha
> Wherein I practice virtuous deeds and gather merits.
>
> The more one has, the more one craves.
> So I forsake my home and renounce my native land.
>
> The country with no boundary-posts is the
>   place near Buddha
> Wherein the faithful one can practice virtuous deeds.
>
> Associates and servants cause more anxiety
>   and craving,
> So I renounce them for all time.

A deep faith arose within the man after he had listened to this song of his former friend, whereupon he offered him many good things. Milarepa was very much pleased by this incident.

From that time on, Shiwa Aui served Milarepa until the day of his Guru's entering into Nirvāṇa. During the course of his life, he learned the complete teachings from Milarepa, and thus was kept from going astray in his meditation experience and understanding.

The nephew, known as the foolish and powerful Sang Jye Jhab, did not act as a good Repa. He held a small temple near the edge of Nya Non. The Jetsun was slightly displeased with him.

After the Nirvāṇa of Milarepa, Shiwa Aui went to the cave of Man Chu in the Goh Valley of Padru to practice meditation. Eventually he attained the Perfect Enlightenment and merits of the Path. He achieved the Accomplishment-of-Freedom-from-Obstacles[49] and so was able to pass through the rocks of the cave and mount to the Pure Land of Goddesses in his lifetime.

This is the story of Milarepa meeting his disciple, the Cotton-clad Shiwa Aui, at Silver Spring.

NOTES

1 Samādhi of Guru-Union (T.T.: bLa.Mahi.rNal.hByor.): A Samādhi of unifying one's mind with those of the Gurus.

2 Weu and Tsang (T.T.:dWus.gTsañ): Weu is a region in Central Tibet, Tsang is a region in southwestern Tibet.

3 Lho Draug Wa was another of Marpa's names.

4 Skillful Path: the Yoga with Form (T.T.: Thabs.Lam.) See the translator's comments in the Appendix.

5 The Four River-like Teachings are probably: (1) the Teaching of the Arising Yoga, (2) the Teaching of the Six Yogas, (3) the Teaching of the advanced Perfecting Yoga, and (4) the Teaching of Mahāmudrā. "River-like" implies that these teachings convey continual grace-waves.

6 See Story 3, Note 2.

7 Ensuing Dhyāna Stage: Every Dhyāna has two stages: the Main, and the Ensuing Stage. In the Main Dhyāna Stage, the mind of the yogi is wholly absorbed in concentration. In the Ensuing Dhyāna Stage, while the yogi continues his daily activities, his mind is still held somewhat in contemplation, i.e., not completely departing from the meditation experience.

8 Three Visualizations: This probably implies the following practices: the vis-

ualization (1) of the Patron Buddha, (2) of the Maṇḍala, and (3) of the inner Cakras.

9 Two Gates: Yoga with Form and Yoga without Form.

10 Prāṇa of Vital-force, or Life Prāṇa (T.T.: Srog.Rluṅ): This is the chief Prāṇa which supports one's life and which also, according to Tibetan Tantra, is the energy-source of the Ālaya (Store) Consciousness.

11 This phrase is not clear to the translator. It probably implies the three favorable times for practicing meditation.

12 Four Rivers: a symbolic term denoting the four stages of Saṃsāric becomings: production, remaining, decaying, and termination.

13 Three Bindings: the term for the teachings directed toward taming the body, word, and mind.

14 Three Key Points: to unite the mind with the Manifestation-Void (T.T.: sNaṅ.sToṅ.), with the Bliss-Void (T.T.: bDe.sToṅ.), and with the Illuminating-Void (T.T.: Rig.sToṅ.).

15 The Sambhogakāya and the Nirmāṇakāya.

16 Passionate Winds: a figurative term to denote the changeable emotions of men.

17 See Story 7, Note 24.

18 Four Cakras: the psychic centers of the head, throat, heart, and navel.

19 Tig Le (Bindu): male semen and female "blood."

20 An important psychic center situated at the top of the head.

21 Retaining Mindfulness: the remembering of meditation-experience during daily activities.

22 Three Companions: Bow, arrow, and sword were the three companions (safeguards) of Tibetan travelers in ancient times.

23 Carrying pouch: The scabbard and quiver were fastened to the belt, along with a pouch in which miscellaneous articles were carried.

24 See Story 7, Note 6.

25 The Four Infinities, or the Four Unlimited Good Wills, i.e., Unlimited Friendliness, Compassion, Sympathetic Joy, and Evenmindness.

26 See Note 23.

27 This probably implies the three standards by which the yogi judges his experience in meditation, i.e., whether the experience is in accord with the Sūtras, whether it enhances or weakens his compassion toward sentient beings, and whether it enlarges his understanding of Śūnyatā.

28. Mandal: The translator presumes that "Mandal," pronounced as "Mandral" by the Tibetans, is a corruption of the Sanskrit word "Maṇḍala." See Story 7, Note 14.

29 Ka Be (T.T.: Kha.Bad.): an architectural ornament of Tibetan houses placed forward by the projecting ends of the beams which support the roof.

30 Dhyānic Warmth: the heat produced in meditation practice.

31 Clear observation (T.T.: lHag.mThoṅ.): deep contemplation on the truth of Prajñāpāramitā.

32 Jomo: the wife of a lay preacher.

33 Illumination-Woman (Tib.: Rig.Ma.): a woman who is well-gifted in understanding and in practicing Tantrism.

34 Mudrā Practice: an advanced form of Heat Yoga.

35 Red and White Elements: the positive and negative energies.

36 Four Blisses: When the Tig Le, the essence of energy, comes down from the Head Center, it successively produces four blisses, namely, the First Bliss, the Superlative Bliss, the Beyond-Reach Bliss, and the Innate-Born Bliss. See the translator's book, "Teachings of Tibetan Yoga."

37 Four Initiations: the Vase, the Secret, the Wisdom, and the Symbolic Initiations. See Story 1, Note 7.

38 The doors of the congregation hall in Tibetan monasteries are kept closed and locked most of the time.

39 Dumo's Fire: the "mystic" fire or heat produced in the Navel Center.

40 The pure wishes for Dharma made in one's previous existence.

41 If two person have made a mutual vow in their previous lives, the force of this vow, or the Karma-of-Wishes will bring its fulfillment in a future life.

42 Pith-Instructions (T.T.: Man.Ñag. or gDams.Ñag.): This may also be rendered as Key-Instructions, which consist of the essence of the Tantric teaching conveyed from Guru to disciple, usually in a very simple, precise, yet practical form, and therefore termed "Pith-Instructions."

43 Sajya (T.T.: Sa.sKya.) Monastery: the main monastery of Sajyaba (the Gray School).

44 Lit. (T.T.): Shu.Yas.Dar.Ma.dWañ.Phyug.

45 Practice Lineage (T.T.: sGrub.brGyud.): This is another name for the Ghagyuba School because this School stresses meditation practice.

46 According to Mahāyāna Buddhism, the Hīnayāna's version of Nirvāṇa and Samādhi is shallow, insufficient, limitative, and negative, in contrast to that of Mahāyāna, which is positive and dynamic. To cling to the blissful serenity of Samādhi is a great danger that may lead one to fall into the Hīnayāna Path.

47 Yogic madness: There is a recognized "stage of insanity" which all yogis should overcome before final or complete Enlightenment. This reference is to the danger of falling into this so-called "spiritual insanity" of advanced yogis.

48 Field of Offering: a term which denotes the qualified receiver of offerings, such as the Guru, Buddha, or the enlightened sages. These offerings will ripen into the giver's merits as seeds sown in good soil.

49 Freedom-from-Obstacles (T.T.: Zan.Thal.): Advanced yogis who have perfectly mastered their Prāṇa-Mind are supposed to be able to pass through all concrete, material obstacles without difficulty. This accomplishment is called Zañ.Thal.

THE SONG OF THE STAFF

Obeisance to all Gurus

Having renounced all worldly belongings and material things, the Jetsun Milarepa's only possession was a cane staff. One day, carrying his staff, Milarepa and his disciple Sevan Repa went to Jen Valley for alms. They came to a barred house, which was near the bank of the river. Except for an old woman, not a living soul was there. Milarepa asked her for alms. She said, "I am a pennyless old woman; but across the field there is a rich man called Shangchub Bar, who is working on his farm. Go there and ask him, and your wish will be granted."

When they arrived at the rich man's house, they saw that he was sorting seeds for sowing. Milarepa said, "My dear patron, we were told that you are a rich man, so we come here to you for alms." The man replied, "It is pleasant to offer you alms; but, if you are a real yogi, you should understand the symbolic meaning of things and be able to preach an exemplary sermon. Now, please use my farming as a parable, and sing me a preaching song." Thereupon, the Jetsun and Sevan sang together:

> Oh, my proud and arrogant patron,
> Listen to me, you rich man of Ngan Tson.
>
> In this month of spring the peasants
> Of Tibet are busy on their farms.
> I, the Yogi, also farm.
>
> Upon the bad field of desires,
> I spread the fertilizer of the Preparatory Practice;[1]
> I wet the field with manure of the Five Nectars;[2]
> I plant the seeds of the Non-confusing Mind,
> Farming with discriminative thought.

190

I plow with Non-dualistic oxen
Harnessed to the Wisdom-Plow,
With Observation of Precepts as the nose-rope,
And Non-distraction Effort as the girth.
Diligence is my whip, and skill my bridle.
With these tools and efforts, the bud of Bodhi sprouts;
In due season ripe will be my fruit.

You are a farmer who grows annual crops;
For eternity I cultivate.
At harvest you are proud and joyful.
Which of us will be happier in the end?

In allegory I have phrased this song of farming.
Though proud and arrogant, be now gay and joyful.
By making many offerings, accumulate
Merits for your own good.

The man countered, "Dear Yogi, I see you have a staff in your hand. What does it mean? Is it for amusement like a child's toy, or is it for lunatics to hold? Please tell me, what is it for?" Milarepa sang in answer:

Listen, my dear, inquisitive patron!
Do you know who I am?
I am the Yogi, Milarepa,
Who follows the ascetic way;
I am a yogi, great in strength and perseverance,
Who has no limitations.

The staff in my hand
Grew on a huge rock.
It was cut by a sickle and became
A companion of wild stags.

It came from Nepal, in the South;
From it I hung the Mahāyāna Sūtras;
I take it with me to the marketplace;
It was offered to me by a faithful follower.
This is the story of my walking-staff.
If you do not understand my meaning,
Listen then with great care:

The stout end, cut from near the root,
Symbolizes being "cut off" from Saṃsāra.
The thin end, cut from near the top,
Symbolizes the "cutting off" of all doubts and
    confusions.
It is two cubits[3] long and represents
The twin qualities of a Buddhist.[4]

Of good quality and pliant, it is like
The original Mind-Essence—good and sound.
The varnish, of a pleasant brown, is like
The great harmony of the "Original Mind Nature."

Straight and supple, it symbolizes
Unmistaken practice and devotion.

The tiny grooves you see, represent
The perfection of the Bodhi-Path,
The four joints in the cane
Are the Four Infinite Wishes,[5]
The three knots symbolize
The Three Bodies of the Buddha.

It never changes color. This represents
The immutable reality of the Root Principle.[6]
Its head, curved and covered, displays
The "beyond-playwords" nature of reality;
Its white and glittering appearance shows
The Dharmakāya—immaculate and pure.

The hollows symbolize the void nature of all beings,
The spots are a symbol of the sole Tig Le.
The scattered black marks indicate
That Tibetan yogis and Repas
Have few disturbing thoughts.

This cane most excellent represents
My devotion and practice in compliance with the Dharma.
Its elegance and loveliness displays
My disciples' sincerity and faith.

The iron ferrule on the tip conveys
The perseverance of yogis in the hermitage.

The handle, wrapped with copper, represents
The mastery and attraction of Ḍākinīs.

The nail attached to the tip displays
The bravery and diligence of yogis;
The hanging brass ring represents
The increase of inner merits.

The ornament of Sha Bran [?] hanging down
Is the flexible understanding of the yogi.
The thong of two twisted ropes represents
The entering of the Two-in-One Path;
The Mother-and-Son thongs intermingling,
The meeting with the Mother of the Three Bodies.

The bone-ornaments hanging on the staff
Mean many travels for the yogi.
The flint and bellows signify
That all he sees and meets
Are the yogi's friends.

The white shell hanging on the staff
Means that I shall turn the Wheel of Dharma.
The rag of leather symbolizes
The yogi's attitude, without fear or shame.

The mirror hanging on the staff
Is the Enlightenment that shines within.
The sharp knife indicates
That the pain of passions will be cut.
The stone-crystal symbolizes
The purifying of defiled habitual thoughts.

The ivory chain hanging on the staff
Is the Chain-of-Regard between Guru and disciple.
The set of bells symbolizes
My widespread reputation;
The woolen cords of red and white,
That my disciples will be numerous.

The handsome staff that now I hold
Is the means and symbol of the conquest over evil
    beings.

Patron, you ask me for the meaning of this staff;
This proves you have sincerity and faith.
This present meeting witnesses
Our pure wishes in a former life.

For mankind and Devas, conceivers of all symbols,
I have sung this "Song of the White Staff."
Revere then and appreciate its Dharma teaching.
Dear patron, I hope you practice Dharma and win
      happiness supreme.

Great faith was engendered in the heart of this rich man. Bowing
down at Milarepa's feet, he said, "Dear Lama, from now until the
day of my death, I shall serve you. Please come and live permanently
in my house." But the Jetsun and Sevan Repa would not promise
to stay more than seven days, saying, "We have no wish to accept
your worldly offerings."

At the end of their sojourn, as they started to take leave, the
patron cried: "Since you have made up your minds to depart, before
you go, please tell us your Experiences and Realizations during meditation." In answer, the Jetsun and his disciple sang together:

Listen to me, faithful patron,
Who are rich but imprudent!
Easy is it to talk of Dharma,
But 'tis hard to practice it.

Oh you confused and worldly beings,
You always waste your leisure, letting time slip by.
Though your mind is ever saying, "I must practice
      Dharma,"
Your life is wasted as the hours slip by.
You should now determine to start practice:

Cool mountain water
Heals the bladder's ills,
But only grouse and mountain birds can reach it;
Beasts of the valley have no chance to drink it.

The Sword of Heavenly Iron[7] falling when it thunders
Is the weapon with which to destroy the foe,
But only the Elephant-Earth-Protector
Can grasp and use it effectively;

Small elephants have not the strength.

The Nectar of Heaven is the essence of long life
Ever keeping the quintessence of body strong,
But only the Holy Guru, Nāgārjuna, could use it—
Not all who practice Dharma.

The golden chest, that gives enjoyment
Is a treasure which cures poverty,
But only "Prince Moonlight" can possess it—
Not the common people.

The wondrous gem beneath the ocean
Is a marvel granting all desires,
But it belongs to the Dragon of Happiness;
Men on the earth cannot obtain it.

Grand scenery, indeed, has the Palace of Joyous
        Heaven,
But only Guru Asaṅga can enjoy it;
Not all human beings can reach or see it.

The medicine of Six Merits
Can cure colds and fever.
'Tis made from Tsan Dan wood,
And not from other trees.

The Ten White Virtues from causation's law
Enable one to roam the higher Realms,
But only those with faith can practice them—
Great sinners are not free.

The Pith-Instructions of the
        Gurus
Enable one to win highest Enlightenment,
But only he with Karma can learn and practice them;
Without capacity or Karma one seldom has the opportunity.

The precious Pith-Instruction of the Oral
        Succession
Enables one, without fail, to become Buddha,
But only determined men can follow it;
Not pleasure-seekers, like yourself.

Poverty is cured by food and wealth
Which the generous and clever soon amass,
But these the miserly can ne'er enjoy.

Generosity is a merit of which one can be proud.
You, the rich man of Ngan Tson, have it;
But not all the wealthy are so generous.

I, Milarepa, and the disciple Se Ston Repa,[8]
Due to wishes made in former lives have stayed
With you, the rich man of Jenlun Ngan Tson,
For seven delightful days. Now we must go.
Health and long life to you and yours!

Milarepa then said, "You offered me food and lodging, and I preached for you. This [relationship] is important. He who reveres and rejoices in the Dharma and has faith in it at all times, is planting the Seed-of-Dharma from which the Innate-born Wisdom will grow in his future lives. He who has rightly made a good wish, does not have to learn many teachings. Nor must he associate [with his Guru] for a long time. If the outer conditions and the inner seeds in one's own mind meet together, though temporarily one may go astray, the power of the seeds-of-the-wish will eventually bring one to the right path. Furthermore, faith and earnestness are most important. Nowadays, because people do not accumulate merits [by practicing virtuous deeds], they seldom see the inner merits of others, but only their outer faults, even though these faults are small and insignificant. If you have faith in me, whether I live near or far from you will make no difference. If we live too close and our relationship becomes too intimate, it will only cause discord and trouble between us. I think it would be too difficult for you, at the present time, to be a perfect practitioner of the Dharma. You must try to understand your own habitual-thinking. In any case, I shall make a good wish for you, and you should also try to pray to, and have faith in me. If you now practice virtuous deeds and put your faith [in the Dharma], you will be reborn in a special, favorable country, with perfect conditions and means [to practice the Dharma]. It is not necessary for a real follower of Dharma to go to many places. Again, he who sees many faults in other people, is liable to be an ignorant person himself. To you worldly beings, your native land is always the best; also, you like grand religious ceremonies. But in fact, if you have good-will and give provisions often and unsparingly to a single beggar, this would be quite sufficient. There is no such thing as 'this teaching is good' and 'that teaching is bad'; you should never be sectarian. It is hard for you to imitate me. The fox can never go where the lion leaps; he would break his back if he tried to copy the lion. It is indeed very difficult for most lovers of the Dharma to follow my way of practicing. I hope that you, the aristocrat, will never lose faith in Dharma."

Having said this to the rich man, Milarepa and his disciple traveled on again for alms, [and soon] came to a town where they met a yogi who appeared to be, and was dressed like, a Tantra-follower. This Tantric yogi said to Milarepa, "Dear Yogi, where have you come from? Judging by your appearance, it seems that you are a person having the Pure View, Pure Practice, and Equal Action.[9] Have you anything to say which may help to further my progress?" Milarepa replied, "Do you have a real understanding of the View, Practice, and Action? If not, I may tell you about mine, but you might not quite appreciate it. It may be better this morning just to establish an auspicious and beneficial Karma-relationship between us." "Never mind," said the yogi, "I shall give you alms. I am a teacher of Tantrism myself, and so have some understanding of these things According to my School, the View, Practice, and Action are like this ...." And he expounded the teachings at length. Then he asked Milarepa, "Does your School agree with mine?" Milarepa replied, "He who does not fear Saṃsāra, renounce the world, and follow the instruction of a qualified Guru, with a very strong desire to attain Buddhahood immediately — driven by his craving and evil instincts is liable to become a mere babbler. Although he talks a great deal about the View, Practice, and Action, he is most likely to go astray." And the Jetsun sang:

> Hearken, you great teacher!
> It is hard to help others
> If one does not renounce this world.
>
> If you do not *realize* Saṃsāra and Nirvāṇa are one,
> And hold a faint idea but dimly in your mind,
> In indulgence you will freely gratify [your senses],
> And be carried away by the torrent of Eight
>   Desires.
>
> [You should carefully observe and ask yourself]:
> "Have I realized the truth of Two-in-One which
>   is beyond extremes,[10]
> Or have I thrown myself over the Four Edges?[11]

Is my practice free of 'mind effort'?
Am I haunted by the ghost of 'form and substance'?
Is my blissful and rapturous Samādhi
A delusive state defiled by 'grasping-craving'?
Have I been shackled by the laws of form
Without grace and blessing?
When I meditate on the identity of manifestation
        and Guru[12]
Does my Awareness wander?
When I illustrate the truth through Tantric symbols,
Have I taught the Truth beyond all symbols?
Have I polluted with 'intentional effort,' and distorted,
The originally pure Self-mind?
Have I done that which I willed
In a way that righteous Lamas ne'er behave?
Did I ever ask myself: 'Am I aware
That wordly prosperity and achievements
Are but the hindrances set up by devils?' "

If you do not understand or practice
The teaching of a Lineage with grace,
The devils will mislead you with their art.
Then you will never free yourself
From the realms of misery and Saṃsāra.
Rely then on a genuine Lineage, and practice
Your devotion without craving and self-indulgence.

Having heard this song, the teacher turned to Milarepa in faith
and reliance, crying, "This is indeed marvelous!" He bowed down at
the feet of the Jetsun and invited him into his house, giving perfect
offerings and service to him. He then asked Milarepa to accept him
as his disciple. The Jetsun knew that he was a destined person, and
granted his request. Thereupon, all three returned to Lashi Snow
Mountain. Having received the Initiation and Pith-instructions from
Milarepa, the teacher later acquired the Accomplishments and reached
the state of Emancipation. He was destined eventually to become
one of the heart-sons of Milarepa, and was known as Shangchub
Jarbo—the Teacher of Ngan Tson.

This is the story of Milarepa singing the "Song of the Staff" at
Jen Valley, and of his meeting with the teacher of Ngan Tson.

NOTES

1 Preparatory Practice (T.T.: sÑon.hGro.): Before engaging in the main meditation practices such as the Arising Yoga, the Perfecting Yoga, and Mahāmudrā, the yogi should first complete all the preparatory practices. The four most common ones are (1) 100,000 prostrations before the symbols of the Three Precious Ones; (2) 100,000 prayers to one's Guru and Patron Buddha; (3) 100,000 prayers of penitence, together with 100,000 Mantras of Vajrasattva; and (4) offering 100,000 "Maṇḍalas."

2 Five Nectars: Five different secretions of the human body.

3 Two Cubits or Two Troos: The Tibetan word "Troo" (T.T.: Khru) denotes a local unit of measure. Its length is from the elbow to the tip of the middle finger.

4 Twin Qualities: probably the merits of Wisdom and of Compassion.

5 Four Infinite Wishes: (1) that all sentient beings may sow the seeds of happiness and attain it; (2) that all sentient beings may avoid suffering and the cause of suffering; (3) that all sentient beings may attain "pure happiness"; (4) that all sentient beings may reach the state of tranquillity. See also Story 17, Note 25.

6 Root Principle: See Story 12, Notes 5, 6, and 7.

7 Heavenly Iron (T.T.: gNam.lCags.): According to Tibetan legends, the weapons made of meteoric metal are extremely strong and valuable.

8 Probably a misprint for "Sevan Repa."

9 Equal Action: Absorbed in the Realm of the "Equality of Saṃsāra-Nirvāṇa," the enlightened being acts fearlessly and indifferently at all times.

10 Lit.: "beyond the Four Edges." See Note 11.

11 The Four Edges or Four Ends (T.T.: mThah.bShi.), are the four basic patterns along which one settles his opinion on reality. They are that reality is (1) positive, or being; (2) negative, or non-being; (3) a combination of both being and non-being; or (4) a state beyond being and non-being. If one clings to any of these four "ends" or "extremes" he is said, according to Buddhism, to have missed the point.

12 A Tantric yogi should know that all manifestations are representations of Absolute Truth, and that the "real Guru" — the embodiment of the Absolute — is his own mind. Thus, to meditate on one's own mind is to realize the identity of the manifestations and Gurus.

THE TWENTY-ONE
EXHORTATIONS

Obeisance to all Gurus

ONE night while meditating on Lashi Snow Mountain, Milarepa dreamt that a most beautiful young girl, adorned with jewels and bone ornaments, came to him and said, "Yogi Milarepa, you should follow your Guru's instruction, go to Di Se Snow Mountain and meditate *there*. On your way, you will meet a well-gifted and destined person whom you should influence and guide according to his need." After saying this she disappeared. When Milarepa awoke, he thought to himself, "This message is sent by the Patron Buddha and Ḍākinī to enable me to repay my Guru's bounty. I must comply with her request and go at once."

On his way from Lashi to Di Se Snow Mountain, he met an inhabitant of Nya Non called Dhamba Jhaupu.

This man invited Milarepa to his house, made great offerings, and gave an elaborate feast in his honor. [At the feast], he said to the Jetsun, "For the sake of the disciples now assembled here, please be kind enough to preach for us the Dharma which blossoms within you. Please put this preaching into a song and sing it for us."

And so Milarepa sang "The Twenty-One Exhortations for Mind":

> Great is the Skillful Path of Tantra
> And the Guru's Pith-Instruction,
> So, too, are perseverance and resolution;
> These are the "Three Greatnesses."
>
> Put the Life-active Prāṇa at the key point,
> The Mind-Essence in its Natural State,

And consciousness under self-examination;
These are the "Three Enterings."

To fulfill the commandments of my Guru,
Achieve the wishes of my heart,
And be altruistic without effort;
These are the "Three Accomplishments."

Outer hindrances and demons disappear,
Inner desires and passions are extinguished,
Disorder and illness of body cease to be;
These are the "Three Absences."

My skill and my resourcefulness in speech,
My eloquence in answering all questions,
My knowledge of the nature and aspects of Mind;
These are the "Three Proficiencies."

I see clearly that bliss is void of substance,
I see all things manifest without discriminating,
I see clearly That which is beyond all words;
These are the "Three Sights."

When men in crowds assemble,
Means and enjoyments are gathered there
And Ḍākinīs congregate;
These are the "Three Gatherings."

These one-and-twenty Exhortations for the Mind
Are fruit of my experience in meditation;
All Dharma seekers should value them,
Especially my followers and sons.

Too much instruction hinders Liberation.
Follow then and practice the precious words
That I have sung to this assembly.

Thereupon Dhamba Jhaupu served Milarepa, who gave him the Initiation and Key Instructions. Having practiced these teachings for some time he attained the Experiences and Realization, and later on became one of the "intimate sons" of the Jetsun.

This is the story of Milarepa's meeting with Dhamba Jhaupu.

MILAREPA'S MEETING WITH KAR CHON REPA

Obeisance to all Gurus

As predicted in Marpa's prophecy, the Jetsun Milarepa set out for Di Se Snow Mountain with several of his disciples. When they reached Lowo Lake, one of the disciples pretended to be ill and would go no farther, so the journey was interrupted. Milarepa then stayed at the Upper Lowo that summer and preached the Dharma there.

When the autumn came and Milarepa was about to go to Di Se Snow Mountain, the disciples and patrons gave him a farewell party. They all circled round and made offerings and obeisance to him. The patrons then besought him for instructions because they all realized that no one could tell when they would meet again. In response, Milarepa sang "The Right Yoga Practice":

> I, Milarepa, the man, the Yogi of Tibet,
> Have little learning, yet are my instructions great.
> I take little sleep, though persevering at my
>   meditation,
> Humble am I in heart, but great is my persistence.
>
> Knowing one thing, I know all;
> Knowing all, I know that they are one.
> I am an expert in Absolute Truth.
>
> My bed is small, yet I am free to stretch my legs.
> My clothes are thin, yet is my body warm.
> I eat but little, yet am satisfied.
>
> I am the one whom all yogis venerate,

To whom all faithful come, a guide
On the dread path of life and death.
Unattached to any home,
I have no fixed dwelling;
Disregarding all, I do my will.

I crave for no possessions. Between clean
And unclean food I do not discriminate.
I suffer little pain from passion's sting.

With little self-importance, I have few desires;
I crave not for objective and subjective things;
Thus can I untie Nirvāṇa's knots.

I console old people when they grieve;
Loving fun, to the young I am a friend.
A yogi, I rove about all regions, wishing
Devas and human beings to live in happiness.

After hearing this song, they said to Milarepa, "To be sure, Revered
One, this is your life and practice; but please tell us what *we* should
do. Be kind enough to give us, your disciples, some instructions and
advice." The Jetsun then emphasized the transiency of all beings, ad-
monishing them to practice Dharma earnestly. And he sang "The Song
of Transience with Eight Similes":

Faithful disciples here assembled [ask yourselves]:
"Have I practiced Dharma with great earnestness?
Has the deepest faith arisen in my heart?"
He who wants to practice Dharma and gain non-regressive
       faith,
Should listen to this explanation of the Mundane
       Truths
And ponder well their meaning.
Listen to these parables and metaphors:

A painting in gold,
Flowers of turquoise blue,
Floods in the vale above,
Rice in the vale below,
Abundance of silk,
A jewel of value,
The crescent moon,

And a precious son—
These are the eight similes.

No one has sung before
Such casual words [on this].
No one can understand their meaning
If he heeds not the whole song.

The gold painting fades when it is completed—
This shows the illusory nature of all beings,
This proves the transient nature of all things.
Think, then, you will practice Dharma.

The lovely flowers of turquoise-blue
Are destroyed in time by frost—
This shows the illusory nature of all beings,
This proves the transient nature of all things.
Think, then, you will practice Dharma.

The flood sweeps strongly down the vale above,
Soon becoming weak and tame in the plain below—
This shows the illusory nature of all beings,
This proves the transient nature of all things.
Think, then, you will practice Dharma.

Rice grows in the vale below;
Soon with a sickle it is reaped —
This shows the illusory nature of all beings,
This proves the transient nature of all things.
Think, then, you will practice Dharma.

Elegant silken cloth
Soon with a knife is cut—
This shows the illusory nature of all beings,
This proves the transient nature of all things.
Think, then, you will practice Dharma.

The precious jewel that you cherish
Soon will belong to others—
This shows the illusory nature of all beings,
This proves the transient nature of all things.
Think, then, you will practice Dharma.

The pale moonbeams
Soon will fade and vanish—
This shows the illusory nature of all beings,
This proves the transient nature of all things.
Think, then, you will practice Dharma.

A precious son is born;
Soon he is lost and gone —
This shows the illusory nature of all beings,
This proves the transient nature of all things.
Think, then, you will practice Dharma.

These are the eight similes I sing.
I hope you will remember and practice them.

Affairs and business will drag on forever,
So lay them down and practice now the Dharma.
If you think tomorrow is the time to practice,
Suddenly you find that life has slipped away.
Who can tell when death will come?

Ever think of this. Devote
Yourselves to Dharma practice.

Hearing this song, all the patrons fell prostrate before Milarepa in their deep faith. Feeling a strong conviction of the truth contained in his admonishments, tears gushed from their eyes like the waters of a spring. Three young men among them asked Milarepa to take them as his disciple-servants. Thereupon, the Jetsun sang of "The Ten Difficulties":

If a Buddhist be without benevolence,
How can he subdue and convert evil people?

If spiritual longing be not awakened,
How can the merits grow within one?

If a "great yogi" has no perseverance,
How can the Experiences and Realization come?

If a monk keeps not the priestly rules,
How can he receive gifts, service, or respect?

If a Tantric yogi violates the Precepts of Samaya,
How can he gain powers or grace?

If a patron be mean and parsimonious,
He can never be of pood repute.

If a yogi jokes and talks of nonsense,
He will never be respected.

He who pays no heed to Karma or to virtue,
Will never understand the truth of Voidness.

If a trusted Lama grows tired of religion,
He finds it hard to readjust to life.

Though faith arises now within you, happy young men,
Self-control will still be hard. Though now you feel
Pressing and urgent need to practice Dharma,
If you go too far, my sons,
Later you will be regretful.

Let us now wish that we meet again—
The power of Karma will bring this to pass.
Till we meet once more, will I, the Yogi,
By my own words steadfastly abide.

All happiness and good fortune,
I wish for you, dear patrons,
Health and freedom from all sickness,
A long life free from injuries,
And may sons and fathers meet again.

I, the Yogi, will wander where I please.
You, young men, so spoiled and happy,
Return now to your homes.

Upon hearing this song, they all surrounded the Jetsun, grasped his clothing, and embraced his body, weeping, bowing down at his feet, and making their wishes.

Among them there was a young man who was extremely sincere. He pleaded again and again with Milarepa in great earnestness; eventually the Jetsun relented and accepted him as a disciple. He then brought the young man back to De Si Snow Mountain, where he gave him the Initiation and Instructions. Later, this young man attained emancipation and became known as Kar Chon Repa, one of Milarepa's "intimate sons."

This is the story of Milarepa's meeting with Kar Chon Repa.

ADMONISHMENTS TO DHARMA WONSHU

Obeisance to all Gurus

ONCE in the early part of the last month of autumn, Milarepa and his disciples went to Bushen Chitang for alms. Many people were gathered there. Milarepa said to them, "Patrons, please give me the alms for which I have come." Now among them was a young, well-dressed girl, who said, "Dear Yogi, who are you? Who are your father and mother, your brother and sister?" Whereupon, the Jetsun sang:

I bow down to all Holy Gurus!
Pray grant me your grace and blessings!

My father is Gungtuzunpo,[1] the All-Perfect One;
My mother, Drowazunpo, the Worthy-Woman.
My brother is called King-of-Knowledge,
My aunt, Lamp-of-Illumination,
And my sister, Dazzling-Faith.
My friend is called Natural-Wisdom,
And my child, Son-of-Illumination.
My book is Foundation-of-the-Universe-and-Manifestation,
My horse, Mount-of-Consciousness-Prāṇa,
And my patrons are the Four-Regions-of-Weu-and-Tsang,[2]
As for me, I am a small white Buddha Stūpa.
I have never practiced singing,
Yet will I sing clearly for you:

My father, the All-Perfect One,
Earns the wages of Knowledge and Practice;

Never do worldly thoughts arise in him.
My mother, Worthy-Woman, always feeds me
The milk of Pith-Instruction from her breast.
Imbibing the Practice-Teachings, I have ne'er felt
        hungry.
My brother, King-of-Knowledge, holds within his hand
The knife of Skill-and-Wisdom,[3]
And with it kills wrong views both coarse and fine.
My aunt, Lamp-of-Illumination, displays her Mirror
        of Self-Mind
Unsullied by the rust of habitual-thought.
My sister, Dazzling-Faith,
Has long been free from meanness.
In her practice of devotion,
She has goods but does not hold them;
What she has, she never hoards.

I and my comrade, Natural-Wisdom,
Like one man live together
And never raise our voice in strife.

My only child, Son-of-Illumination,
Is heir and holder of the Buddha's Line;
I have never raised a child
Who needed washing or change of diapers.

My book, Foundation-of-Universe-and-Manifestation,
Illustrates for me the Principles and Meanings;
Never have I read books with printed words.

My horse, Mount-of-Consciousness-Prāṇa,
Carries me swiftly where e'er I want to go.
I never need a horse of flesh and blood.

My patrons in the Four Regions of Weu and Tsang,
Offer me provisions when I ask for them.
I never weigh or press my bag of flour.
When I offer, it is to the Precious Ones;
When I rely, it is upon my own Guru.

I say that I am white, because I practice deeds of
        whiteness.
I say that I am small, for few are my desires.

Therefore, I say that I'm a Stūpa, small and white.

"These sayings are indeed very wonderful," remarked the girl. "But do you also have any Saṃsāric companions, sons, and belongings?"
Milarepa then sang in reply:

> At first my experiences in Saṃsāra
> Seemed most pleasant and delightful;
> Later, I learned about its lessons;
> In the end, I found a Devil's Prison.
> These are my thoughts and feelings on Saṃsāra.
> So I made my mind up to renounce it.

> At first, one's friend is like a smiling angel;
> Later, she turns into a fierce, exasperated woman;
> But in the end a demoness is she.
> These are my thoughts and feelings on companions.
> So I made my mind up to renounce a friend.

> At first, the sweet boy smiles, a Babe of Heaven;
> Later, he makes trouble with the neighbors;
> In the end, he is my creditor and foe.
> These are my thoughts and feelings about children.
> So I renounced both sons and nephews.

> At first, money is like the Wish-fulfilling Gem;
> Later, one cannot do without it;
> In the end, one feels a pennyless beggar.
> These are my thoughts and feelings about money.
> So I renounced both wealth and goods.

> When I think of these experiences,
> I cannot help but practice Dharma;
> When I think of Dharma,
> I cannot help but offer it to others.
> When death approaches,
> I shall then have no regret.

Hearing the Jetsun's song, the light of faith was aroused in the girl. She invited Milarepa and his disciples to her house, and gave them perfect service and offerings. She was then given the Instruction, and entered the Path.

Milarepa and his disciples then went together to Dre Tze Snow Mountain. One day, many patrons came to visit him. Among them there was a well-gifted, aristocratic young man — a descendant of the Jowo family, who had the greatest faith in Milarepa. He said "Dear Lama, all your doings are inconceivably marvelous! Please grant us a teaching which we can always practice."

In response to his request, Milarepa sang:

> Listen, all you faithful patrons.
> When you walk, identify your perceptions with Mind-
> Essence;[4]
> This is self-liberation when you walk.
>
> When you sit, relax and be at ease;
> This is the Heart-Teaching of how to sit.
>
> When you sleep, sleep in the Realm of Equality;
> This is the way to sleep in the Great Light.
>
> When you eat, eat in the Realm of Voidness;
> This is the way to eat without dichotomy.
>
> When you drink, drink the water of Skill and Wisdom;
> This is the way to drink without cessation.
>
> When you walk, sit, or sleep, always look at your mind;
> This is a worthy practice without pause or interruption.

"We are incompetent people and do not know how to practice this profound teaching," exclaimed the patrons, "Oh, those who know how to do so are fortunate indeed!" Milarepa replied, "When you say you do not know how to practice this teaching, that only means you want to shun it; this is also the very sign of incapability for devotion. If you *determine* to practice it, you will know how to do it and really understand it. Now, listen to the profit of this teaching in my song":

> My gifted patrons, in the transient,
> Flask-like human body dwells
> An innate-born Buddha Kāya.[5]
> If one can display the lamp of Great Light,
> The outer and inner Dharmakāya will shine brightly!
>
> In the Saṃsāric house of Complex-Thought

Dwells a baby eagle—the Bodhi-Mind,
If once she flaps her wings of Wisdom-Skill,
Surely she will fly up to the Sky of All-Knowing!

In the Victorious Snow Mountain of Self-Body
Dwells a baby lion of consciousness.
He who can practice [Dharma] without clinging
To the Six-Consciousnesses-Group,
Surely will conquer both Saṃsāra and Nirvāṇa!

On the blind ocean of Saṃsāra float
The seagoing merchants of the Six Realms.
He who never parts from the Trikāya,[6]
Surely will conquer the raging seas!

In the illusive house of the Five Poisons
Dwells a group of bandits to prevent one's liberation.
He who can hold secure the Rope of Skill, will
Surely overcome these dreadful outlaws.

The Absolute Body, Dharmakāya, is like the firmament;
The Wish-fulfilling Gem may there be found.
He who can meditate on it without distraction,
Surely will attain the Trikāya of Buddhahood.

In the cities of the Three Kingdoms of Saṃsāra
Lie the iron chains that bind us in the Six Realms.
He who can untie them through the Guru's teachings,
Surely will tread the Path of Liberation.

From the gem-like, precious Guru
Springs the fountain of the Pith-Instruction.
He who quaffs it with unshaken faith
Surely will be freed from sinful thirsting.

Thus he sang; and the patrons were all confirmed in their belief, and departed. But the young aristocrat determined to devote himself to the pursuit of Dharma, thinking: "One day I must come to this Lama and offer myself as his servant-disciple." Meanwhile, the Jetsun and his disciples decided to remain at that place, enjoying the offerings and services from both human and non-human beings. They worked on furthering their patron's progress until the end of spring.

When they were about to return to Di Se Snow Mountain, the patron

gave them a grand festival. Arising from the assembly, the young aristocrat, who had the utmost faith toward Milarepa, said, "Dear Lama, I
have heard that you, the Dharma practitioner, have the teaching called
the 'View, Practice, Action, and Fruit.' Would you please be kind
enough to tell us your own experience of them?"

In answer, Milarepa sang:

> Because I see the self-face of the View,
> The thought of contrast by itself dissolves;
> How then can I have the Idea-of-Two—
>   the self and others?
> The View is void of limit and discrimination.
>
> When in the Practice I become absorbed,
> Good and evil are reduced to self-liberation;
> How then can I have the Idea-of-Two—
>   happiness and suffering?
> The Practice is devoid of limitary feelings and
>   experience.
>
> When I adhere to the self-continuance of Action,
> Dislike is reduced to self-liberation;
> How then can I have the Impulse-of-Two—
>   craving and aversion?
> The Action is free from limitary attachment.
>
> Since self-liberation is the Fruit,
> Both Nirvāna and Saṃsāra are reduced to it.
> How then can I have the Idea-of-Two—
>   getting and abandoning?
>
> Absence of fear and hope is
> The Fruit of this great Practice.

The young aristocrat then said to Milarepa, "Dear Lama, I have
made up my mind to devote myself to the practice of Dharma. But
I do not dare to start without the permission of my parents and relatives. Although I will have to ask their permission first, please be kind
enough to accept me as your disciple-servant and take me with you."
Milarepa replied, "He who wants to practice the Dharma, should think
of the miseries of Saṃsāra. Then, if he still cannot make up his mind
and, instead, looks for permission or recommendation from others, he
will never succeed. Listen to my song":

If a pious person, who wants to practice Dharma,
Cannot cut off the tie of influence,
How can he break through others' domination?

If one cannot live on the alms of Non-attachment,
How can he free himself from the bonds of
      honor and pride?

If, knowing the transiency of all being,
He has no sense of contentment,
How can he be content with his amassed wealth?

How can one understand the truth beyond words,
By talking and discussing without first-hand
      experience?
How can he who does not realize
The truth beyond all symbols,
Describe It with a darkened mind?

How can he who shuns not the evils of bad partnership
Avoid the painful consequences?

If one cannot utilize this suffering
To further his spiritual growth,
How can he overcome all griefs and blind striving?

If one knows not that disturbing thoughts themselves
      are Dharmakāya,
How can he reduce them
By corrective measures?

If one renounces not all concerns and undertakings,
How in moderation can he practice his devotion?

How can he who does not resign from all activities
And cut off all attachments, achieve success
In Dharma by doing this and that, or by mere thinking?

How can he who renounces not all ties,
Practice meditation without worldly thoughts in mind?

If he does not renounce at once,
How can he hope to do so later?

If he thinks he need not strive for improvement now,
But can do so later, he must fail.

If he does not strengthen now his will,
Success from hope and expectation will not spring.

Upon hearing Milarepa's song, the young aristocrat was deeply moved and convinced of the truth contained in it. He decided at once to practice the Dharma, and his parents also gave their permission. After serving his apprenticeship with Milarepa, he was given the Initiation and Pith-Instructions, and eventually attained success and Liberation. He was known as Ngogom Repa Dharma Wonshu Shawa, one of the "close sons" of Milarepa.

This is the story of Milarepa meeting his disciple Repa Dharma Wonshu at Bu Shen.

NOTES

1 Gungtuzunpo (T.T.: Kun.Du.bZañ.Po.; Skt.: Samantabhadra): The "Ādi Buddha," or "Primordial Buddha," which, according to most Tibetan scholars, is a symbolic name to denote the Primordial Buddha-nature within all sentient beings, but not a name to denote a person or deity whose existence is prior to all beings.

2 Weu and Tsang: Central and Southwestern Tibet.

3 Skillfulness and Wisdom (T.T.: Thabs.Dañ.Çes.Rab.; Skt.: Upāya [and] Prajñā): Upāya means the skillful or ingenious methods and conduct with which a Bodhisattva applies his altruistic deeds to benefit sentient beings. Prajñā means the transcendental Wisdom shared only by enlightened beings. Upāya in its most general application denotes the first five Pāramitās, i.e., Charity, Discipline, Patience, Diligence, and Meditation; Prajñā denotes the last Pāramitā, i.e., the Prajñāpāramitā, the Perfection of Wisdom.

4 Lit.: "Bring all manifestation to the Path."

5 Kāya: meaning Body.

6 Trikāya: the three Bodies of Buddha, i.e., the Body of Truth (Dharmakāya); the Body of Divinity or Reward (Sambhogakāya); and the Body of Manifestation (Nirmāṇakāya).

22

THE MIRACLE CONTEST
ON DI SE SNOW MOUNTAIN

Obeisance to all Gurus

O NCE when the Jetsun with many of his disciples were on their way
to Di Se Snow Mountain from Bu Shen, the local deities of Di Se
and Ma Päm came out with a great retinue to welcome them. They
bowed down to Milarepa, and made offerings to him on a grand
scale. They welcomed him sincerely and pointed out the local meditation hermitages, all of which were places distinguished in history and
legend. They also swore to protect his followers, and then returned
to their own abodes.

When Milarepa and his disciples reached the banks of Lake Ma Päm,
there came a Bon[1] Priest called Naro Bhun Chon. This man, having
heard a great deal about Milarepa, and having learned that he was
coming to Di Se, went with his brothers and sisters to Lake Ma Päm
to meet the Jetsun and his disciples. Pretending that he did not know
who they were, the Bon priest asked, "From whence have you come
and where might you be going?" Milarepa replied, "We are going to Di
Se Snow Mountain to practice meditation. Our destination is a hermitage there." The priest then asked, "Who are you, and what is your
name?"

"My name is Milarepa."

"Oh, in that case," replied the priest, "you are just like Ma Päm—it
has a great reputation in far-away places, but when one reaches it one
finds it not really so wonderful as reputed. Perhaps the lake *is* quite
marvelous, but it and the encircling mountains nearby are all dominated
by us, followers of Bon. If you want to stay here, you must follow our
teachings and sow your seeds [in Bon]."

Milarepa replied, "Generally speaking, this mountain was prophesied
by Buddha Himself to be a place of the Doctrine-holders. For me, in

particular, it has great significance, for it was spoken of by my Guru Marpa. You Bonists, who have been staying here so far, are indeed very fortunate! If you want to remain here in future, you should follow the teachings of *my* religion; otherwise, you had better go elsewhere."

"It seems to me that you have a dual personality," said the Bon priest. "From a far distance I heard that you were indeed great; but when one comes close to you, you look small and insignificant. If you are really the remarkable person that people say, you should not mind having a contest with me. We will *see* whose miraculous powers are superior. The one who wins shall remain here and be considered as the legitimate owner of the place, and the one who loses shall leave." Saying this, the priest straddled the Ma Päm lake and sang:

> The Di Se Snow Mountain [of the Himalayas] is
>   most famous,
> But its summit is covered deep in snow!
>
> The lake of Ma Päm is indeed well-known,
> But the power of water breaks through it!
>
> Milarepa's reputation is indeed most great,
> Yet he is an old eccentric who sleeps naked.
> From his mouth he chants melodious songs,
> But he holds in his hands a metal staff.[2]
> There is nothing great about him!
>
> In our Bon religion,
> The Immutable One is the Swastika-Body[3] —
> The Lord Ye Shin Dsu Pud, and other heavenly beings.
> The fierce blood-drinking Deity with gaping mouth
> Has nine heads, eighteen arms, and many miraculous
>   powers.
> Yes, His Transformation Body has nine heads!
>
> His sister is the World-Conquering Mother.
> I, the Bon novice, am her disciple.
> Look at me! See how I demonstrate miraculous power!

In reply, Milarepa seated himself above the lake and, without his body growing any bigger or the lake any smaller, he appeared to cover it all. He sang:

Listen to me, you heavenly and human beings here
    assembled.

On the summit of the Eagle Mountain
Upon the Seat of Eight Non-Fears[4]
Sits the Victorious One, Buddha Śākyamuni.

In the Dharma Palace of the Heaven of Og Men[5]
Abides the Sixth Buddha, Great Dorje-Chang, the
    Wisdom Body of Not-Two.

The great Mother, the Goddess, is Dagmema;
The Transformation Body of the Inborn is the great
    Tilopa;
The Teacher, the Door-Protector,[6] is the great Nāropa;
The Buddha-like Translator is the great Marpa.
From these four Deities, I receive grace and blessings.

I, Milarepa, the renowned and celebrated one,
Following the order of my Guru, Marpa,
For the welfare of all men
Meditate on Di Se Snow Mountain.

To you, the wrong-view-holder Bonist,
I now give answer with this song:

The famous Di Se Mountain blanketed with snow
Symbolizes the pure, white Buddhist doctrine.
The streams flowing into the famous Blue Lake of
    Ma Päm
Symbolize one's deliverance to the Realm of
    the Absolute.

I, the famous Milarepa, the old man who sleeps naked,
Am he who now transcends the dualistic realm!

The little songs springing from my mouth
Are but the natural outflow of my heart;
They tell of, and describe the Sūtras of the Buddha.

The staff held in my hand
Symbolizes the crossing of the ocean of Saṃsāra.
I have mastered both the mind and forms;

Unaided by worldly deities
I can perform all miracles.

Di Se, where dwell worldly Devas with crude bodies,[7]
Is the king of all snow mountains on this earth.
This place belongs to Buddhists,
To the followers of Milarepa.

If you, Bon priests and heretics, will now practice
      the Dharma,
You, too, will soon be able to benefit all;
If not, you should depart and go elsewhere,
Because my powers of magic are greater far than yours.
Watch closely now and see what I can do!

At this, Milarepa performed another miracle by putting the whole
Ma Päm Lake on his finger-tip, without doing the slightest harm to the
living beings in it. The Bon priest said, "In this first contest, your miracle was better than mine. But I came here first. We must have another
contest to see which of us is the more powerful." Milarepa replied, "I
shall not emulate you, the magician who smears drugs on his body in
order to deceive others by conjuring up delusive visions. I will not enter
into any contest with such a person. If you do not wish to follow the
teachings of the Buddha, you may go elsewhere." The Bon priest countered, "I will not renounce the teaching of the Swastica-Bon. If you
win the contest, I will give up and go away. Otherwise, I will never
leave here. According to the Buddhist precepts, you may not kill or
harm me. Is this not so? Now let us fight with our supernatural powers."
Thereupon, the Bon priest started to circle Di Se Snow Mountain
from right to left, while Milarepa and his followers circled it clockwise.
They met on a big rock in the northeastern valley of Di Se. The Bonist said to Milarepa, "It is very good that you [pay homage to this holy
place] by circumambulating it. Now, you should follow the Bon way
of circling the mountain." Saying this, he took Milarepa by the hand
and dragged him in his direction. The Jetsun retorted, "I will not follow
your wrong path and reverse the Buddhist tradition. I think it better
that you follow me and adopt the Buddhist way of making the circle."
Saying this, Milarepa in turn grabbed the Bon priest's hand and dragged
him in *his* direction. Pulling each other back and forth on the rock,
both the Jetsun and the Bon priest left many of their footprints there.
But because the power of Milarepa was much greater than that of the
priest, he was forced to follow Milarepa's direction.
When they reached the north side of Di Se, the priest said, "Later,

we should follow the Bon way, go in the opposite direction, and make another circle." "Well, that will depend on how great your power is," replied Milarepa. The priest then said, "It seems that your power is greater than mine this time. But we should still try our strength further." Saying this, he lifted up a huge rock, as big as a yak, in front of the hill. Then Milarepa came forward and lifted up the priest as well as the rock. The priest then said, "This time you win again. But to win once or twice means nothing. We should continue our contest." Milarepa replied, "The stars may try to emulate the light of the moon and sun, but the darkness covering the Four Continents will be dispelled only by the sun and moon. You may try to emulate me, but you can never match me. Now, Di Se Mountain belongs to me. It was to please you that I revealed my miraculous power. Everyone can now see that the Buddhist practice is superior."

Thereupon, the Jetsun sat in the Lotus Cave on the western side of Castle Valley, while the Bon priest sat in a cave on the eastern side. Milarepa stretched his leg from the west side of the valley and reached right in front of the cave where the priest was sitting. He then called, "Now, you do the same thing!" The priest also stretched out his leg, but it did not even reach the brook! Whereupon, the Non-men spectators in the sky all laughed heartily at him.

Although the priest was now a little ashamed and embarrassed, he cried out, "I still want to fight on!" Saying this, he again started circling the mountain in the Bon way. The Jetsun also resumed the circling in the Buddhist way. This time they met on the south side of Di Se. When it began to rain, Milarepa said, "We need a shelter to protect us. Let us now build a house. Would you like to lay the foundation stone and floor, or do you prefer to put on the roof?" The priest said, "I prefer to put on the roof. You do the foundation work." Milarepa agreed. Then he pointed to a rock as big as three persons standing up together, and said, "Let us go over there." When they reached it, the Jetsun began to lay the foundation. He saw that the Bon priest had split a giant rock, as big as the body of an eight-year-old child. Whereupon, Milarepa made a sign, a mudrā of Conquering, and the rock held by the priest split down the middle and broke in half. Milarepa then said, "Now, you can bring the roof here." "But you have already broken it!" cried the priest. "Well, it was because of our contest of miracle-working that I did it," replied Milarepa, "but this time I shall let you prepare another rock and will not repeat the gesture of breaking. This time you may bring me the prepared rock." Accordingly, the priest split another rock and was about to lift it up, when Milarepa immediately made a gesture of pressing-down. The priest was surprised, as he tried to lift the rock, to find that it had become extremely heavy. So he stopped trying and made an excuse, saying, "I have already prepared the rock-roof. Now it is your turn to carry it to the other side." Milarepa replied, "My job is to lay the foundation; yours is to put on the roof. Now try to lift it up and bring it here." So the Bon priest tried again. He used all his strength, struggling with distended eyes to lift the rock, but he could not move it an inch. Seeing this, Milarepa said, "I am a yogi who has attained both the Common and Ultimate Accomplishments. My miraculous powers are different from yours. Though you have achieved the miraculous power of the Common Accomplishment, it can never emulate mine. If I make another subduing-gesture, you will not even be able to split the rock any more. The reason that I did not do so in the beginning was simply because I wanted to amuse the spectators. Now look at me and see how I lift it up!" So saying, Milarepa merely used one hand to pick up the giant rock and put it on his shoulder. Thereby, his handprint was found impressed in the rock. Then he stood on it and left his footprints. Finally he put the rock on his head and left his headprint and [more] handprints upon it. Later on, this cave was called the Cave of Miracle-Working and became very famous. It was then that the Bon priest admitted his defeat.

The Jetsun had many other contests with Naro Bhun Chon. His performances were far superior to, and much more wonderful, than the priest's. Finally, Naro Bhun Chon said, "You said that I am a magician; but from what I can see, *you* are the magician. I am not convinced by your miracle-working. Now, on the fifteen of this month, we shall have a race to see who can first reach the summit of Di Se Mountain. The winner will be recognized as the host of the mountain. This will also decide, beyond dispute, the one who has really attained the Ultimate Accomplishment." "Very well," replied Milarepa, "we will do as you wish. But what a pity that you Bon priests think your little bit of mystical inner experience is the Ultimate Accomplishment! To attain the Ultimate Accomplishment one has to behold the nature of his own mind. If one wants to realize this, he should follow and meditate on the teachings of my School — the Practice Succession." The Bon priest replied, "What difference is there between your mind and mine? Is yours good and mine bad? What difference is there between Bonism and Buddhism? Although your practice and mine are alike, you may be more proficient in the art of delusive magic. Therefore, so far, it looks as if you are superior. Anway, the race to Di Se will settle everything once and for all." Milarepa replied, "All right! Very good! That will settle everything."

Whereupon, Naro Bhun Chon concentrated his mind to pray to his god diligently and undistractedly, while Milarepa just carried on naturally. When it came to the fifteenth day, in the very early morning, Naro Bhun Chon, wearing a green cloak and playing a Bon musical instrument, flew through the sky on a drum towards Di Se. Milarepa's disciples all saw this, but Milarepa was still sound asleep. Thereupon, Rechungpa called out: "Dear Jetsun, wake up! Look! Though it is still so early in the morning, Naro Bhun Chon is flying on a drum to Di Se! He has reached the waist of the mountain now!"

The Jetsun still lay there as if nothing had happened, and finally said slowly, "Has our Bon friend arrived there already?" Then all the disciples pressed Milarepa to take immediate action. He said, "Very well. Look!", and he made a gesture toward the Bon priest. When the disciples looked at the priest again, they found that despite all his efforts to mount higher, he could only circle round and round the mountain.

When the day broke, and the sun appeared, Milarepa snapped his fingers, donned a cloak for wings, and flew over toward Di Se. In a second he arrived at the summit of the mountain, reaching it just at the time when the sunlight also shone upon it. There the Jetsun beheld the Gurus of the Transmission, and the tutelary deities. Buddha Dem Chog and his retinues all appeared, rejoicing before him. Although he knew that in essence all are equal — that the nature of Equality is imbued in all — Milarepa was nevertheless very pleased at his victory.

Meanwhile Naro Bhun Chon had reached the neck of the mountain. When he saw the Jetsun, lofty and compassionate, sitting at ease on the summit, he was dumbfounded and fell down from the heights, his riding-drum rolling down the southern slope of Di Se. As his pride and arrogance were now utterly subdued, he humbly cried to Milarepa, "Your power and miracle-working are indeed superior to mine! Now you are the master of Di Se. I will leave, but go to a place from where I can still see Di Se Snow Mountain."

Milarepa then said, "Although you are blessed by the worldly gods and have attained a smattering of Common Accomplishment, I, on the other hand, am a person who has fully realized the Innate Wisdom and attained the Ultimate Accomplishment. How can you possibly emulate me? The summit of Di Se Snow Mountain is the Mystic Vajra garden wherein the Wisdom Buddha, Korlo Dompa [Saṃvara], dwells. You have no merit to reach there. For the sake of the Buddhists who are assembled here, I asked permission of the deities, and showed it to all. Because I wanted to suppress your pride, I made you fall down from the mountain and lose your drum. From now on, even if you want to reach the foot of Di Se, you will have to rely on my power to get there. I will now tell you why I possess such power:

I bow down to my Guru, the gracious Marpa!

Through His mercy and the compassion of all Buddhas

I heard the wondrous Lord Buddha Sākyamuni,
He who subdued the heretics and followers of the
     Six Schools[8]
With the rightful teaching of Dharma.
The doctrine of Buddhism has thus been spread over
     the world.

On the Mountain, the Snow Di Se,
I, the Yogi of Tibet, with the Dharma conquer Bon,
And make the Buddha's Practice Lineage illuminate
     Tibet.

My miraculous powers come from superstrength,
Which I have many reasons to possess:
Belonging to a Lineage with great blessing and grace
Is one of the sources of this strength.

The primordial Buddha, Dorje-Chang, is a strength;
The compassionate Guru, the Master of all Pith-
     Instructions, is another;
From the Translator Marpa comes a third.

The Mind-Beyond, with its boundless knowledge, is a
     strength;
The Originally Pure[9] is another;
So is the unwavering meditation practice of
     Non-discrimination,
And so also is the Great Light.

If, when relaxed completely,[10] one observes what
     happens,
This very act in itself produces strength.

The All-flowing, All-abundant, and All-embracing,
And the self-face of the Being-Nature all bring
     strength.

The self-liberation of all forms is a strength.
If one follows the orders of his Guru,
The observation of precepts becomes a
     strength.

To be without sinful deeds and transgression is a
    strength.
If one can meditate in all one does,
This very practice will bring strength.
When all manifestations become your friends,[11]
A Great Strength will emerge;
Strong perseverance and determination do the same.

This is my strength, the strength of Milarepa.
With it have I now conquered heretics.
Hereafter I shall be the master of Di Se Snow Mountain,
Whence I shall propagate the Buddha's teachings.
To you, oh Wisdom-Deities, I give worship, and pray.

So went his song. "I am now fully convinced of your miraculous strength and powers." said the Bon priest, "They are indeed superior and marvelous. I sincerely beg you to allow me to stay where I can still see Di Se Snow Mountain." Milarepa replied, "In that case, you might live on the mountain over there." Saying which, he grasped a handful of snow and threw it to the top of a mountain to the east. Since that time a lump of snow has always been seen on the top of that mountain. Then, by Milarepa's power, both he and the Bon priest came to the neck of Di Se. The priest said: "In future I would like to circumambulate Di Se to pay my homage, but I will need a place to stay during my pilgrimage." "You may stop over there — the mountain opposite Di Se," replied the Jetsun. Afterwards, the Bonists built a stūpa in a cave there, and used it as a dwelling place during their pilgrimages to Di Se. Thus the followers in Milarepa's Lineage controlled all the region of the three lakes in the snow mountains.

This is the story of how Milarepa subdued Naro Bhun Chon at Di Se Snow Mountain.

NOTES

1 The aboriginal religion of Tibet.

2 Milarepa's staff was made of cane, but certain parts were probably covered by metal.

3 Swastika-Body; Swastica-Bon: The Swastika sign is a holy symbol of the Bon religion.

4 The Seat of Eight Non-Fears: This perhaps implies liberation from the Eight Worldly Desires.

5 Og Men (T.T.: Hog.Min.) Heaven: the central Heaven where Buddha Dorje-Chang resides.

6 Nāropa, the Door-Protector: Because Nāropa was one of the six famous professors of Vikramasila Monastery, in charge of one section (the North Section) of the School, he was so named.

7 The crude bodies of Devas: Though the heavenly bodies of Devas are illuminating and magnificent, in comparison with the splendor of the "Reward-Body of Buddha" (Sambhogakāya) they are crude and vulgar.

8 This implies the six main Schools of Hinduism: (1) Nyāya, (2) Vaiśesika, (3) Sāṁkhya, (4) Yoga, (5) Mīmāṁsā, and (6) Vedānta.

9 The "Originally Pure": This is another term denoting the innate and pure Buddha-nature.

10 The most important Key-Instruction of Mahāmudrā is relaxation. Only through complete relaxation of mind may the Mind-Essence be seen.

11 The enlightened being feels that all becomings are conducive, and not obstructive, to his spiritual growth.

23

THE ENLIGHTENMENT
OF RECHUNGPA

Obeisance to all Gurus

HAVING circled Di Se Snow Mountain, Milarepa and his disciples returned to the Gray Cave of Dorje Tson of Gu Tang. The former patrons all came to visit the Jetsun, and asked him about his welfare and health. He told them that he felt extremely well and in turn inquired after their health. They replied: "It is by good fortune that under your protection and blessing we, too, are all very well and have not suffered from sickness or loss of life. Our livestock also thrives. We, on our side, are very glad to learn that you have successfully made the pilgrimage to Di Se without having met with any difficulties on your way. Please be kind enough to sing us a song of your well-being." Milarepa answered, "I am as happy as this — listen!" And he sang of the "Twelve Happinesses of Yoga":

> Like avoiding the pitfalls of evil,
> Happy is it to practice the Yoga of Renouncing-
>   One's-Own-Land.

> Like a good horse freeing itself from the bridle,
> Happy is it to practice the Yoga Free-from-Subject-
>   and-Object!

> Like wild beasts creeping on low ground,
> Happy is it to practice Yoga in solitude!

> Like the eagle flying freely in the heavens,
> Happy is it to practice the Yoga of Conviction!

Like vultures gliding freely through the sky,
Happy is it to practice Yoga without hindrances.

Like a shepherd restfully watching his sheep,
Happy it is, in Yoga practice,
To experience the Illuminating Void.

Like the huge Mount Sumeru standing firm
On the ground at the world's center,
Happy it is to practice the steadfast Yoga without
    disturbance.

Like the wide rivers flowing freely,
Happy is the continual sensation of the Yoga
    Experience.

Like a corpse lying quiet in the cemetery
Doing nothing and having no worries,
Happy is the Yoga of Non-action.

Like a stone thrown in the ocean, that never returns,
Happy is the Yoga of No-returning.[1]

Like the sun shining in the sky,
All other lights o'ershadowing,
Happy it is to practice the Yoga
Brighter than all lights.

Like leaves falling from the Dali tree,
That can never grow again,
Happy it is to practice the Yoga of No-birth.

This is the song of the "Twelve Happinesses of Yoga."
I now present it to you, my patrons, as a gift of
    Dharma.

After listening to this song, the patrons all returned home with deep faith in their hearts.

      ...   .

To test the accomplishment and experience of Rechungpa, and also to find out how strong was his spirit of renunciation, one day Milarepa casually sang for him the song of the "Twelve Deceptions":

Worldly affairs are all deceptive;
So I seek the Truth Divine.

Excitements and distractions are illusion;
So I meditate on the Non-dual Truth.

Companions and servants are deceptive;
So I remain in solitude.

Money and possessions are also deceptive;
So if I have them, I give them away.

Things in the outer world are all illusion;
The Inner Mind is that which I observe.

Wandering thoughts are all deceptive
So I only tread the Path of Wisdom.

Deceptive are the teachings of Expedient Truth;[2]
The Final Truth is that on which I meditate.

Books written in black ink are all misleading;
I only meditate on the Pith-Instructions of the
     Whispered Lineage.

Words and sayings, too, are but illusion;
At ease, I rest my mind in the effortless state.

Birth and death are both illusions;
I observe but the truth of No-Arising.

The common mind is in every way misleading;
And so I practice how to animate Awareness.

The Mind-holding Practice[3] is misleading and
     deceptive;
And so I rest in the realm of Reality.

Rechungpa thought to himself: "My Guru is Buddha Himself; there
is no illusory idea in his mind. But because of my incapacity for devotion, as well as that of others, he has sung me this song." And Rechungpa sang in answer to explain to his Guru his understanding on the teaching of View, Practice, and Action.

Hearken to me, please, my Father Guru,
My darkened mind is full of ignorance.
Hold me fast with the rope of your compassion.

At the crossroad where Realism and Nihilism meet
I have lost my way in seeking the View of
          Non-Extremes;
So no assurance have I in the knowledge of the Truth.

Drowsy and distracted all the while,
Bliss and Illumination are not yet my lot.
And so I have not conquered all attachment.

I cannot free myself from taking and abandoning,
And needlessly I continue my impulsive acts;
So I have not yet destroyed all delusions.

I was unable to shun all deeds of fraud
And observe the Tantric Precepts without flaw;
So I have yet to conquer all temptations.

The illusory distinction between Saṃsāra
          and Nirvāṇa
I have not realized as the Self-Mind Buddha;
So I have yet to find my way to Dharmakāya!

I was not able to equate hope with fear
And my own face behold;
So I have yet to win the Four Bodies of Buddha.

I have been protected by your compassion in
          the past;
Now, putting my whole being in your hands,
Pray, still grant me more of your blessings.

Thereupon, Milarepa [sent his compassionate grace-wave to bless
Rechungpa, and] said to him, pretendingly, "Oh, Rechungpa, you have
had more understandings and experiences than those you have just told
me. You should not hide anything from me. Be frank and candid." *As
Milarepa said this, Rechungpa suddenly became enlightened.* At once
he sang "The Seven Discoveries":

Through the grace of my Father Guru, the holy Jetsun,

I now have realized the Truth in Seven Discoveries.

In manifestations have I found the Void;
Now, I have no thought that anything exists.

In the Voidness have I found the Dharmakāya;
Now, I have no thought of action.

In myriad manifestations the Non-Dual have I found;
Now, I have no thought of gathering or dispersing.

In the Elements of Red and White,[4]
Have I found the essence of equality;
Now, I have no thought of accepting or rejecting.

In the Body of Illusion[5] I have found great bliss;
Now, in my mind, there is no suffering.

I have found the Transcendental in the world;
Now, delusion has no hold upon my mind.

In the Self-Mind I have found the Buddha;
Now, in my mind Saṃsāra no more exists.

Milarepa then said to Rechungpa, "Your experience and understanding is close to real Enlightenment, but it is still not quite the same. Real Experience and true understanding should be like this." And he sang "The Eight [Supreme] Realms":

He who sees the world and Voidness as the same,
Has reached the realm of the True View.

He who feels no difference between dream
    and waking,
Has reached the realm of True Practice.

He who feels no difference between Bliss
    and Voidness,
Has reached the realm of True Action.

He who feels no difference between "now"
    and "then,"
Has reached the realm of Reality.

He who sees that Mind and Voidness are the same,
Has reached the realm of Dharmakāya.

He who feels no difference between pain and pleasure,
Has reached the realm of the True Teaching.

He who sees human wishes and Buddha's Wisdom as
    the same,
Has reached the realm of supreme Enlightenment.

He who sees that Self-Mind and Buddha are alike,
Has reached the realm of True Accomplishment.

Thereafter, through the mercy and blessing of his Guru, Rechungpa gradually improved in understanding and Realization. He then composed "The Song of the Six Bardos,"[6] in which he presented to Milarepa his insight and final understanding:

I bow before the holy Gurus.

In the Bardo where the great Void manifests
There is no realisitic or nihilistic view;
I do not share the thoughts of human sectaries.

Beyond all apprehension is Non-existence now;
Of the View this is my firm conviction.

In the Bardo of Voidness and Bliss there is
No object on which the mind can meditate,
And so I have no need to practice concentration.
I rest my mind without distraction in the natural
    state.
This is my understanding of the Practice,
I no longer feel ashamed before enlightened friends.

In the Bardo with lust and without lust
I see no Saṃsāric bliss;
And so, no more a hypocrite, I meet no bad companions.
Whate'er I see before me I take as my companion.
This is my conviction of the Action,
No longer feel I shame before a gathering of great
    yogis.

Between vice and virtue I no more discriminate;
The pure and impure are now to me the same.
Thus, never shall I be untruthful or pretentious.
Now have I wholly mastered the Self-Mind.
This is my understanding of Morality,
No longer feel I shame before the Saints' assembly.

In the [new-found] realm of Samsāra and Nirvāna
Sentient beings and the Buddha are to me the same;
And so I neither hope nor yearn for Buddhahood.
At this moment, all my sufferings have become a
    pleasure.
This is my understanding of Enlightenment,
No longer feel I shame before enlightened beings.

Having freed myself from words and meanings
I speak no more the language of all scholars.
I have no more doubts in my mind.
The universe and all its forms
Now appear but as the Dharmakāya.
This is the conviction I have realized.
No longer feel I shame before a gathering of great
    scholars.

Milarepa was highly delighted, and said, "Rechungpa, this is indeed
the real Experience and knowledge. You can truly be called a well-
gifted disciple. Now there are three ways in which one may please one's
Guru: First, the disciple should employ his faith and intelligence to
gratify his Guru; then, through unmistakable learning and contemplation, he should enter the gate of Mahāyāna and Vajrayāna, and practice them diligently with great determination; then finally, he can please
his Guru with his real experiences of Enlightenment, which are produced step by step through his devotion. I do not like the disciple
who talks much; the actual practice is far more important. Until the
full Realization of Truth is gained, he should shut his mouth and
work at his meditation. My Guru, Marpa, said to me: 'It does not
matter much whether one knows a great deal about Sūtras and Tantras. One should not merely follow the words and books, but should
shut his mouth, unmistakably follow his Guru's verbal instructions, and
meditate.' Therefore, you should also follow this admonishment, forgetting it not, and putting it into practice. If you can leave all Samsāric
affairs behind you, the great merits and accomplishments will all become yours."

Rechungpa replied, "Dear Jetsun, please be kind enough to tell what Marpa said." Milarepa then sang "The Thirty Admonishments of my Guru":

Dear son, these are the words He said to me:

> "Of all refuges, the Buddha's is the best;
> Of all friends, faith is most important;
> Of all evils, Nhamdog is the worst;
> Of all devils, pride;
> Of all vices, slander."

He said:

> "He who does not purify his sins with the Four
>   Powers[7]
> Is bound to wander in Saṃsāra.
> He who with diligence stores not merit,
> Will never gain the bliss of Liberation.
> He who refrains not from committing the Ten Evils,
> Is bound to suffer pains along the Path.
> He who does not meditate on Voidness and
>   Compassion,
> Will never reach the state of Buddhahood."

He said:

> "If in this life you want Buddhahood,
> Observe your mind without diversion
> And practice the Six Yogas,
> The essence and final teaching of all Tantras.
> Practice, too, the Skillful Path of Tantra,
> The essence, the final teaching of the Pith-
>   Instruction.
> If you look for fame, goods, and recognition,
> You throw yourself into the mouth of devils.
> If others you revile, and praise yourself,
> You will fall into the abyss.
> If you tame not your elephantine mind,
> The teachings and Pith-Instruction will be useless.
> The greatest merit is to raise the Heart-for-
>   Bodhi;
> To understand the Non-arising is the highest View.

Profound meditation is the teaching of the
Skillful Path.
The Nāḍī and breathing exercises should be prac-
ticed too."

He said:

"Behold and recognize the face of the Innate-Born!
Put yourself in the hands of holy beings!
Do not dissipate your life by doing worthless
things."

He said:

"Behold and watch your unborn mind,
Look not for pleasures in Saṃsāra,
Think not that all sufferings are ill."

He also said:

"When you realize your mind, you become a Buddha.
It is unnecessary to talk and do a lot!
There is no other teaching more profound than
this.
Follow and practice, then, all these
instructions!"

After hearing this song, Rechungpa, improved greatly in Realization
and Understanding.

. . . .

Later when Milarepa and his disciples were living ascetically during
their retreat, many Ḍākinīs came and offered them a sacramental
feast. They addressed Milarepa thus: "It is good for you during your
devotions to accept food and clothing from human beings, and also
to receive a little heavenly nourishment from the Ḍākinīs. We will
always bring provisions for you." Milarepa replied, "The possessions,
facilities, and food of the common people can never match the merits
of Enlightenment and the power of Realization. Therefore, worldly
needs are dispensible. Now, hearken to my song":

I bow down to all Gurus.

From the realm of Absolute Reality
I, the Yogi Milarepa, sing this song;
From the realm of Universal Non-existence
I, Milarepa, chant this hymn.
Please listen, Mothers and Ḍākinīs.

The Law of Cause and Effect is e'er supreme —
The convincing Buddhist doctrine.
How can common faiths e'er match it?

Supreme it is to live and meditate alone;
How can trance compare with this?

Samādhi is supreme, free from "this" and "that";
How can common knowledge e'er attain it?

"Essence" is supreme in the state of "After-
    Meditation";
How can common practices ever equal it?

Mindfulness beyond all words also is supreme;
How can common actions e'er attain it?

The unison of Love and Voidness is supreme;
How can common accomplishment e'er reach it?

Supreme, too, is my cotton robe that's never cold;
How can the gaudy clothes of common people match it?

Supreme is my Samādhi that's never hungry;
How can meat and wine compare with it?

This drink of mine comes from the stream of Bodhi;
How can common drinks compare with it?

Within, my heart is brimming with contentment;
How can food and wealth o'ershadow it?

My Guru, the Translator Marpa, is supreme;
How can other yogis equal Him?

Seeing the Buddha-face of the Self-Mind is supreme;

How can the common "patron Buddha" meditation
    match it?

I, the Yogi Milarepa, am supreme;
How can other yogis match me?

My body is immune from pain and illness;
How can drugs or doctors so insure it?

Please listen and give judgement, oh Ḍākinīs,
Where there is no light, I see but brightness;
The light itself is very radiant too.
Where there is no warmth, I feel well-heated;
This single cotton robe has warmth in plenty.
Where'er discomfort is, I rest in ease;
This body of illusion is most comfortable.
Where there is no joy, I feel most joyful;
This life of dreams is itself delightful!
I, the Yogi, feel but happiness and joy!

Is not the Drajadorje Mountain high enough?
If not, why would vultures float above it?

If the cold December wind is not severe enough,
How can it freeze the waterfalls and rivers?

If my cotton clothing is not warmed by Inner-Heat,
How can a single robe shut out the coldness?

If Samādhi food does not sustain me,
How can I e'er endure insatiate hunger?

If there is no Stream-of-Bodhi for my drinking,
How can I live without water and not thirst?

If my Guru's Pith-Instructions are not profound enough,
How can I conquer hindrances and devils?

If a yogi has no Realization and Experience
[To make him confident and full of joy]
How can he ever meditate in solitude?

These accomplishments are gained through the grace
    of my Guru.
Thus should one concentrate on meditation practice.

Having heard this song, the Ḍākinīs exclaimed, "What you have said
is indeed wonderful! Tomorrow, a well-destined disciple will come here.
Please take care of him." With these words, they all disappeared like the
rainbow.

The next day, a few patrons came on a visit from Gu Tang. They
asked Milarepa to preach the Dharma for them. Whereupon, the Jetsun imparted to them the Prayer of Taking Refuge, together with explanations on the benefits of practicing the Dharma. The patrons asked,
"Do you also practice this Prayer of Taking Refuge?" Milarepa replied,
"Yes. This prayer is my sole shelter, and I depend upon it alone in my
devotion and practice. You should also pray earnestly to your Guru and
the Three Precious Ones, not merely by words but by sincerely taking
them as your true Refuge. The benefit of this is very great as I have
told you before. All of you should therefore be very happy and satisfied
with this prayer." Milarepa then sang a song in which he described the
different frames of reference in which the Refuges are set, and urged
them to practice the Dharma.

Obeisance to all Gurus.

The Buddha, the Dharma, and the Saṅgha
Are the three outer Refuges;
Even I take them as my shelter.
By putting all my trust in them,
I have gained joy and satisfaction.
Fortune will come, if in them you take your refuge.

The Guru, the Patron Buddha, and the Ḍākinīs
Are the three inner Refuges.
Even I take them as my shelter.
By putting all my trust in them,
I have gained joy and satisfaction.
Fortune will come, if in them you take your refuge.

The Nāḍīs, Prāṇa, and Bindu are the three secret
    Refuges;
Even I take them as my shelter.
By putting all my trust in them,
I have gained joy and satisfaction.

Fortune will come, if in them you take your refuge.

Form, Voidness, and Non-distinction
Are the three real Refuges;
By putting all my trust in them,
I have gained joy and satisfaction.
Fortune will come, if in them you take your refuge.

If you look not to the Refuges,
Who will protect you from eternal suffering?

Day and night the rotting house of your body
Is invaded by the [Four] Elements.
Through months and years,
Rain brings it to dissolution.

To the dying these eroding drops
Bring neither joy nor pleasure.

'Tis like the shadow of the setting sun;
You may try to fly away from it
But never can you escape.

Observation of death is a Buddhist's "teacher,"
From whom one learns to practice worthy deeds.
One should always think, and remember,
That joy is absent at the time of dying.

If a sinner sees the nature of death,
He learns a good lesson of truth.
He will then ponder on the thought,
"How regretful I will be when that moment comes!"

If a man of wealth sees death around him,
He has learned a good lesson of truth —
That goods and money are his great foes.
Let him then ponder on the thought,
"I should try always to be generous!"

If an old man feels that death is near him,
He has learned a good lesson of truth —
That life is short and transient.
Let him then ponder on the thought,

"Life is, after all, a sad dream."

If a young man sees death around him,
He has learned a good lesson of truth —
That life is short and fades soon to oblivion.
Let him then practice his devotions!

Our parents bear the burdens of our worries,
But orphans must endure them by themselves.

A smooth, fine leather coat is indeed a comfort —
But, beyond imagination, for him who never wore one.

Crops on the farm are the cure for poverty,
But those who do not work can ne'er enjoy them.

[A couplet is omitted here as the text is corrupt. Tr.]

He who practices the Dharma will be joyful;
But those who practice not, can never share it.

Give more away in gifts, and you will ne'er be hungry.
If you want to conquer drowsiness and sleep,
Practice more good deeds.[8]

Remembering the miseries of the lower Realms
Helps one and all to practice Buddhism.

After hearing this song, many patrons became devoted Buddhists. Among the group, there was one young man who had confirmed within him an immutable faith towards Milarepa. He asked permission to follow him in order to give him service. Milarepa thought, "This is the man whom the Ḍākinīs predicted. I should take him as my disciple." And he imparted the Initiation and instructions to him. After practicing these teachings, the young man attained Accomplishment and Liberation. He was known as Ron Chon Repa, one of the close sons of Milarepa.

This is the story of Milarepa meeting Ron Chon Repa on his later trip to Drajadorje Tson.

NOTES

1 Yoga of No-returning (T.T.: Phyir.Mi.lDog.Pahi.rNal.hByor.): implying an advanced stage on the Path. When a yogi reaches it he will never regress in his spiritual development or fall back again into Saṃsāra.

2 The Expedient Truth, or the Expedient Teachings: There are two very important terms in Mahāyāna Buddhism which explicitly reflect the Mahāyāna Buddhist view and its evaluation into the various conflicting doctrines as upheld by different Schools of Buddhism, and by other religions. One is known as the "Expedient Teaching" (T.T.: Draṅ.Don.), and the other, as the "Ultimate," or "Final Teaching" (T.T.: Ñes.Don.). The "Expedient Teachings" are those doctrines arranged and preached for the unevolved or not-yet-ripened devotees who are not ready to receive the higher form of teaching. The "Final Teachings" are those which may be described as supreme and ultimate.

The myriads of Buddhas see only one final Reality in the realm of Supreme Enlightenment. However, to enable all sentient beings to realize this Reality, various approaches, teachings, or steps appropriate to different groups and individuals are necessary because all sentient beings do not share the same dispositions, capacities, and Karmas. A teaching that is beneficial to one group or to one individual may not be helpful to another; hence, a variety of approaches is needed to ripen these innumerable types of people. For the Hīnayāna-bent, Hīnayāna Buddhism is taught; for the Mahāyāna-bent, Mahāyāna Buddhism. This approach is also true for Christians, Hindus, and other religionists — an appropriate teaching, even in the guise of a different faith, is wisely given to all and sundry who may require it.

Because of this all-embracing attitude, Mahāyāna Buddhism is impregnated with an extremely inclusive and tolerant spirit, which has been unmistakably demonstrated throughout Buddhist history. This recognition of the value and usefulness of all religions is typically reflected in the popular Buddhist proverb, "Since sentient beings suffer many different sicknesses, Buddha, the King of Physicians, has to prescribe for them various treatments and medicines; hence all the teachings of the different Schools and religions are merely the differing remedies prescribed by Him for the benefit of each case."

Although the Expedient Teachings are necessary for those who have not evolved to a level advanced enough to accept the highest teachings (the Final Truth), they do lay a foundation for approaching it; without these Expedient Teachings, it would not be possible for many who, for the time being, do not yet possess the capacity, to appreciate and practice the higher teachings.

3 Mind-holding Practice: Most of the meditation practices are devised for the development of mental concentration, i.e., to hold onto an object in one's mind's-eye. In other words, a mental effort is required in all of them. But the meditation of Mahāmudrā is of a quite different nature. It is effortless and natural; in its practice no object whatsoever is held in the yogi's mind. In comparison with the teaching of Mahāmudrā, all others are temporal and expedient.

4 The White Element is the positive, and the Red Element the negative force of the body.

5 Body of Illusion: Any body possessing form and attributes is illusory; this applies to both Saṃsāric and Nirvāṇic bodies, including the Reward Body and Transformation Body of Buddha.

6 Bardo here does not mean the state after death, it means "in-between" states of all kinds.

7 The Four Powers through which one's sins can be purified are:
  (1) The Power of sincere repentance.
  (2) The Power of determination not to commit the same sin again.
  (3) The Power of undertaking good deeds to compensate for the wrong deeds previously committed.
  (4) The Power of contemplating on the void nature of being.

8 To lessen one's drowsiness by practicing good deeds: Some people constantly feel drowsy while they are practicing meditation. As soon as they cease meditating, drowsiness disappears. If all methods of curing drowsiness are tried without success, it is due, according to many Gurus, to sins committed in the past. The remedy for this is to practice confession-prayers and perform diligently various meritorious deeds.

24

THE CONVERSION OF
A DYING BONIST

Obeisance to all Gurus

E ARLY one morning on the eighth day of a lunar month, when Jetsun Milarepa was meditating at Drajadorje Tson and observing silence, a number of Ḍākinīs dressed as earthly ladies came to him and prophesied:

> Oh, silent yogi with great power of will
> Who practices austerity,
> The sole lion in the midst of all this snow,
> Who sees, alone, Saṃsāra in Nirvāṇa,
> Listen to us — the four Ḍākinī sisters
> Who come to prophesy.

> Tomorrow, in the early morning,
> Go to the eastern shore of Baltang Lake,
> Where people sin and sport in wanton pleasures.
> You, the Lion of the snow mountain,
> Should help them back into the path of virtue,
> Guiding those who have lost their way to the
>   right Path.

After conveying this message to the Jetsun, the Ḍākinīs vanished.

Accordingly the next day Milarepa journeyed eastward. On the way, he met a shepherd. When the shepherd saw him walking above the ground — his feet never touching the earth — an unshakable faith toward Milarepa arose within him. He offered the Jetsun his own food, and asked for the teachings of Dharma. Whereupon Milarepa preached on the Law of Kharma; on the errors of Saṃsāra; on the difficulties of obtaining favorable human birth, body, and environment; and lastly, on the unpredictableness and inevitability of death. Convinced by these teachings, the shepherd said, "Dear Lama, your preaching has been a reminder of the great sufferings of Saṃsāra. On thinking it over, [I find] I have no more desire for any gain or loss, happiness or misery in this life. The sufferings which you have mentioned, distress me so much that I feel I cannot bear them any longer. Please give me some instruction that can help me." "Very well," said Milarepa, "I shall teach you." The shepherd then confided to him, "I — and I alone — know of a secret cave called Mamo Tson. Please, let us go there."

When they arrived at the cave, the shepherd offered food and gave service to the Jetsun, and then asked for the teachings that would release him from Saṃsāric suffering. Milarepa then taught him how to meditate. [Not long after], the shepherd confided, "When I am concentrating, I feel very peaceful and there is no suffering whatsoever. But when my mind begins to wander, pictures of the miseries in Saṃsāra all appear before me; I can hardly bear the distressing experience of seeing them. With your great compassion, please bring me to the state of eternal happiness." Milarepa replied, "If you want to be always happy, you must ever avoid sinful deeds and follow my example by practicing all the virtues." The shepherd answered, "I am willing to do so for the sake of attaining the longed for perpetual happiness. I would like to become your servant. Please take me with you."

Milarepa recognized that this shepherd was a destined disciple, so he took him in and granted him the Initiation and Pith-Instructions. Later on, the shepherd was known as Tsiwo Repa, the most oustanding student among those "Disciples-with-Realization."

On the morning of the day that the Jetsun met Tsiwo Repa, the Ḍākinīs said to him, "There is a place called Lapu; you should go there." And so Milarepa went to Lapu where lived a very rich old man, a pious follower of Bon, who had many sons. Recently he had contracted a very serious disease. On the day of Milarepa's visit, one of this man's sons had just returned home from consulting a diviner, who had said that the remedy was to kill one hundred yaks, one hundred goats, and one hundred sheep, and with the meat to hold a great festival and sacrifice for the Bon monks. Following this instruction, the rich man's sons had made all the arrangements for the feast and were just about to slaughter the animals when the Jetsun arrived.

Milarepa, on first reaching Lapu, had met a girl on her way to fetch water and had asked alms from her. She informed him of the great Bon festival to be held for the sick rich man, saying that she was sure he would find alms if he went there. As Milarepa approached the rich man's house he saw all kinds of people entering it. It seemed that anyone could walk in, even the dogs. Nevertheless, the hosts said, "Dear Lama, our father is very sick. Please leave us." Milarepa replied, "All I want is something to eat. Please give me food." The sons then prepared a little food for him, and were about to send him away, when the sick man's relatives and doctors began to gather round to observe his illness. Milarepa went to them asking for charity.

When the rich man beheld Milarepa's face, a great faith arose in him, and somehow a change took place in his mind. He clutched Milarepa's robe and besought him, saying, "Dear Lama, I am a [living] man for only today or tomorrow. Look on me with your compassion!" Thus he implored, while tears streamed down his face. Milarepa said, "It is a good omen that you have such faith in me. If I cure your illness, will you renounce the world and practice Dharma?" The rich man replied, "If I'm relieved of this illness, I shall do whatever you say. Not only will I practice Dharma, but I will also cause my sons to become Buddhists." The Jetsun thought to himself, "The Ḍākinīs prophesied that I should convert certain evil and pleasure-loving men and thus accomplish benevolent deeds and give blessings to all. This must be the opportunity [they] meant, so I shall act accordingly." Whereupon he said to the rich man, "You may slaughter all the yaks and goats you wish, but that will not cure your illness. In fact, it will only make your situation worse. Rather, you should set all those cattle free. On the other hand, I know a method that will definitely cure you; but first — what religion do you profess?" The sick man answered, "While I do not disbelieve in Buddhism, I have always loved and placed my faith in Bon." "In that case," said Milarepa, "You should now dismiss all these Bon monks and doctors. I will perform a 'Bon' ceremony for you which will certainly help your recovery." To which the eldest son of the rich man added, "I propose that both the Bon monks and this Lama perform their ceremonies together. Cannot this be done?" "Your suggestion is apt," the Jetsun replied, "but there are already too many doctors and too much hocus-pocus here. All this does not help. It would be better to dismiss them all." The sick man supported him by adding, "We should do what the Lama says." Accordingly, both the ritualists and the physicians were dismissed. Learning of this, the people began to murmur, "Are not the ceremony-makers and doctors capable? Surely, this foreign yogi can neither diagnose nor help. The sick man will probably die soon." After voicing such thoughts, they became all the more worried and distressed.

The sick man asked Milarepa, "What animal, then, should we slaughter for an offering?" The Jetsun said, "In the performance of my ceremony, no sacrifice is necessary. I have a 'Bon'[1] prayer of my own. Listen attentively!" Thereupon, Milarepa, chanting a Bon melody after the Bon manner, sang for the sick man "The Parable of the Twenty-two Family Members":

"Sou, yon yon, yon, yon, yon yon ngo . . . . .[2]
In the beginning of time, arose a manifestation.
At that moment, as the first of all happenings,
The outer objects appeared as something with
          attributes.

The assembling of elements, the Aggregations,
[Formed] the great city, the Three Realms of Saṃsāra
The inner mind, which discerns, was comprehended
          as one with qualities;
In the Illuminating-Void Awareness,
Thereby sprang up a myriad ideas and perceptions.
This is the source of all Karma and Kleśas!

All dwellings in this distressed world are illusory,
For they are built upon forms of delusion.
Because of clinging to the god and father image,
One fashions his active mind as the ego.
Because of clinging to the mother and goddess image,
One's mind pursues a myriad things.

When the mother and father united,
Then were born the twelve Nidāna sons[3]
And the eight Consciousness daughters.
These brothers and sisters, with their parents,
Totaled twenty-two.

From the arising of this family
Came the four-and-eighty thousand Kleśas
And the three hundred and sixty Distractions.
Thus arose the eighty thousand Evils and Hindrances,
And the four hundred and four kinds of disease.

This is the first chapter of my song,
The Chapter of the Members of the Family.

All the two-and-twenty members are beset with illness,
They are wrapped in the sickness of a blinded mind
And they suffer from a myriad afflictions.

Fever inflames their upper parts,
The fire of anger ever burns within them,
While like yaks distraught they deeply groan.
Chills plague their lower parts
And churning pools of lust
Drive them to lechery.

Skran-blindness[4] afflicts their middle parts;
The dropsy of ego-clinging swells and distends them.
Troubled are they by sub-Prāna sickness
And choked by swollen pride;
Diseased in heart,
They denounce others while they praise themselves.
They make their bed among the Five Poisonous
     [Desires].

Surrendering their minds
To the nonsense of "this" and "that,"
They lose all appetite for being virtuous.
For the waters of sin they thirst
And vomit virtue's medicine.

To the Ten Directions they spit the saliva of
     worthless talk;
They take the Eight Worldly Claims for clothing,
Relatives of the Ten Evils surround their beds.
Minds clouded, they wander in the realms
Of distraction, longing for food and wealth.
Dark and hopeless are these diseases.

This is the second chapter of my song,
The Chapter Describing Sicknesses.

For diseases such as these what is the cure?
"Bon" will help, and divination too;
Thus, I, the Yogi, will divine for you.

A messenger, the transiency of all lives,
Was sent to ask a divination.
An expert diviner was then called,
And a cushion of faith unshakable provided.
The beverage of trust was mixed
And a barley-heap for augury arranged

In veneration of the Dharma.
The question, the inquiry into the profound teaching
     of Dharma,
Was presented to the soothsayer.

The augur, a proficient Guru, charts
A horoscope of the Four Elements.
He counts the rounds of years, the Twelve Nidānas,
And also numbers the Eight Trigrams — or
     Consciousnesses.
The diagrams of the Nine Vehicles[5] are drawn.
A prediction of good or evil is thus made.

This is the third chapter of my song,
The Chapter of Divining by the Stars.

Reading the chart, the soothsayer prophesies:
For these two-and-twenty people,
The omen is bad indeed.
From the time of no-beginning,
On the foundation of Saṃsāra and Nirvāṇa
Was set up a stove of mental blindness.

The host, pure manifestation, was singed by words.
The burners, hate and lust, left behind a burning-spot.
Because of stove, fire, and burning-spot,
The Wisdom-Father god left the house and went to
     Heaven;
The local god of the Great Bliss withdrew and
     disappeared;
The conquering god of Self-Awareness also went away.

Because these three great gods withdrew,
The demons could send forth afflictions.
Hence arose the Eight Dharmas of the world,
And the pain of life came into being in Saṃsāra.
Burning anger — the most dreadful demon;
Stirring lust — that pernicious demoness;
Blind ignorance — the fierce dragon demon;
Stinging jealousy — the demon called Tsan Rigs;[6]
Egotism and prejudice — another, named Rtor Legs,[7]
Self-praise and self-inflation — the demon styled
     Mamo;[8]

Evil deeds and habitual-thinking — the dread demon
    called Shen Dre[9] —
My host, these are the demons which afflict you.

According to the divination,
Your life is in great danger,
For whoe'er is born, will die.
According to the divination,
Your family affairs are not auspicious;
At the end of a gathering there must be departure.
According to the divination,
Your monetary affairs do not prosper,
For the end of gain is loss.
According to the divination,
Your dealings with your foes are not lucky,
For no longer can you take the upper hand.
To reverse these evil omens,
Let us hold a "Bon" service.

This is the fourth chapter of my song,
The Ominous Divination of your Life.

Now I, the Yogi, will chant a "Bon" prayer for you.
"Bon," in its deeper teaching, says:
"In the morning of the first day was laid
The foundation of Heaven's Tripiṭaka;[10]
The ransom was given of hearing, practice, and
    contemplation."
The sacramental offerings of pure precept are now
    prepared,
And the hymns of the four Tantras now are chanted.
The initiatory gift which frees from craving is
    presented.

For the disappearance of the Father into Heaven,
The recognition of basic blindness
Is the remedy I offer.
For the withdrawal of the local gods of the Great
    Bliss,
Victory over the Four Demons is the remedy I offer.
For the absence of the conquering god of Self-
    Awareness,
The ransom of Self-Renunciation is my offer.

The evil thoughts of the Eight Worldly Affairs,
I amputate with the Awareness-knife that is free
    from craving.
To cure the lives of pain in this distressing world,
I offer the balm of Universal Bliss.
The fire-like, angry demon
I poison with the Wisdom of the Void;
The lust-stirring demoness
I conquer with Mind-Essence.

To quell the dragon demon of blind ignorance,
I summon the eight dragons, Self-liberating Forms.
To the king of demons, suffocating pride,
I give the hart's horn of the Wisdom of the Void.
To conquer the Tsan demon, stinging jealousy,
I raise the arrow-scarf, the Wisdom of Accomplishment.
To the bragging, self-praising demon called Mamo,
I recite the prayer of the Non-existence-of-Self-and-
    Others.
To cleanse clinging to self and egotisms,
I make altruistic offerings.
To nullify the evil of habitual-thinking, the
    Shen Dre demon,
I perform the conquering demon dance, the Voidness
    of Mental Functions.

If there be harmful demons,
These remedies will dispel them.
If there be ghosts of prosperity,
These acts will capture them.
If you make sacramental offerings,
Do so in this way.

Mind-Nature has nor birth nor death;
Through this "Bon" understanding
Threats to life are overcome.

The companion of Self-Manifestation
Gathers not nor separates,
But overcomes all threats of family strife.

Transcendental property cannot be exhausted;
By knowing this is the fear of poverty dispelled.

Through the teaching of this "Bon" doctrine,
Ill omens and divination are reversed.
If one understands [the Dharma] truly,
Even the sufferings he undergoes
Will appear to him as Divine Instructions.
Through this "Bon" teaching,
All evil encounters are transformed.

This is the fifth chapter of my song,
The Chapter of Subduing Devil-demons.

Oh, family of two-and-twenty members!
The ill of your mind-blindness has been cured,
The painful groaning of self-clinging ended.
Oh sick man! Upon your face appears
A fair complexion — the Illuminating-Void;
Food and drink — the illuminating and blissful Samādhi —
Become delicious and appetizing to you!

The sick man is now grateful for his cure;
With heartfelt sincerity, he renders thanks
And makes propitiation.
He sends his son, Self-Awareness,
To the mountain of the Great Perfection.[11]
The shepherd boy, Constant-Mindfulness,
Then takes a yak — the Nine Successive Vehicles,
A sheep — the Four Tantras, and a goat — the Three
    Canons.

Thence, upon the plain of Universal Equality
Guests are summoned to a feast of Myriad Wisdoms.
The oblation with butter is anointed,
Together with the food of Sūnyatā.
The arrow-scarf of Learning and Contemplation is
    spread out.
Appreciation is expressed to all the company.

Before the Guru, the soothsayer of skill,
Is hung the human skull of Faith, Veneration, and
    Sincerity,
For, with the holy teaching of "Bon" he rides
The horse of Skillful-Wisdom.
To the all-perfect "Bon" Body

He offers a yak of the Nine Successive Vehicles.
To the conquering gods, the Five Nirmāṇakāyas,
He offers a sheep of the Four Tantras.
To the Life-god, the Transformation Body of Tathāgata,
He offers a Tripiṭaka goat.
To the Goddess of Medicine who cures all diseases,
He offers a sacrificial meal of the Four Immeasurables.[12]
Such are the sacrifices and propitiations.

This is the sixth chapter of my song,
The Chapter of Propitiation and Sacrificial Offering.

In the wide courtyard of the "Bon,"
Are tethered yak and sheep and goat.
The butcher, All-Knowing Wisdom,
Sharpens the sword of Knowledge
And opens the life hole of Two Preparations.[13]
The butcher then severs the liferoot [spine] of
        the Two Hindrances[14]
And flays the skin of all-disturbing thoughts.
Understanding the meaning of the Sūtras and Tantras,
The butcher, knowingly, cleaves the limbs.
Relying on the holy sayings and sound judgment,
He divides the various parts
With the cleaver of the Pith-Instructions,
Chopping into pieces all the flesh.
The various portions of the meat, the "Bon" form,
Are piled into a cauldron, the "Bon" essence.
The three firestones of Primordial Trikāya are laid,
And the fire of Four Infinites is lit.
He boils well the meat 'til it is sweet and tender —
The consummation of Experience and Enlightenment.
Then he takes out the meat, the unison of Meditation
        and Activity.

In the great mansion of "Bon" essence,
In the illusory city of Six Realms,
To the feast throng crowds of guests.

The banquet is arranged by skillful hands —
Those of the Five Great Wisdoms.
The food and drinks — many yet one —
Are offered to all guests without discrimination.

To the wise Succession Gurus who have the power to
    bless,
The upper-body is offered in complete perfection.

To the Guru who illustrates the holy words and
    Pith-Instructions,
The liferoot [spine] of Bodhi, the Skillful Path,
    is served.

To the Guru who frees all beings from Saṃsāra
The pure eyeballs are given.

To the Guru who knows the words and meanings
    [of the Buddhist teaching],
The tongue that tastes all flavors then is given.

To the virtuous, precept-observing monks,
Are served the pleasant parts, pure and pacified.

To the men of "Bon" who know the Law of Karma,
Are given the meat and wine of "benevolent deeds."

To the yogi who knows the truth of Non-existence,
The fat of the Great Bliss is presented.

To the firm protector of the Buddhist doctrine,
Is given the gullet which brings benefits to all.

To the meditator of the Skillful Tantric Path,
The upper breast of greatest rapture is presented.

To the great yogi who meditates on the transiency
    of being,
The lower breast of the Skillful Bodhi-Path, is
    served.

To the yogi without sectarian ideas,
Is offered the castrated ram of all delight.

To the yogi with compassion that embraces all,
The knuckles and joints of the Four Infinities are
    given.

To the man who is disgusted with this world,
Is presented the breastbone, free from acts and craving.

To the one who practices the main teaching of "Bon,"
The four limbs, indispensible to life, are served.

To the physician, the nourishing Bodhi-Mind,
The backbone of this life and that beyond, is offered.

To all followers who are faithful and sincere
The heart, the essence of instruction, is presented.

To the steadfast one who ne'er forsakes the Path of
      Virtue,
Is given the liver — Cause-and-Effect that never fails.

To the industrious follower, are presented
The kidneys, Skill and Wisdom.

To beginners in the Dharma are presented
The feet, the well-designed Expedient Truths.

To the yogi, who always heeds his meditation practice,
Is given the herdsman's meat, the essential
      Pith-Instruction.

This is the seventh chapter of my song,
The Chapter that invites Superior Beings to a Feast.

Such was the feast that Milarepa served,
And then, the worthy guests went home.

. . .   .

Though the universal foundation [Ālaya] of all men
      is one,
Their conduct and dispositions vary greatly.
Therefore, to arrogant and pretentious monks,
Is given the penis that e'er clings to form.

To the teacher who follows nought but words,
The skinless and decayed part of the legs is served.

To proud, pompous, and evil priests
The meatless nape is offered.

To proud black magicians, who practice sorcery,
The neck grease, maker of black-bitterness, is given.

To bigoted and sectarian monks
Is given the spinal marrow of disputation.

To greedy and contemptible solicitors,
The barren nose-tip of vanity is given.

To the yogi who strolls about the village,
The rumor-hungry ears are presented.

To disciples of small faith but with gross heresies,
The ill-rewarding spleen is served.

To the person who upsets and subverts the Brotherhood,
The bitter gall is given.

To the "grand" teachers, who have not realized
      Mind-Essence,
The midriff, the ostentatious but vain Maṇḍala, is
      offered.

To the yogi whose meditation practice is merely of
      the mouth,
The lung, so tasteless yet so large in size, is
      served.

To the yogi who knows little but boasts much,
The skin of the stomach is presented.

To town-dwellers, "Bon" monks who eat up life,
The gullet, which fosters lust and hate, is given.

To fraudulent forecasters who throw lots,
The water-holding bladders are presented.

To the presumptuous man who claims there is no Karma,
Is served the tail, symbol of erroneous views.

To those who lack both modesty and scruple
Is served the anus, which ruins them and others.

To yogis, who cling to mind in meditation,
The brain, the source of blindness and folly, is
        offered.

To charlatans who claim that they have special
        teachings,
Are served the intestines, rounded like Saṃsāra.

To those who lust and crave, is given
The goiter, with which all are sore afflicted.

To those indifferent to the truth of Voidness
The cartilage,[15] which is neither meat nor fat, is
        served.

To people with small merit but great ambition
The tasteless and useless throat is given.

To persons who know little but want to
        teach
Are served the entrails from the lower parts.

To foolish yogis who blindly dwell in caves,
Tripe, smooth outside but coarse within, is given.

To him whose chief desire is to gather riches,
Is served the lower portion of the gullet.

To mean and brawling women
The head, with all its holes, is given.

To mean but wealthy men,
The round and storing belly is presented.

To people who see nothing but this life,
The testicles are served, fair on the surface but
        all foul within.

To the patron with sweet words but sullied heart,
The worthless, black intestines are presented.

To women who confuse themselves while still
    reviling others,
The teeth, of stony hardness, are served up.

To parents who at home have many mouths to feed,
Skin, both tough and meatless, is presented.

To the person who has nothing whatsoever,
But toils and struggles for his family,
The useless bowels are given.

Incapable disciples who rebel
Are served with thin and meatless soup.

To those who e'er postpone their Dharma practice,
Are given the remnants, symbol of their laziness.

To the countless sentient beings in the plane of
    Bardo
Are thrown the final scraps of meat.

The Four Initiations[16] of self-liberation from the
    Five Gates[17]
Are given by the butcher of All-Knowing Wisdom;
And with the jug of Wisdom that is immutable,
Sweet wine is offered to all guests without
    discrimination.

I, the rich man, have now prepared a feast for you,
So eat and drink, dear guests, just as you please.

This is the eighth chapter of my song,
The Chapter of Dining at the Feast with Guests.

    . . .   .

Now is the time to speak a few propitious words;
Words, surely to be heard by all the Buddhas.
The Precious Ones do not appear on earth but stay
    in Dharmadhātu,
While my Guru adorns me by sitting on my head
And my brothers in the Dharma sit in rows [before me].

The first thing one should remember is the
    transiency of life;
Then he should read the lives of holy Saints.
Next, he should study the simple or comprehensive
    Sūtras,
Choosing them to meet his own requirements.
Then he should contemplate on the Instructions.

If in this song I have hidden anything from you,
If my preaching has been unsound or incomplete,
If I have transgressed or misrepresented anything,
I beg forgiveness from the Holy Ones.

[Milarepa then continued]:

Now, it is time for me, your host, to sing a
    song of pride.

At first, when I had contracted this disease,
I sent for a diviner, a yogi of devotion.
As he revealed the divination,
Unsparingly I offered the sacrificial ransom.

When he performed the ritual of offering,
    I realized
He was indeed a free-handed yogi
For his riches were truly inexhaustible.
Then he served the feast and entertained
His guests with all propriety.
I became aware he was an experienced yogi;
When he spoke, after the dinner,
He proved that he could teach us all.

When the feast was over, he gracefully gave thanks.
Lastly, he wished for final liberation of all men.
Oh, who is this "Bon"? Of whose "Bon" is he?
He is the "Bon" whose family numbers two-and-twenty,
He calms the fears of those who are besieged,
He is the "Bon" who removes malignant pressures.

This is my little after-dinner song.
Oh guests, drink ye and be drunk with the wine
    of Reality!

In a happy mood, let us sing and sport and play!

It is happy to be blessed, and a joy to meditate!
Cheerful, cheerful, are these after-dinner words.
May all rejoice, be gay and full of mirth.
Happy it is to vomit when drunk with devotion,
Happy to shout and cry under the blessing.
Ever, then, be joyful under the grace of your Gurus!

This is the ninth chapter of my song,
The Chapter of the Sermon After Feasting.

So Milarepa sang, mimicking the Bon way of chanting. Hearing it, the sick man was blessed and cured. Sons, daughters, servants, and friends, including some learned Lamas, were so delighted that one could hardly describe their joy. The villagers declared, "It is indeed miraculous to revive a dying man. The blessing of Dharma is surely greater than that of the Bons!" An unalterable faith in the Jetsun arose in them all. The rich man then addressed the Jetsun, saying, "Dear Lama, your preachings were all Buddhist; they were not of Bon. I have always been a follower of Bon and believed its teachings, but now I will become a Buddhist and put my whole faith in Buddhism — I, and my sons, and all my family and household." The Jetsun gave assent, and thus the whole family, including the father with his eight sons, became Buddhists.

Among the sons was one who had been an expert in Bon, which he had mastered to a perfect degree and in which he thoroughly believed. But after his father's cure, an immutable faith toward the Jetsun and Dharma awoke in him. He said to Milarepa, "Outwardly, the practice and words used by Bon and Dharma appear alike, but the compassion and grace are different and so are the achievements. Bon practices are greedy and covetous. In whatever ceremony is held, at least one living being will be slaughtered as an offering. The gods we worship are all worldly. When a follower is about to die, he has no real assurance within himself. His heart is filled with fear and confusion. From now on, I will renounce Bon and become a Buddhist. Please accept me as your servant-disciple and allow me to go with you." It occurred to Milarepa that this man was a well-destined person. He, therefore, took him for a disciple and granted him the Initiations and Pith-Instructions. Eventually, this young man attained Liberation and all the Accomplishments. He became known as Shen Gom Repa, one of the close disciples of Milarepa. His father and his brothers all gave their best service and offerings to the Jetsun while he dwelt at Langgo Ludu Tson, Bepu Mamo Tson, and Barkon Gi Tson. They entered the Gate of Liberation and followed the

Path of the All-Knowing Ones, thus preventing themselves from falling into the miserable realms of Saṃsāra.

This is the story of Milarepa meeting Tsiwo Repa, the outstanding enlightened Yogi, and Shen Gom Repa, the close son-disciple of Milarepa, at Bepu Mamo Tson and Lapu Paima Tson.

NOTES

1 Milarepa did not, of course, perform a Bon ritual; he merely mimicked the Bon cult in fun.

2 This is the first line of a chant in which the Bon monks intone their hymns. Milarepa derisively mimicked the Bon way of singing in this song.

3 The Twelve Nidānas: The general twelve successive stages that characterize Saṃsāric becomings are: (1) ignorance, (2) action, (3) consciousness, (4) name and form, (5) the six sense organs, (6) contact, (7) sensation, (8) craving, (9) grasping, (10) existing, (11) birth, (12) old age and death.

4 The name of a disease.

5 The Nine Vehicles (T.T.: Theg.Pa.Rim.Pa.dGu.): The Ningmaba (T.T.: rÑiñ.Ma.Pa.) School of Tibetan Buddhism classifies all Buddhist doctrines into nine different approaches or Vehicles. They are : (1) the Sravākayāna, (2) the Pratyekayāna, (3) the Bodhisattvayāna, (4) the Kriyātantra, (5) the Caryātantra, (6) the Yogatantra, (7) the Mahāyoga, (8) the Anuyoga, and (9) the Ādiyoga. The first three belong to the exoteric (Sūtra) doctrine, and the last six to the esoteric (Tantric) doctrine. (The 7th, 8th, and 9th are subdivisions of the Anuttara Tantra.) The new schools of Tibetan Buddhism, i.e., Ghagyuba, Sajyaba, and Geluba do not follow these classifications. It is interesting to note that Milarepa, a founder and follower of Ghagyuba tradition, used the Ningmaba terminology on this occasion.

6, 7, 8, 9 The four main types of demons found in Tibetan legends.

10 Tripiṭaka: the Buddhist Canon, which consists of three main bodies: Sūtra, Sāstra, and Vināya.

11 Great Perfection (T.T.: rDsogs.Pa.Chin.Po.): the Ningmaba version of the teaching of Mahāmudrā.

12 The Four Immeasurables, or the Four Infinite Thoughts: friendliness, compassion, sympathetic joy, and evenmindedness.

13 Two Preparations (T.T.: Tsogs.Lam.gÑis.): This refers to the preliminary and advanced stages of preparation in the Bodhisattva's spiritual development.

14 The Two Hindrances: the Hindrance of Passions and the Hindrance of Knowledge. Perfect Buddhahood is achieved through the complete annihilation of these two hindrances.

15 T.T.: Krab-Krab, a term probably denoting cartilage.

16 The Four Initiations: See Story 1, Note 7, and Story 17, Note 37.

17 The Five Gates: the five senses and sense organs.

25

CHALLENGE FROM
A CLEVER MAIDEN

Obeisance to all Gurus

WHEN Milarepa and his heart-son-disciple Rechungpa were begging alms and helping sentient beings at the place of the Five Small Lakes in the Dritsam region, their reputation ran high. People said, "Look! The Jetsun Milarepa and his son Rechungpa are now meditating at Di Se Snow Mountain and Ma Päm Lake!" Influenced by their great fame, all the people of Joro Dritsam were convinced that Milarepa and Rechungpa were truly marvelous and unusual yogis. As their respect and admiration grew, they said, "Let us go to visit these two acomplished yogis!"

So one day, a number of patrons came to see the Jetsun, and brought with them provisions and oblations. Among them was a young girl called Rechungma, who was intelligent, compassionate, and had great faith in the Dharma. Actually, she was a Ḍākinī who had incarnated in human form. Having heard the life-story of Milarepa, the faith of this well-gifted girl was confirmed, and she came today with four young girl friends to visit him. But in order to test, and thus verify the reputation of the Jetsun and his son, she and her friends challenged Milarepa by singing this song:

> We take refuge in the Three Precious Ones;
> Pray, bless us with your great compassion.
>
> Oh, you two exalted Repa Yogis,
> You have a great reputation from afar!
> Oh, ye faithful here assembled,
> Please be silent now and listen to our song.
>
> We five young girls from good families,

Now sing for you our offering;
Please judge our words and ponder on our parables.
For you two Repas, this our song is sung!

The fame of Di Se Snow Mountain is great
When one sees it not, but hears much of it.
People say, "Look, the snow of Di Se
Is like a crystal stūpa."
But when one comes near and sees it clearly,
Nothing great or wonderful is found.

The top of Di Se is wrapped in drifts
Of snow, its body is snow-clad.
In this we see nothing great or wonderful,
Except that these mountains round about
Are rather nice and charming.

The fame of Lake Ma Päm is great
When one sees it not, but hears much of it.
People say, "Look! Lake Ma Päm
Is like a Maṇḍala of greenish gems!"
But when one nears it and sees it clearly,
Nothing great or wonderful can be seen.

'Tis but a lake filled by the rain,
A place where water trickles.
Encircling it are rocks and meadows.
In this we see nothing great or wonderful.

Great is the fame of the height of Red-Rock
When one hears about it from far away.
People say, "This rock is like a precious jewel!"
But when one comes near and sees it clearly,
It is but a great stone jutting out.

Upon it bushes and trees are growing,
And round it brooks and small streams flow;
In it there is nothing great or wonderful.

You, the elder and the younger Repa,
Have a fame that spreads to far-off places;
From far away we have heard much of you.
People say, "They are indeed accomplished beings!"

But when one comes near and scans you closely,
One sees an old man and a callow youth
Who chant, and hum, and sing together,
Exhibiting their bodies, nude and shameless.

He sees two common people wearing cotton,
Two beggars who eat the food of alms;
He sees two unscrupulous rascals
Who roam unrestrained at large.

There is nothing wonderful or good about you;
There is nothing great that we can find.

To us sisters who have wandered everywhere,
Our morning's pilgrimage has wasted time.
To us sisters who have traveled the world over,
Our morning's journey is meaningless;
The trip was never worth sore feet.

To us sisters who in this world have seen everything,
To see an old and young man like you two, is a
        waste of time.
To us sisters who have heard all things in this world,
The claims of your good name are but empty clamor.
You two, either a pair of Buddhist puppets,
Or devil-possessed agents,
Will cause but evil hindrances.

If you understand what we are singing,
You may answer us with verses.
If you cannot understand, you may
Get up and go, for we do not want you!

Thus they sang. The Jetsun said, "Oh Rechungpa, the three lakes of the Snow Mountain were prophesied by the Buddha Himself to be a superb place for devotion. If we do not answer those who disparage them, not only will these slanderers be damned, but also the merits of such holy places will be misconstrued. We yogis who act candidly with our bodies, mouths, and minds, should also answer the slanders made against us. Thus, not only will the merits and rightness of yogic action be illustrated, but the slanderers will also be corrected. Now, Rechungpa, sing in chorus with your father for these young women!"

Oh, faithful patrons here assembled,
And you young people who love to chant and sing,
Especially you five loquacious maidens,
Listen to this reply, the song that I shall sing.

Know ye who we are?
We are the older and younger Repas.
I, the old man on the right side singing,
Am the Yogi Milarepa;
He, the young man chanting on the left,
Is Dor Draug Rechung.

With a good tune and words of meaning,
I sing to you my patrons here assembled,
The song which flows from my enlightened spirit.
Think, as you hear it, and listen mindfully.

The fame of Di Se Snow Mountain is far-spreading;
People say of it in distant places,
"Di Se is a crystal-like pagoda!"
When one approaches closer,
One sees the summit is snow-covered.

The prophecy of Buddha says [most truly],
That this snow mountain is the navel of the world,
A place where the snow leopards dance.
The mountain top, the crystal-like pagoda,
Is the [white and glistening] palace of Dem-Chog.

The great snow mountains which Di Se encircle,
Are the dwelling places of five-hundred Arhats.[1]
Here all deities of the Eight Divisions pay their
    homage!
Surrounding it are hills and marshes.
The region abounds with "incense" plants,
The source of nectar-producing drugs.
This is the great place of accomplished yogis;
Here one attains transcendental Samādhis.
There is no place more wonderful than this,
There is no place more marvelous than here.

The fame of Ma Päm Lake is indeed far-spreading;
People say of it in distant places,

"Ma Päm Lake is like a green-gemmed Maṇḍala!"
When one approaches closer,
One sees there waters [cold and] plentiful.
As prophesied by the Buddha in past ages,
This lake is called "The Lake-That's-Never-
    Warm,"[2]
The fountainhead of four great rivers,
A place where fish and otters swim.

Because it is the Eight Nāgas' dwelling,
It appears to be a Maṇḍala made of gems.
The water falling in it from the heavens
Is like a stream of milk, a rain of nectar;
It is the Hundred Devas' bathing place,
The water with eight merits.

The lovely plains and rocks this lake encircling,
Are treasuries of the lesser Nāgas.
Here grows superb Tsanbudrisha wood.
The Southern Continent, Tsanbu,
For this reason has its name.
There is no place more wonderful than this,
There is no place more marvelous than here.

The fame of the height of Red-Rock is far-spreading;
People say of it in distant places,
"That huge rock is like a heap of jewels!"
When one approaches closer,
One sees a great rock towering above a meadow.
As prophesied by Buddha in past ages,
It is the Black Hill, the rock of Bije Mountain Range.
It is the central place, north of the woodlands
On the border between Tibet and India,
Where Indian tigers freely roam.

The medicine trees, Tsandan and Zundru,
Are found here growing wild.
The rock looks like a heap of glistening jewels;
It is the palace where live the heavenly saints;
It is a seat of hermits, blessed by the Ḍākinīs,
And where accomplished yogis live.

Here the river all the hill encircles,

Making [a solitary] place, forbidden.
There is no place more wonderful than this;
There is no place more truly marvelous!

The fame of the elder and younger Repas is far-
          spreading;
People say of us in distant places,
"They are truly the accomplished beings!"
When one approaches closer,
One sees only an old man and a younger fellow,
With nothing wonderful about them!
The plain looks of these two
Show the complete exhaustion
Of form-clinging and discriminating thoughts!

Lying with our bodies naked, shows
That we need not clothes of the Two Clingings.
Heedlessly exposing our male organs proves
That we have no self-made shameful feelings.

These little verses flowing from our mouths
Come from our inner Experience.
The cotton clothes we wear
Show blissful inner heat a'burning.

That we eat left-over food as beggars
Proves our abnegation of desires and pleasures,
Shows our spirit, unconcerned and fearless.
Thus we live with our six senses in a
Way most natural and ingenuous!

I am the Guru of the faithful and well-gifted,
The source whence their Pith-Instructions came.
I am the symbol to which patrons pay their homage,
The exemplar of all the saints and sages.

To me, great yogis tell their understandings;
Through me, wrong views may be eliminated.
I am the source from which Truth is illumined —
The one who has realized the Law of Non-existence.

I am the one whose mind remains [in peace],
Who leads others on the Path's Experiences.

I am the one who realized himself as Dharmakāya,
Who with compassion works for others.
There is nothing else more wonderful than this;
There is no one else more marvelous than I.
Young lady visitors,
You have pilgrimaged to every land,
But your journeys were but toil and drudgery.
If you want to make a pilgrimage of value,
Travel to the holy Shrine of Paugba Wadi.[3]

It may be true that you have journeyed everywhere,
But all of this was waste of time,
And made you feel footsore and weary.
If you want to make a [worthwhile] journey
Visit holy Bodhgaya!

There may be no place that you have not visited,
But they are all of little meaning.
If you want to make a [real] pilgrimage,
Visit Lhasa Chrunon Temple![4]

There may be nothing of which you have not heard,
Yet all that has been without significance.
If you want something truly meaningful
Listen to the Pith-Instructions of the Oral
      Lineage.
You may have relied on many people,
Yet they were but your kinsfolk.
If you seek a person on whom you can rely,
Find a capable Guru!

You may have done all things, everywhere,
But most of them were deeds of Karma.
If you want your deeds to be truly worthy,
You should practice the teaching of the holy Dharma.

This is the old man's answer to you maidens;
If you can understand it, these are the real teachings.
Otherwise you may regard it as a common song.
The time has now come for you to leave.
We are the yogis who do whate'er we will —
You visitors may go and do the same!

Rechungma, who was the leader of the girls, and who stood in the center, was thereupon confirmed in her great faith. As tears rolled down her cheeks, she untied the jade from her belt and took off the jeweled ornaments from her head. Prostrating herself before Milarepa she cried: "We five girls all sincerely ask you to grant us the teaching of Dharma. Also we beg that you give us the profound Pith-Instructions, for we have now made up our minds to meditate in a hermitage." And she sang prayerfully:

As one light is kindled from another,
The teaching has been transmitted down
From Dharmakāya, the great Dorje-Chang.

The [holders] of this great Succession
Are compassionate and enlightened;
Are they not the great Tilopa and Nāropa?
He who journeyed to India with such hardship,
Was he not great Marpa the Translator?
He who underwent such trials for his teacher, Marpa,
Is he not the great and faithful Milarepa?
His naked body is full of splendor,
His speech rich and melodious,
His loving mind shines forth with radiant light.
I bow down to the body, speech, and mind of my
        Father Repa.

We five girls who have come to this meeting,
Must have had small merit in our previous lives.
We have attained human bodies, but are lowly born;
We have no self-control in practicing the Dharma.
To-day, because of your blessing, most precious Jetsun,
Deep faith from our hearts up-wells.

This precious jade upon my belt,
And the jeweled headdress,
I now untie, and offer to you.
Pray grant us Buddha's teaching,
Pray tell us your life-story!

Milarepa replied, "I have no use for your gems and ornaments. If you sincerely intend to practice Dharma, there are many better and wiser Gurus than I. Go and ask the Dharma from them. I am a person who pays no heed to clothes and food, and always dwells in no-man's land.

You could not follow my way of living, and it is doubtful whether you would be able to endure want of food and clothing. Please, then, listen to my song":

> The Marvelous One, who underwent
> Such hardships for Nāropa,
> The one blessed by the great Tilopa and Dorje-Chang,
> Is he not the Father Translator who speaks two tongues,
> The Father Translator, Guru Marpa?
>
> I am Milarepa blessed by His mercy.
> My father was Mila Shirab Jhantsan,
> My mother Nyantsa Karjan,
> And I was called Tubhaga ["Delightful-to-Hear"].
>
> Because our merits and virtues were of small account,
> And the Cause-Effect Karma of the past spares no one,
> My father Mila passed away [too early in his life].
> The deceiving goods and belongings of our household
> Were plundered by my aunt and uncle,
> Whom I and my mother had to serve.
> They gave us food fit only for dogs;
> The cold wind pierced our ragged clothing;
> Our skin froze and our bodies were benumbed.
> Often was I beaten by my uncle,
> And endured his cruel punishment.
> Hard was it to avoid my aunt's ill temper.
> I lived as best I could, a lowly servant,
> And shrugged my shoulders [in bitter resignation].
> Misfortunes descended one after the other;
> We suffered so our hearts despaired.
>
> In desperation, I went to Lamas Yundun and Rondunlaga,
> From whom I mastered the magic arts of Tu, Ser,
>   and Ded.[5]
> Witnessed by my aunt and uncle, I brought
> Great disaster on their villagers and kinsmen.
> For which, later, I suffered deep remorse.
>
> Then I heard the fame of Marpa, the renowned Translator,
> Who, blessed by the saints Nāropa and Medripa,[6]
> Was living in the upper village of South River.

After a hard journey I arrived there.
For six years and eight months[7] [I stayed]
With him, my gracious Father Guru, Marpa.
For him I built many houses,
One with courtyards and nine stories;
Only after this did he accept me.

From him I received the Pointing-out Instruction.
Thus I truly understood Mahāmudrā,
The view of the profound Absolute.

He also taught me the Six Yogas of Nāropa,
The final teaching of the Path of Means.[8]
I was ripened through the Four Initiations,
And obtained a true, decisive understanding
Of the great Guru Nāropa's teaching.

Having received the Pith-Instructions from Marpa,
I renounced all the affairs of this life;
And, no longer lazy, devoted myself to Dharma.
Thus have I reached the State of Eternal Bliss.
Such is the story of my life.

I wish you five young ladies
All good fortune and great joy.
Leave us now and go home.

Hearing the Jetsun's life story, all the maidens' faith was strengthened
anew. They begged Milarepa to accept them as his servants. He said,
"You are spoiled girls from rich families, and if you come with me, you
will never be able to endure the hardships of my life. If you want to
practice the Dharma, you should live ascetically, as I do. But I doubt if you
can." Then he sang a song called "The Self-Examination":

I bow down at the feet of Marpa, the Translator.

If you, the five young sisters,
Really want to practice Dharma
And insist on coming with me,
Think this song over carefully
And obtain the answer for yourselves.

You should ask yourselves: "Have I

The persistence to endure the hardships
Of the ascetic life?
Have I a will strong and dominant enough
To renounce all Saṃsāric desires,
And follow the instructions of my Guru?"

Though you leave your native land,
The prison of all evils,
Can you persevere alone in rugged places?

Though you renounce your kinsmen, the noose of devils,
And realize their detriments,
Can you depend upon a qualified Guru?

Though you realize that properties and goods
Are poisonous, the enticing bait of demons,
Can you live in destitution and endure hardship?

Though you forsake soft woolen clothes from Weu,
Can you produce the warm and blissful Dumo
        [Inner-Heat]?

If you renounce a city life
And forsake your friends and lovers,
Can you live alone in no-man's land?

Though you disavow the Eight Desires,
Can you live in a humble and lowly way?

Though you understand the transiency of this life,
Do you realize the precariousness of [all] life?

This is the tradition of the Ghagya Lama,
The way of Practice in our Lineage.
You may come with me if you can answer "Yea."
I shall then give you the Tantric teaching
And the Pith-Instruction of the Skillful Path.
Then shall I bless you and grant you the Initiations.

Having heard this song, the girls all became very happy. Their leader, Rechungma, said, "Though we were born in a female form, which is considered to be inferior, nevertheless, so far as the Ālaya [Store]Consciousness is concerned, there is no discrimination between man and woman. We are convinced of the faults of Saṃsāra, and shall try to follow our Guru's instructions. But, in view of our inability to practice the Dharma in a perfect way, we beg you to accept us as your servants. No matter whether we have, or have not, the ability to practice the Dharma, please do not forsake us!" Then in song she expressed her confidence in being able to practice the Jetsun's teachings, and besought him to accept her as his servant:

> Father, Qualified Guru, Precious One,
> Your naked body is full of splendor!
> I bow down at your feet, Jetsun Repa,
> Through ascetic practice you help all sentient beings!
>
> We five sisters who come to this assembly,
> May have a lower body-form as women,
> But in the Bodhi-Mind, there is neither man nor woman!
> Thinking of the defects of Saṃsāra, please allow
> Us to practice austerities and follow your instruction!
> Let us leave our country, the prison of demons,
> And remain forever in a hermitage!
> Let us leave for good our relatives, the trouble-
>   makers,
> And rely solely upon our Guru!
>
> Property and possessions are the lure of devils.
> Let us fore'er renounce them and practice austerity!
> Let us give up fine woolen clothes from Weu,
> And kindle the blissful, wondrous Inner Heat!
> Let us leave our native land and lovers
> And remain in no-man's land.
>
> Let us each act humbly with our body, speech, and mind;
> Let us depart from the Eight Worldly Claims and realize
> That all is transitory.
>
> Let us remember the uncertainty of coming death!
> Let us follow the instructions of our Lama.
> Oh, most perfect Guru, most precious one!
> Please be kind and grant to us the Dharma,
> Please accept us, the five sisters, as your servants!

Milarepa realized that they were well-destined disciples, and so accepted them.

At that time, Milarepa and his son-disciples were still dwelling at the Five Small Lakes. There he imparted the Initiations and Pith-Instructions to the five girls, and set them to meditating. Rechungma attained the warm and blissful experiences and other merits of Dumo within three days.

Later Rechungma became ill. In order to test her perseverance in remaining in solitude, Milarepa told her that she might go wherever she liked. But the girl replied, "Although I am ill, I will stay in the hermitage," thus proving that she had the persistence to endure misfortunes.

One day, Rechungma went to see Milarepa when he was sojourning elsewhere, and met him in a great assembly. In order to test her faith and see whether she had full confidence in him, he sang before the assembly a song with two meanings:

> I pray to all the holy Gurus,
> I take refuge in the Patron Buddha.
>
> Listen, faithful patrons,
> If you cannot renounce the Eighty Worldly Desires,
> Never say that you are men with faith;
> Your faith may so be lost when adverse conditions come.
>
> If you do not avoid the Ten Evil Deeds,
> Never call yourselves men of discipline,
> Lest you should fall down to the lower paths.
>
> If distracted thoughts still haunt your mind,
> Never claim that you observe the Tantric Precepts,
> Lest you should fall into the Vajra Hell.[9]
>
> Never criticize the teachings of other Schools
> If you have not made impartial and wide studies,
> Else you will violate the principle of Dharma
> And scorch your own mind badly.
>
> If you have not realized the illusory nature of
>   all beings,
> Never neglect virtuous deeds, and avoid all sinning,
> Lest you should fall into the Three Lower Realms!
>
> If you do not understand the minds of others,
> Never slander others or condemn their views,

Lest you be misled by self-conceit and egotism.

If you have not unified your mind with Dharma-Essence,
Do not boast of your meditation experiences,
Lest devils interrupt your progress.

If you have not reached the state of beyond-talking,
Do not boast of your great understanding,
Lest you be left in a pitiable position —
Longing for, but ne'er obtaining the tantalizing Fruit.

If you have not reached the realm of spontaneous
          action,
Do not do what you will or neglect your self-control,
Lest the sling-stone that you throw rebound upon
          your head.

Through my mouth the Dharma has been preached;
It should be treasured in your hearts.
Comprehend it clearly, and bear it in your minds!

Among the audience [only] Rechungma fully understood the meaning of this song. She rose from the crowd and said to Milarepa: "Regarding the accomplishments of my Guru, his acts and deeds, I have never
had a single moment of doubt nor the slightest skepticism. Please listen
to my song," Whereupon, she chanted "The Fifteen Realizations":

I bow down to all holy Gurus!
Toward the Jetsun, my Father Guru,
I have steadfast reverence and faith immutable!

The Three Precious Ones are but one Entity;
Amongst [the deities] I cannot discriminate.
In the Pith-Instructions of the Whispered Lineage
          given by my Guru
There are no playwords or vain babblings.
In the practice of the Yidham Yoga,
Whose essence is the Jetsun,
There are no periods of time or intervals.
Things as they manifest are by nature magic-like;
I do not deem them to be substantial,
Nor do I cling to them with habitual thoughts!

In the Mind-Essence, the quintessential "light,"
There is no adulteration by distracting thoughts.
In the real nature of beings, the realm of Mind,
There is no subject-object difilement.
In the natural state of the Mind-Essence
There is no ground from which habitual thought may
     rise.

The nature of the mind is Dharmakāya;
It is not defiled by forms
And from attributes is free.

Our bodies are the meeting-place of the Four Diseases,
And so we should not quarrel with our friends.

Devils and misfortunes should be used to help in
     our devotions;
There is no need to seek imaginary divinations.

Dreams are delusory emanations of habitual thoughts;
One should not deem them to be true or cling to them.

Forgive the foe, who is your real teacher,
For you should never cherish vengeful thoughts.
Toward the behavior of an accomplished being
Do not raise doubts and criticism.
Self-manifestation is the Buddha, the One originally
     existing;
So do not seek the Accomplished One in other places.

My holy Guru, gracious teacher,
Pray always bless all capable disciples,
[Bathing them ever] in the stream of love and grace!

Pray, always remember me, this ignorant disciple!
Pray embrace me ever with your great compassion!

    Milarepa was very pleased; he decided that Rechungma was a quali-
fied female yogi, fitted to be a companion in [Tantric devotion]. And so
he imparted to her all the Pith-Instructions without reservation.

    Then he said to Rechungpa, "You are very good at teaching the disci-
ples. You should take care of this girl." And he handed her over to Rechungpa, who for a time took her as a companion in devotion. Thereafter,

she went to meditate at Semodo of Namtsoshumo in the North, observing absolute silence for eight years. Eventually she gained the Ten Experiences and Eight Merits, and perfected all spiritual Purifications and Realizations of the Path; and in this life she went to the Pure Land of the Ḍākinīs.

This is the story of Milarepa meeting Rechungma, one of his four [foremost] female disciples, at Five Small Lakes of Joro Dritsam.

NOTES

1 Arhat: an (enlightened) being who has forever annihilated all desires and passions; the name for the enlightened being of the Hīnayāna Path.

2 The Lake-That's-Never-Warm (T.T.: mTso.Ma.Dros.Pa.): "The Lake of Ma Päm, in Nari. The Hindus describe it as something like the northern ocean, inhabited by Nāgas, and Tibetans in good faith repeat such legends, at least in their literature, although they know better. This lake has a reputation of being extremely cold all the year round." (Quoted from Jaschke's Dictionary.)

3 Paugba Wadi: a sanctuary in Nepal containing the image of a Buddha called Wadi-zunpo, the good or holy Wadi.

4 Lhasa Chrunon: a famous temple built by King Sron.bTsan.sGam.Po.

5 Tu, Ser, and Ded (T.T.: mThu., Ser., [and] gTad.): three different arts of black magic.

6 Medripa (Skt.: Maitrpa).

7 According to the general belief among Tibetan Lamas, Milarepa apparently stayed with Marpa, his Guru, for much longer than six years and eight months as this text suggests. It is possible that some mistake has slipped in here.

8 Path of Means: See the translator's comments in the Appendix; see also Story 7, Note 7, and Story 5, Notes 18 and 19.

9 Vajra Hell: the horrible hell to which the precept-violator of Tantrism goes.

26

THE HUNTSMAN
AND THE DEER

Obeisance to all Gurus

Having directed his disciple to remain at different hermitages for their devotions, Jetsun Milarepa went to a secluded place at Nyi Shang Gur Da Mountain on the border between Nepal and Tibet. The upper slopes were very rugged, cloudy, foggy, and continuously deluged with rain. To the right of the mountain towered a precipitous hill where one could always hear the cries of wild animals and watch vultures hovering above. To its left stood a hill clothed with soft, luxuriant meadows, where deer and antelopes played. Below there was a luxurious forest with all kinds of trees and flowers and within which lived many monkeys, peacocks, turkeys, and other beautiful birds. The monkeys amused themselves by swinging and leaping among the trees, the birds darted here and there with a great display of wing, while warblers chirped and sang. In front of the hermitage flowed a stream, fed by melting snow and filled with rocks and boulders. A fresh, clear, bubbling sound could always be heard as one passed by.

This hermitage was called Ghadaya. It was a very quiet and delightful place with every favorable condition for devotees. And so it was here that Jetsun Milarepa indulged in the River-Flow Samādhi, while all the benevolent local deities rendered him services and oblations.

One day, Milarepa heard a dog barking [in the distance], after that a great noise arose. He thought, "Hitherto, this place has been very favorable for meditation. Is some disturbance on the way?" So he left the cave, came to a huge rock, and sat upon it absorbed in the Compassion of Non-discrimination.[1] Before long, a black, many-spotted deer ran up, badly frightened. Seeing this, an unbearable compassion arose within the Jetsun. He thought, "It is because of the evil Karmas this deer has acquired in the past that he was born in such a pitiable form. Though

275

he has not committed any sinful deeds in this life, he must still undergo great suffering. What a pity! I shall preach to him the Dharma of Mahāyāna, and lead him to eternal bliss." Thinking thus, he sang to the deer:

> I bow down at the feet of Marpa;
> Pray, relieve the sufferings of all beings!
>
> Listen to me, you deer with sharp antlers!
> Because you want to escape
> From something in the outer world,
> You have no chance to free yourself
> From inner blindness and delusions.
>
> With no regret or sadness
> Forget your mind and outer body —
> The time has come for you
> To renounce all blindness and delusion.
>
> The Ripening Karma is fearful and compelling,
> But how can you escape from it
> By fleeing with your delusory body?
>
> If escape is what you want,
> Hide within Mind-Essence;
> If you want to run away,
> Flee to the place of Bodhi.
> There is no other place of safe refuge.
>
> Uprooting all confusion from your mind,
> Stay with me here in rest and quiet.
> At this very moment the fear of death is full upon you;
> You are thinking, "Safety lies on the far side
>   of the hill;
> If I stay here I shall be caught!"
> This fear and hope is why you wander in Saṃsāra.
>
> I shall now teach you the Six Yogas of Nāropa,
> And set you to practicing the Mahāmudrā.

Thus he sang in a tuneful voice like that of the God Brahmā. Had there been anyone to hear, he could not have helped feeling charmed and delighted.

Affected by the Jetsun's compassion, the deer was relieved from its painful fear of capture. With tears streaming from its eyes, it came near to Milarepa, licked his clothes, and then lay down at his left side. He thought, "This deer must be hunted by a ferocious dog, the one whose barking I heard just now."

As Milarepa was wondering what kind of a dog it could be, a red bitch with a black tail and a collar round her neck, ran toward him. She was a hunting dog — such a savage and fearful creature that her tongue was hanging out like a blazing ribbon, while the sharp claws on her feet could rend any prey, and her threatening growl was like thunder. Milarepa thought, "It must be this bitch that has been chasing the deer. She is indeed ferocious. Full of anger she regards whatever she sees as her enemy. It would be good if I could calm her and quench her hatred." Great pity for the bitch rose in him and he sang with great compassion:

> I bow down at the feet of Marpa;
> I pray you, pacify the hate of all beings.
>
> Oh you bitch with a wolf's face,
> Listen to this song of Milarepa!
>
> Whatever you see, you deem it to be your foe;
> Your heart is full of hatred and ill thoughts.
> Because of your bad Karma you were born a bitch,
> Ever suffering from hunger, and agonized by passion.
>
> If you do not try to catch the Self-mind within,
> What good is it to catch prey outside?
> The time has come for you to capture your Self-mind;
> Now is the time to renounce your fury,
> And with me sit here restfully.
>
> Your mind is full of greed and anger,
> Thinking, "If I go that way, I shall lose him,
> But I will catch him if I go forward on this side."
> This hope and fear is why you wander in Saṃsāra!
>
> I shall now teach you the Six Yogas of Nāropa,
> And set you to practicing the Mahāmudrā.

Hearing this song of Dharma, sung in a heavenly voice and with immense compassion, the bitch was greatly moved and her fury subsided. She then made signs to the Jetsun by whining, wagging her tail, and licking his clothes. Then she put her muzzle under her two front paws and prostrated herself before him. Tears fell from her eyes, and she lay down peacefully with the deer.

Milarepa thought, "There must be a sinful person who is following these two animals. He will probably be here any moment." Before long a man appeared looking very proud and violent; from under his lashes his eyes glared fiercely, his hair was knotted on the top of his head, and his long sleeves flapped from side to side as he ran toward the Jetsun. In one hand he held a bow and arrow, and in the other a long lasso for catching game. As he dashed up, one could hear his breath coming in suffocating gasps and see streams of sweat pouring down his face and almost choking him to death. When he saw the Jetsun with the bitch and deer lying beside him, like a mother with her sons, he thought, "Are the deer and my bitch both bewitched by this yogi?" He then cried angrily to Milarepa, "You fat, greasy repas and yogis! I see you here, there, and everywhere! High in the mountain snows you come to kill game; low on lake-shores you come to hook fish; on the plains you visit towns to trade in dogs and fight with people. It does not matter if one or two like you die. You may have the power of keeping my bitch and my deer, but now see whether your clothes can also keep out my arrow." So saying, the hunter drew his long bow, aimed at Milarepa, and shot. But the arrow went high and missed. The Jetsun thought, "If even ignorant animals understand my preaching, he should be able to understand it too, for after all he is a man."

So he said: "You need not hurry to shoot me, as you will have plenty of time to do so later. Take your time, and listen to my song." Whereupon, in a tuneful voice like that of the God Brahmā, the Jetsun sang to the hunter, whose name was Chirawa Gwunbo Dorje:

> I pray to all accomplished beings;
> I pray you to extinguish the Five Poisonous Kleśas.
>
> You man with a human body but a demon's face,
> Listen to me. Listen to the song of Milarepa!
>
> Men say the human body is most precious, like a gem;
> There is nothing that is precious about you.
> You sinful man with a demon's look,
> Though you desire the pleasures of this life,
> Because of your sins, you will never gain them.
> But if you renounce desires within,
> You will win the Great Accomplishment.

It is difficult to conquer oneself
While vanquishing the outer world;
Conquer now your own Self-mind.
To slay this deer will never please you,
But if you kill the Five Poisons within,
All your wishes will be fulfilled.

If one tries to vanquish foes in the outer world,
They increase in greater measure.
If one conquers his Self-mind within,
All his foes soon disappear.

Do not spend your life committing sinful deeds;
It is good for you to practice holy Dharma.
I shall now teach you the Six Yogas of Nāropa,
And set you to practicing the Mahāmudrā.

While the Jetsun was singing this, the hunter waited and listened. He thought, "There is nothing to prove that what this yogi has just said is true. Usually, a deer is very frightened, and my bitch very wild and savage. Today, however, they lie peacefully together, one on his left and the other on his right, like a mother with her sons. Hitherto I have never missed a shot during my winter hunting in the snow mountains, but today I could not hit him. He must be a black magician, or a very great and unusual Lama. I will find out how he lives."

Thinking thus, the hunter entered the cave, where he found nothing but some inedible herbs; [seeing such evidence of austerity], a great faith suddenly arose within him. He said, "Revered Lama, who is your Guru and what teachings do you practice? Where did you come from? Who is your companion, and what do you own? If I am acceptable to you, I should like to be your servant; also I will offer you the life of this deer."

Milarepa replied, "I shall tell you of my companion, from whence I come, and how I live. If you can follow my way of life, you may come with me." And he sang to Chirawa Gwunbo Dorje:

The Lamas, Tilopa, Nāropa, and Marpa —
These three are my Gurus;
If you they satisfy,
You may come with me.

The Guru, the Yidham,[2] and the Ḍākinī —
To these three Mila pays his homage;

If you they satisfy,
You may come with me.

The Buddha, the Dharma, and the Sangha —
These three are Mila's refuge;
If you they satisfy,
You may come with me.

The View, the Practice, and the Action
These three are the Dharmas Mila practices;
If you can absorb these teachings,
You may come with me.

The snow, the rocks, and the clay mountains —
These three are where Mila meditates;
If you they satisfy,
You may come with me.

The deer, the argali, and the antelope —
These three are Mila's cattle;
If you they satisfy,
You may come with me.

The lynx, the wild dog, and the wolf —
These three are Mila's watchdogs;
If you they satisfy,
You may come with me.

The grouse, the vulture, and the singing Jolmo —
These three are Mila's poultry;
If you they satisfy,
You may come with me.

The sun, the moon, and the stars —
These three are Mila's pictures;
If you they satisfy,
You may come with me.

The gods, the ghosts, and the sages —
These three are Mila's neighbors;
If you they satisfy,
You may come with me.

The hyena, the ape, and the monkey —
These three are Mila's playmates;
If you they satisfy,
You may come with me.

Bliss, Illumination, and Non-thought —
These three are my companions;
If you they satisfy,
You may come with me.

Porridge, roots, and nettles —
These three are Mila's food;
If you they satisfy,
You may come with me.

Water from snow, and spring, and brook —
These three are Mila's drink;
If you they satisfy,
You may come with me.

The Nāḍīs, Breaths, and Bindus —
These three are Mila's clothing:
If you they satisfy,
You may come with me.

The hunter thought, "His words, thoughts, and actions are truly consistent." The uttermost faith thus arose within him. He shed many tears and bowed down at Mila's feet, crying, "Oh precious Jetsun! I now offer you my deer, my bitch, my bow and arrows, and my lasso. I and my bitch have committed many sins. I pray you to free my bitch, Red Lightning Lady, thus delivering her to the higher Realms; and [I pray you] to bring this black deer to the Path of Great Happiness. I pray you grant me, the huntsman Chirawa Gwunbo Dorje, the teaching of the Dharma and lead me to the Path of Liberation." Then he sang:

Sitting on my right side is the deer
With horns as white as snow.
The markings round his mouth are his adornment.
If I slay him, my ravenous appetite
For seven days might be satisfied.
Now I do not need him and offer him to you.
Pray deliver this black deer to the Path of
      Great Happiness,

Pray lead Red Lightning Lady to the Path of Bodhi,
Pray bring me, Gwunbo Dorje, to the Land of Liberation.

This black rope with its metal ring
Is fit to bind wild yaks on Great North Plain;
Now I do not need it and offer it to you.
Pray deliver this black deer to the Path of Great
     Happiness,
Pray lead Red Lightning Lady to the Path of Bodhi,
Pray bring me, Gwunbo Dorje, to the Land of Liberation.

To wear this goat-skin with spotted pattern
Will keep one warm, however high the mountain;
Now I do not need it and offer it to you.
Pray deliver this black deer to the Path of
     Great Happiness,
Pray lead Red Lighning Lady to the Path of Bodhi,
Pray bring me, Gwunbo Dorje, to the Land of Liberation.

In my right hand I hold arrows,
Each shaft adorned with feathers four;
When I shoot them with a "Phei!",
They always hit the target;
Now I do not need them and offer them to you.
Pray deliver this black deer to the Path of
     Great Happiness,
Pray lead Red Lightning Lady to the Path of Bodhi,
Pray bring me, Gwunbo Dorje, to the Land of Liberation.

This superb white bow in my left hand
With white bark [of birch] is decked;
When you bend it, e'en the dragon
In the sky will roar [with fear];
Now I do not need it and offer it to you.
Pray deliver this black deer to the Path of
     Great Happiness,
Pray lead Red Lightning Lady to the Path of Bodhi,
Pray bring me, Gwunbo Dorje, to the Land of Liberation.

In this manner Chirawa Gwunbo Dorje, the huntsman, offered the
deer, his bitch, and all his belongings to Milarepa. He then said, "Oh
Lama! Please accept me as your servant. I will go home to get provisions
from my children and then return. Do you intend to remain here? Please

tell me clearly, where are you going to stay?" The Jetsun, very pleased with his offering of the deer and with his change of heart towards the Dharma, then said, "Huntsman, it is very wonderful that you have determined to renounce your sinful activities and perform virtuous deeds. But it will be difficult for you to rely on me completely. Though you may have confidence in me, it will be difficult for you to find me, because I have no permanent residence. Nevertheless, if you want to practice the Dharma, you should cut off all attachment to your family and follow my example at once. I will tell you why I have no definite dwelling place, so listen to my song":

> I, the strange Repa in my hermitage,
> For three months in the summer
> Meditate on the Snow Mountain.
> That refreshes body, mind, and inspiration.
> For three months in the autumn I go out for alms —
> Begging grain for sustenance.
> For three months in the winter
> I meditate in forests,
> And so am free from bad and untamed Prāṇas.
> For three months in the spring
> I haunt meadows, hills, and brooks,
> Keeping in good health my lungs and gall.
> In all seasons of the year,
> I meditate without distraction.
>
> Our bodies, formed from the Four Elements,
> Are subject to affliction and decay.
> Ever must one watch and meditate;
> This is the only way to conquer the Five Kleśas!
>
> I eat whatever food is there;
> This is the way to be content,
> To quench desires and their consequences.
> The sign of the great diligence of yogis
> Is their constant practice of the Dharma.

The huntsman then said: "A Lama like you is indeed marvelous and unique. From the bottom of my heart I want to practice the Dharma. I am going home to say a few words to my family and also to get some provisions with which to sustain my devotion. I will soon be back. Please remain here until then."

The Jetsun replied, "If you really want to practice the Dharma, there is no need to see your family. Following the ascetic way of practice, one does not have to look for provisions for his devotion, because he can live on fruits and vegetables. No one can be sure when death will come. Besides, your present meritorious thought and earnestness may change, so it is better to stay here. Listen to me before you talk with your family." And Milarepa sang:

> Hearken, hearken, huntsman!
> Though the thunder crashes,
> It is but empty sound;
> Though the rainbow is richly colored,
> It soon will fade away.
> The pleasures of this world are like dream-visions;
> Though one enjoy them, they are the source of sin.
> Though all we see may seem to be eternal,
> It soon will fall to pieces and will disappear.
>
> Yesterday perhaps one had enough or more,
> Today it is all gone and nothing's left;
> Last year one was alive, this year one dies.
> Good food turns out to be poisonous,
> And the beloved companion turns into a foe.
>
> Harsh words and complaints requite
> Good will and gratitude.
> Your sins hurt no one but yourself.
> Among one hundred heads, you value most your own.
> In all ten fingers, if one's cut, you feel the pain.
> Among all things you value, yourself is valued most.
> The time has come for you to help yourself.
>
> Life flees fast. Soon death
> Will knock upon your door.
> It is foolish, therefore, one's devotion to postpone.
> What else can loving kinsmen do
> But throw one into Saṃsāra?
> To strive for happiness hereafter
> Is more important than to seek it now.
> The time has come for you to rely on a Guru,
> The time has come to practice Dharma.

Hearing this song, Chirawa Gwunbo Dorje was completely converted to the Dharma. He then remained with Milarepa and did not return home. After meditating for some time, he had several experiences, which he told Milarepa, and then asked for further instruction. Milarepa was very pleased, and said, "You have already begun to produce merits [within you], so you should follow these instructions":

> To rely on a Guru,
> One should pray to him often and sincerely.
> When one practices the devotion of the Yidham and
>   Ḍākinī,
> Clearly and often should he meditate on the Arising
>   Yoga.
> When one meditates on transiency and the approach
>   of death,
> He should e'er remember
> That death cannot be predicted or avoided.
>
> When one practices Mahāmudrā,
> He should cultivate it step by step.
> When one meditates on parent-like sentient beings[3]
> He should e'er remember to repay his gratitude to them.
> When one meditates on the deep teaching of the
>   Whispered Lineage,
> He should persevere with great determination.
>
> When one reaches the consummation of Dharma,
> He should avoid ups-and-downs and make it stable.
> When one examines his devotions
> To see if they agree with Dharma,
> He should not waver nor be fickle,
> But should bring them to one-pointedness.
> When one cultivates the holy Dharma,
> He should renounce the world.
>
> When food is offered by the deities,
> One does not need to find food for himself.
> If like a miser one is ever hoarding goods,
> He never can succeed in gaining more;
> This is witnessed in the oath of all Ḍākinīs,
> Hence you should abandon worldly play.

Thereupon, the Jetsun gave to Chirawa Gwunbo Dorje the complete Initation and Pith-Instructions. Through practicing them, the huntsman eventually became one of the heart-sons of Milarepa and was known as

Chira Repa — The Cotton-clad Huntsman. The deer and the bitch were also forever removed from the Paths of Sorrow. It is said that the bow and the arrows which the huntsman offered to the Jetsun are still in that cave.

This is the story of Milarepa meeting his heart-son, Chira Repa, at Nyi Shang Gur Da.

NOTES

1 Compassion of Non-discrimination or Non-discernment (T.T.: dMigs.Pa. Mei.Pahi.sÑyiñ.rJe.), is a spontaneous, non-discriminating, and infinite love embodied in the Uncreated Voidness — the exclusive Compassion of Buddhahood. From the human point of view, compassion cannot arise without an object about which it is concerned. Compassion or love seems necessarily to be involved in a dualistic or subject-object mode. But according to Mahāyāna Buddhism, the highest compassion is one that transcends both subject and object, and is brought forth through the realization of Voidness. It is, in essence, identical with the intuitive Wisdom-of-Voidness. This is one of the most inscrutible mysteries of Buddhahood.

2 Yidham: the Patron Buddha of a Tantric Yogi. See Story 7, Note 29.

3 As sentient beings have been wandering in Saṃsāra throughout beginningless, infinite time, they must all have had parental relationships with one another in one or more of their innumerable past incarnations.

THE INVITATION FROM
THE KING OF NEPAL

Obeisance to all Gurus

WHEN the Jetsun Milarepa was practicing the River-Flow Samādhi and observing silence in the Riga Daya Cave of Nyi Shang of Mon, a few local huntsmen came that way. Seeing the Jetsun sitting motionless, they were all struck with wonder and doubt. After staring at him for a while, they suddenly became frightened and ran away. After a time they crept back one by one. Drawing their bows, they asked the motionless Jetsun: "Are you a human or a ghost? If you are a man, answer us." But the Jetsun still sat motionless without uttering a word. The huntsmen then shot many poisonous arrows at Milarepa, but none of them could hit him. They tried to throw him into the river, but they could not lift his body. Then they lit a fire, but even this could not burn him. Finally, they moved his body [by lifting the seat and ground he sat on] and heaved it over a steep cliff into the great turbulent river below. Yet, still in a serene lotus posture, the Jetsun's body did not touch the water, but floated above the river. Then it started moving upward and finally came back to rest in its original place, all this without Milarepa having uttered a single word.

All the huntsmen were amazed and hastily departed. On their way home, talking loudly about the incident, they approached the foot of a hill. Chira Repa, being nearby, heard their talk and appeared before them, saying, "That was my Guru, the supreme Yogi of Tibet. These miracles have proved him to be an accomplished being; even animals understand his preaching!" Then he told them the story of Milarepa and the deer and bitch, also how he had been practicing the Dharma through the Jetsun's influence. At this, great faith and reverence toward the Jetsun arose within the huntsmen, and from then on the name of Milarepa was heard throughout Nepal.

At that time, the reputation of, and the tales about, Milarepa reached the ear of the King of Ye Rang and Ko Kom, who also became filled with great faith and reverence toward him. One day, the All-Merciful Mother Tārā revealed Herself to the King and said, "The cloth of Ka Shi Ka and the supreme Ahrura [myrobalan — a universal medicine] which are now stored in your treasury should be offered to the great Tibetan Yogi, a Bodhisattva of the tenth [and final] stage, who is now at the mountain cave of Nyi Shang Gadaya north of Nepal. This will have great significance for the future." Thus She prophesied. The King then sent a man who spoke Tibetan to visit Milarepa. When the man saw the ascetic way in which the Jetsun was living, and how he had renounced all the necessities and affairs of this life, he was greatly impressed and struck with wonder. A great faith arose within him. Thinking, "This yogi is undoubtedly Milarepa himself, however I must make sure," he said to the Jetsun, "Oh Guru! What is your name? Don't you find it hard to live thus without taking nourishing food? What does this mean? Why is it necessary to abandon all belongings and material possessions?" Milarepa then answered the envoy, "I am the Tibetan Yogi, Milarepa. 'Without belongings' means 'without sufferings.' Now, listen to my song":

> I bow down to all holy Gurus.
>
> I am the man called Milarepa.
> For possessions I have no desire.
> Since I never strive to make money,
> First I do not suffer
> Because of making it;
> Then I do not suffer
> Because of keeping it;
> In the end, I do not suffer
> Because of hoarding it.
> Better far and happier is it
> Not to have possessions.
>
> Without attachment to kinsmen and companions,
> I do not seek affection in companionship.
> First I do not suffer
> Because of heart-clinging;
> Then I do not suffer
> From any quarreling;
> In the end I do not suffer
> Because of separation.

It is far better to have no affectionate companions.

Since I have no pride and egotism,
I do not look for fame and glory.
First I do not suffer
Because of seeking them;
Then I do not suffer
In trying to preserve them;
In the end I do not suffer
For fear of losing them.
It is far better to have no fame nor glory.

Since I have no desire for any place,
I crave not to be here, or there.
First I do not worry
About my home's protection;
Then I do not suffer
From a fervent passion for it;
In the end I am not anxious to defend it.
It is far better to have no home nor land.

With great faith in Milarepa, the envoy went back to the King of Ye Rang and Ko Kom and informed him in detail about the Jetsun. Then the King's faith and reverence were also confirmed. He said to the envoy, "Go and see whether you can persuade him to come here. If he does not accept the invitation, you may offer him this cloth of Ka Shi Ka and also this supreme drug, Ahrura."

Accordingly, the envoy went back to Milarepa and said, "I was sent by the King of Ye Rang and Ko Kom, a ruler with great faith in the Dharma, to invite you, the Tibetan Yogi, to come to his country." Milarepa replied, "In general, I do not look up to people and do not stay in cities; in particular, I do not know how to entertain kings, nor do I need good food or worldly pleasures. It is not mere words or à myth that a man practicing the Dharma should be indifferent to hunger and cold, and should hold the knife-of-starving to his death. You, envoy of the King, may return to your country. I will follow the order of my Guru, Marpa, to meditate in solitude." The envoy then said to the Jetsun, "So be it, if you insist. But would it not be a sorry case indeed that a great king, having sent a special envoy to fetch a common yogi, got nothing back but the return of his own envoy's empty hands and thorn-pricked feet?" To this the Jetsun replied, "I am the great Universal Emperor. There is no other emperor who is happier, richer, and more powerful than I." The envoy retorted, "If you claim that you are the great Universal Emperor himself, then you must have the Seven Precious Articles of Royalty.[1] Please show me one of them." The Jetsun replied, "If you worldly kings and officers will follow my Royal Way, each of you may also become the Supreme Emperor, and thus be rich and noble." Whereupon he sang:

> If you kings and courtiers who seek pleasures,
> Follow the Royal Succession of Milarepa,
> Eventually you will obtain them.
> This is the Royal Succession of Milarepa:
>
> My faith is the Royal Precious Wheel
> Revolving around the Virtues day and night.
> My wisdom is the Royal Precious Gem
> Fulfilling all the wishes of the self and others.
>
> The observance of discipline is my Royal Precious
>   Queen;
> She is my adornment, one most beautiful.
> Meditation is my Royal Precious Minister;
> With him I accumulate the Two Provisions![2]
> Self-respect is my Royal Precious Elephant,
> Which takes responsibility for the Buddhist Dharma.
>
> Diligence is my Royal Precious Horse,
> Which bears the Kleśas to Non-ego Land.
> Study-and-contemplation is my Royal Precious General,
> Who destroys the enemy of vicious thoughts.
>
> If you have these Royal Precious Trappings,
> You will gain a king's fame and prosperity,
> And conquer all your foes.
> You then may spread the Ten Virtues in your dominion,
> And urge all mother-like sentient beings
> To follow my noble teachings.

"This is indeed the tradition of Dharma," cried the envoy. "It is truly wonderful. If you insist upon not coming with me, I have here two precious things to offer you. They are sent by my King; one is the cloth of Ka Shi Ka, and the other is the supreme drug, Ahrura."

The Jetsun accepted these two gifts and then duly offered good wishes and dedications for the King.

About this time, Rechungpa and Shen Gom Repa set out to find the Jetsun in order to invite him [to return to Tibet]. While on their journey, they encountered a band of brigands from Nyi Shang and Nepal. When the bandits were about to rob them, they cried out that they were yogis, and asked to be spared. But the bandits replied, "Only the San Chia Yogi [Milarepa] can be considered as a real yogi. He is one whom poisoned arrows cannot harm, fire cannot burn, and water cannot drown. When one throws him over a cliff, he flies up again. He even refused the invitation of the King of Ko Kom."

Rechungpa then told the bandits that it was just for the sake of finding the Jetsun that they had come to this place. The bandits then directed them to Milarepa's abode.[3]

When the two Repas finally found the Jetsun, they saw that he was dressed in the cloth of Ka Shi Ka and that upon a stone plate [before him] was laid the supreme drug, Ahrura. They bowed down to him and asked, "How have you fared, dear Guru? How is your health?" The Jetsun replied, "I am very well indeed. Let me tell you how well I am! Now, hearken to my song":

> This is a place where flowers bloom,
> And many kinds of trees dance and sway;
> The birds here sing their tuneful melodies,
> And monkeys gambol in the woods.
> It is pleasant and delightful to stay here alone.
> Truly this is a quiet and peaceful place.
>
> With my Guru above my head, it is joyful here to
>   meditate;
> It is pleasant here to enjoy the Inner Heat;
> It is happy here to practice the Illusory Body,
> The spontaneous liberation from all worldly desires.
>
> Happy is the melting away of the dream of confusion;
> Joyous is absorption in the Great Illumination;
> Happy is the sight of the dark Blindness leaving;
> Joyful it is to become Buddha Himself
> Without practicing Transformation Yoga.
>
> It is happy to realize completely
> The true nature of Bardo and to remain
> In the transcendental realm of the Great Bliss.
>
> Your Father finds so much happiness and pleasure

In enjoying his invaluable blessings —
The joy of eating luscious fruits grown on the mountain,
And drinking sweet cool water from the springs.
Reflect upon my words, and you will understand my
        meaning.

Were you robbed, my sons, by bandits on your way here?
If so, credit it to your previous Karma.
You should realize that no money means no foe.
Never, oh my sons, hoard or pile up wealth.

If you can tame your mind,
You will have no foe!
Never, oh my children, hold hate in your hearts.

If you can tame your mind
You will have no foe!
Look up to the face of Buddha!
If your compassion ever grows,
You will have no enemy!

My sons, you should regard others as dearer than
        yourself.

Shen Gom Repa then said, "It is just because a yogi like you, dear
Jetsun, can have such happiness and tolerance toward his enemies, that
we have come here to invite you [to return to our own country]. We
see no need for you to remain in the solitude of a hermitage. Please
come to Tibet to help sentient beings there." The Jetsun replied, "To
stay in a hermitage is, in itself, to help all sentient beings. I may come
to Tibet; however, even there I will still remain alone in a hermitage.
You must not think that this is an ill practice; I am merely observing
my Guru's orders. Besides, the merits of all stages in the Path are acquired in the hermitage. Even if you have very advanced Experiences
and Realization, it is better to stay in the land of no-man, because this
is the glory and tradition of a yogi. Therefore you, also, should seek
lonely places and practice strict meditation. Now, hearken to my song":

Thanks to my Guru must still be paid,
And sentient beings still liberated.
I meditate in gratitude to Him,
Not because He, the Jetsun, is in need;

This is the oath and act of accomplished beings.

The wild ass, with white mouth, in the North,
Never bends low his head, even at threat of death.
It is not because he desires to die;
This is but his act and way —
The natural function of this wild beast!

The flesh-eating tigress, in the South,
Never eats her own breed's flesh, even when she starves,
Not because there is a principle to follow;
This is but her act and way —
The natural function of this great beast!

The white lioness, in the West,
Never leaves the snow mountain, even when she freezes,
Not because she cannot go elsewhere;
This is but her act and way —
The natural function of this queen of beasts!

The great eagle, in the East,
Strains his wings whenever he is flying;
But never in his mind is there the fear of falling.
To hover in the sky,
Is the natural way and action
For this king of birds!

When in meditation Milarepa perseveres
And renounces all wordly things,
He is not a prey to base ambition;
To abjure craving is his natural function.

Liberated yogis remain in seclusion,
Not because they fear disturbance and distraction;
It is the way and the tradition
Of all accomplished beings.

When monks and lay disciples
Discipline themselves in meditation,
It is not to gain in precedence o'er others;
It is the way and the tradition
Of all liberation-seekers.

For you, faithful and well-gifted disciples,
I sing these Pith-Instructions;
This is not for sport or pleasure —
It is the tradition of my Lineage.

Rechungpa then said, "I will keep these admonitions in my heart. You, dear Jetsun, are indeed different from other people. By the way, who offered this fine cloth and superb Ahrura to you?"

Milarepa then replied in this song, "The Gift from Man and Deity":

In the country of Ye Rang and Ko Kom
Lives a pious king, a Bodhisattva,
Victorious in the Dharma.
A prophecy from the Mother of All Mercy
To him was given in revelation.

Said the Mother of All Mercy,
"Invite Milarepa to see you.
He is now meditating
In the cave Gadaya of Nepal."

Knowing the uncertainty of death,
I refused the invitation.
I was then offered this cloth of Ka Shi Ka,
Made from fine bark of the Bal Dkar,
Now a sweet companion for my Dumo[4] meditation!

I was also offered the superb drug, Ahrura,
Which cures all ills of the Four Elements.
Because of this worthy gift,
I foresee that in the next seven years
All people in this King's country
Will be immune from sickness and disease.

Both Repas said to the Jetsun, "We will not indulge in the Eight Worldly Desires and will sincerely practice our devotions. Now for the welfare of sentient beings, please come to Tibet." Because of their earnest and repeated requests, the Jetsun finally agreed and went to the Nyan Yuan Cave of Chu Mdo on Lashi Snow Mountain, and resided there.

. . .   .

One day Tserinma, a local goddess, came to molest Milarepa while he was enjoying the company of some low-born fairies in the forest of Sen Ding, but in a silver mirror he saw and recognized Tserinma [in her true form]. Thereupon she vanished into the sky.

The next year, when the Jetsun was staying at Chon Lun, Tserinma again tried to intrude. She saw Milarepa riding on a lion, painted with cinnabar, dressed in sun and moon clothes, and holding a canopy and a victorious banner in his hands — then vanishing into the sky. Having failed again to trap Milarepa she withdrew.

This is the story of Milarepa receiving offerings from the King of Ko Kom in Mon, together with a brief account of the intrusion of [the goddess] Tserinma.

NOTES

1 Seven Precious Articles of Royalty: These are the wheel, gem, queen, minister, elephant, spirited horse, and commander-in-chief — the symbols, or necessary possessions, of a king.

2 The Two Provisions (T.T.: Tshogs.gÑis.): Journeying along the Path toward Buddhahood, one needs a supply of two "spiritual provisions." One is the Provision of Wisdom and the other is the Provision of Merits. The former is the study, understanding, and practice of the Prajñāpāramitā, the latter is the study and practice of all meritorious deeds, including charity, discipline, diligence, tolerance, and meditation.

3 The meaning of the passage here is very obscure. This is only a approximate translation.

4 Dumo (T.T.: gTum.Mo): the mystic heat produced by the practice of Heat Yoga.

THE GODDESS
TSERINMA'S ATTACK

Obeisance to all Gurus

> He, who is born in the Snow Country,
> Free from all worldly taints,
> Blessed by the Succession of Nāropa —
> The wondrous one who has conquered pain
>   and trials —
> The cure, the supreme remedy
> For the ills of sentient beings,
> Revered by all like sun and moon,
> He is the Holy One, the famous Mila.
> I bow to Him, the Father Repa, with great veneration.

· · ·   · · ·   · · ·

In the snow country to the North, on the border between Tibet and Nepal, where the people speak different languages, there was once a magnificent and prosperous trading center where one could find all kinds of merchandise. There stood the palace of the King of the Nāgas, and there the sound of the conch-trumpet could be heard. It was a place where wealth and fortunes spontaneously increased. On the east side of the gem rock rising like a leaping lion, at the left corner where the Heavenly Nun, the Propitious Goddess of Long Life [Tserinma] lives, there was a quiet spot where dwelt the great Repa Yogi, Milarepa. It was a place encircled by the deities of the snow mountains, and abounding in pastures and meadows where many healing herbs could be found. It was a place of blessing, situated near the bank of the Lohida [Lodahan?] River — the quiet hermitage of Medicine Valley.

In the year of the Water Dragon, while Jetsun Milarepa was practic-

296

ing the Flowing-River Yoga, just past midnight of the eighth day of the first month of the summer season, the eighteen Great Demons, leading all the ghosts and spirits in the whole Universe, came to attack him in order to hinder his devotion. By their great power they shook the earth, changed [the appearance of] the sky, and made their magic. Among them there were five extremely dreadful, wild-looking, flesh-eating female demons who displayed themselves in a number of ugly and ferocious forms conjured up to distract the Jetsun from his meditation. Whereupon, Milarepa sang a song, "Calling the Buddhas and Dākinīs for [my] Army":

> I pray to you, precious Guru,
> The famous Lho Draug Wa with Three Perfections.
> I, the destined disciple, sincerely pray to you.
>
> Father from the Realm of No-form
> You see all that happens.
>
> In this quiet place on the way to Drin River,
> I, the Tibetan Repa Yogi, have been deep in meditation.
> The visions, produced by concentrating Prāṇa
>   [in my body][1]
> Amuse and fascinate me
> Like a fantastic play!
>
> The ghosts and Devas in the Realms of Form
> Are all assembled here; none is left out.
> Most eminent among them are the five female demons
> Who into dread and hideous shapes have turned.
> They have come to hinder my devotion,
> And seek occasion [to distract me].
> I see a demoness grin like a skeleton,
> And lift up Mount Sumeru;
> I see a red one put out her tongue which drips with
>   blood
> And swallow the ocean waters.
> The most dreadful one appears as Yamāntaka,[2]
> Clashing a pair of sun-and-moon-like cymbals.
> I see an ash-smeared demoness dancing
> On the stars and planets, while she loudly laughs.
> I see a beautiful coquettish goddess,
> Whose looks incite one's ardor to extremes.
> With her enticing smile and captivating features,

She is most attractive and alluring.

There are also other vicious demons,
Stretching out huge arms, without their bodies showing,
They bend the forest trees,
Toss rocks, and shake the earth.
I see them digging trenches in the Four Directions
      [to surround me];
I see the four borders guarded by four giants;
I see fires aflame throughout the heavens,
And floods all the Four Continents submerging.
The sky is crowded with Non-men demons
With loud and piercing voices.
They shout, "Out! Out! Get out of here!"
Sending down a rain of dread diseases,
They laugh: "Ha, ha! The foundation of his
      wisdom is collapsing!"

When such hindrances descend upon me
I pray you, oh my gracious Gurus
And Patron Buddha, bestowers of accomplishment,
I pray you, holy Bha Wo and Bha Mo[3]
Who dwell in the Region of Reality —
I pray you, guards of Dharma, protectors from all
      hindrances,
Who have great magic power and mighty armies —
Protect, support, and help me;
Bless me and consecrate my mouth and body;
Display your anger, bare your canine teeth,
      and show your fearful faces;
Pray manifest in your most dreadful forms.
Oh Father and Mother deities,
Display the ghostly form of Yamāntaka —
He who is most prideful and most insolent.
I pray you, Wrathful Deities in the heavens,
Let from your mouths the lightning flash;
With thunder growl, "Hūṃ! Pai!" midst sheets of rain.
Arrogantly laughing in twelve different ways,
Destroy the nets and snares of all these demons!

That which hinders body is thus destroyed without;
That which hinders mind is thus destroyed within;
The unfavorable conditions are thus transmuted

Into the practices and teachings of the Bodhi-Path.
Pray drown these vicious demons in your floods.
Do you not hear me, holy, supreme Yidham and Ḍākinīs?

Thus the Jetsun sang and prayed fervently to the Gurus and Patron
Buddhas [Yidham]. In the meantime, the eighteen Devas and demons,
the main party among the adversaries, thought: "Judging by the words
he has just spoken, he appears to have lost his peace of mind and to
have been disturbed by us. We will soon have a chance [to destroy
him.]." This thought pleased them, but they were still uncertain about
[the extent of] Milarepa's inner Realization and Enlightenment. With
hesitation and misgivings, they decided to attack him with many insulting and threatening words in order to test his achievement in Yoga.
Whereupon, the Devas and demons sang together a song called "Procla-
mation of the Hindrances":

Oh you, the deep-voiced singer,
Who chants loudly and lyrically
Like the humming of Vedic sages!

You, the Yogi, who remains alone in the hermitage,
You, who have sent for Deva and Ḍākinī armies,
Are you not the great Repa ascetic?
But when your body is deprived of all assistance,
You will be shaken and alarmed.

Though you are in a state of panic now,
Listen to our song while we show our lenient faces.

The gem-dragon with a pair of golden wings
Is called the Ruler of Nam Lo.
When he flies up in the sky he sees beneath his wings
A propitious forest growing on the cliff.
Embraced by ranges of snow mountains,
Lies Medicine Valley on the high plateau.
Upon this auspicious eighth day in the lunar month,
Eighty-thousand trouble-makers are here assembled.
The sky is overshadowed by this demon army.

From the great Devas and mighty spirits of the Cosmos,
Down to the small and low earth-crawling serpent
     spirits,
All have appeared in their conjured wrathful forms.

With miraculous power and insatiable yearning
We have come to confuse you and to hurt you.

The Eighteen Great Demons are the leaders;
The guards in the Ten Directions are the Ten
    Retinue Demons;
We have with us the fifteen great Child Demons,
And the five unique Flesh-eating Demonesses.
We have with us the Bha Mo Demoness;
She eats the flesh of humans and drinks blood.
She lives on [sacrificial] odors and eats stones.
We have with us the Srinmo Demoness,
Who can demonstrate all actions in the world.
We, all the Devas and spirits here assembled,
Cast dice for lots before we came.
The divination said, "Now it is your turn
To be slaughtered, Yogi."

There is no way of your escaping!
You have no power, no freedom.
We have come to take your life, your soul, and spirit;
To stop your breath and take consciousness from
      your body,
To drink your blood and eat your flesh and Skandhas.[4]
Now your life has come to its final ending —
Your Karma and all your merits are exhausted.
Now the Lord of Death will eat you,
And the black rope of Karma bind you fast.
Tonight you leave this world.

Do you regret your deeds done in this lifetime?
When the army of the Lord of Death arrests you,
Will you be certain of escaping,
Or prepared without fear to die?
Are you confident of not falling
Into the Three Miserable Realms?
This we ask you.

Tonight you shall follow in our footsteps;
A guide sent by the Lord of Death will lead you.
Most dreadful are the dark realms of the Bardo —
To these new places, unfamiliar,
You now must go.

For your body, have you a protector?
For your mouth, have you the Horse of Wishing?
For your mind, are you ready to go to other realms?

Alas, poor Yogi, you have neither friends nor kinsmen,
This remote place is dark and perilous,
This lonely path is difficult and hazardous,
For you must proceed alone without companions.
Here you should not stay —
You should depart at once.

Thus sang the Devas and ghosts. The Jetsun then thought, "You demons and all the manifestations in the cosmos are merely conjurations of one's own mind; this is explicitly taught in all the holy Sūtras and Śāstras. According to the nectar-like teaching, clearly pointed out by my holy Guru, the nature of mind is the Illuminating Essence, beyond all extremes of playwords. It is never born and it never dies. Even though the myriad armies of the Lord of Death encircle it, and rain weapons upon it, they cannot harm, destroy, or sully it. Even though all the Buddhas in the Ten Directions and the Three Times should gather all their merits, and ray their infinite beams of light upon it, they could not make it better; nor could they color it or form it into substance. It will remain as it is, and can never be destroyed. This fetter-like body of mine was made out of subject-object clingings, and is destined to die. If these Devas and demons want it, I will give it to them. All life is transient and changeable. Now I have the opportunity to give my body away; if I do so, I shall make a worthy offering. It is owing to wrong subject-object thoughts that I see the shadows of Devas and ghosts as they now appear before me; the perception of the afflicter and the afflicted is as delusory as clouds, mist, and flickering mirages seen through impaired eyes. These delusory visions are like 'veils' created by wavering thoughts, which themselves have been produced by habitual-thinking derived from Original Blindness since beginningless time in Saṃsāra. In these phantom visions there is nothing to be afraid of." With this thought in mind Milarepa began to absorb himself into the Realm of Reality. Fearlessly, and with unshakable confidence, he sang a song:

This is the well-known place called Dinma Drin —
A town to which both Hindus and Tibetans come,
A market-place where many traders gather.
Here you live, Queen of Heaven.
Oh cruel Lady Tserinma of the Snow Lakes,
Your hair is decked with the mountain snow;

Embroidered on your skirt in all their beauty,
Are the verdant fields of Medicine Valley.
In this place, encircled by the river,
Have now assembled eighty thousand trouble-makers.

From the Heaven of Conjuration[5] above,
To the Realm of Hungry Ghosts below —
All the Devas and spirits here are gathered,
Singing their stupid songs [to hurt and confuse me].

Floating in the sky above are the fragrance-eating,
The rotten, the man-like, the hungry,
The vampire-ghoulish, the cannibalistic, the harmful,
The corpse-raising, and the Jung Po demons . . . .
Oh these unthinkable myriad demons!
Hardly can I recall their names!
Especially fierce among them
Are the five cannibal demonesses
Who, with abusive language, curse me,
And shout, "Die you shall, you must!"

Because of my [human] fear of death
I meditate on Immortal Mind,
Absorbed in the Uncreated Realm.
The keystone of the principle I practice
Is self-liberation from Saṃsāra.
With this quintessence of all teachings,
I clearly see Awareness, naked and unsubstantial.

My confidence in the View is the transparency of flux;
Since I know the Illuminating Void,
I fear not life or death.

Due to my [human] fear of the Eight Non-freedoms
I meditate on flux and on Saṃsāra's faults,
And train myself to watch the Law of Karma.
Then I take refuge in the [Three] Precious Ones.

Through constant meditation on the Bodhi-Mind
I eradicate forever the obscuring
Shadows of habitual thoughts.
Whatever may appear before me,
I see as false illusions;

Thus I fear not the Three Miserable Paths.

Fearful of life's uncertainty,
I have developed skill in Nāḍī-Prāṇa practice.
Through practicing the Key-instruction
Of the Three Identifying Exercises,[6]
I have checked my understanding of the Six Groups
        [of sense].
Thus, am I sure to see the Dharmakāya,
And lead myself to the Path Divine.

Since my mind has been totally absorbed
In the uncreated Dharmadhātu,
I have no regret nor fear of dying even now.

You, the worldly Devas and foolish demons
Who steal the lives of sentient men and women,
Listen closely to my words.
This human body, composed of Skandhas,
Is transient, mortal, and delusory.
Since in time I must discard it,
He who would, may take it now.

May the offering of my body serve as ransom
For all mankind and sentient beings.
May this offering serve as dedication
For the benefit and blessing of my parents.[7]

Since I have offered this, my body,
With sincerest dedication,
May you all be satisfied and happy.
I hope, through this one virtuous deed,
That the debts and Karmas I have owed
From time-without-beginning in Saṃsāra
May all be cleared and settled finally.

The running mind is void and unsubstantial —
I see this more clearly than you demons.
You thought that I would easily be frightened
When you raised the hosts of demon armies
From the Eighteen Hells and Lokas to attack me.
But I am a yogi of the Void,
Who clearly sees the nature of Ignorance.

I do not fear you demons —
Fictions conjured up by mind,
Manifest yet non-existent.
Oh, how fascinating is the play,
How fantastic are the dramas of Saṃsāra!

Thus, without the slightest fear in his mind, the Jetsun sang. Then he cried out to the demons in these truthful words: "From beginningless time in the past until now, we all have taken myriads of bodily forms in our past incarnations, comparable only to the total sum of grains of sand in the great Universe. Nevertheless, we have seldom utilized these bodies for a worthwhile purpose. Instead, we have wasted them by doing meaningless things [over and over again], thus accumulating more and more Skandhas and pains. If you Devas and demons are interested in taking my body, which is made of the Four Elements and worldly Skandhas and filled with thirty-two kinds of filthy things, I can give it to you right now. Why not? Furthermore, all the sentient beings in the Six Realms are either my mother or my father. For the sake of clearing the debts I owe them, I now give my body away, from the top of my head to the toes on my feet — the twelve limbs, including the head, the five organs, the five essentials, the six internal contents, the flesh and bones, the feet and fat, the brain and cortex, the grease and blood, the hair and nails, the skin and dirt, the breathing, the life, the semen, and the vital energy — I now offer all of them to you. Whatever part you may desire, take it with you and enjoy it. I hope, through this merit of offering my own body, that from now on all demons and malignant spirits will be relieved of the hatred and ill-will in their hearts. Let this Merit become the very seed of their great compassion, and may it grow forever in their hearts! May the seed of this compassion, combining with the nourishment of Innate-Born Wisdom, free all demons forever from malignance and bitterness. May you all become very merciful, lenient, and kind. I now dedicate this Merit as a boon to all sentient beings, for their perfect happiness, goodness, and contentment."

Upon hearing the Jetsun's words and sincere wish, all the Devas and demons [felt great remorse], and became very respectful to him. They ceased their hostile conjurations and remained there peacefully. The five extremely fierce flesh-eating Ḍākinīs, who had displayed such dreadful forms, exclaimed, "The fact that you have no attachment or concern for your body is truly marvelous! We did not come here with so much hatred and determination really to harm you. We came only to test your Realization and understanding. Generally speaking, all the outer hindrances created by demons depend on one's inner clinging-thoughts.

When we first arrived, we saw you displaying a certain amount of apprehension, and heard you calling to the deities and Ḍākinīs for help. Seeing this, we thought you might still have fears and desires in your mind. Consequently, we have been threatening you and ridiculing you with outrageous words. But, since we have heard your sincere and truthful replies, we regret our wrongdoing. Hereafter, whenever you run into danger or find your mind running wild, you should meditate on the Mind-Essence in an effortless manner. You will then surely conquer all hindrances. By so doing, even if all the Cosmos, from the [Heaven of] Brahmā to the earth, should be shaken and overturned, you will not be frightened or overwhelmed." Having given this good advice to the Jetsun, the five intemperate demonesses sang together from the upper sky:

> Oh great Yogi Repa,
> Because of your accumulated merits
> You were born in a human body.
> You are well-gifted, endowed
> With leisure and favorable conditions.
> As the glad time ripens for fulfilling
> The wishes made in your past lives,
> You have found the teaching of holy Dharma,
> Thus enabling you to practice its devotion.
> You are a good man, a superior being,
> While we are only low and worldly creatures.
> Our intelligence is small, and great our ignorance;
> Our births are in the lowly forms of women.
> Having little merit,
> We ever nurse malignant thoughts;
> Because of our sinful deeds, we in the sky must travel.
> As you may not understand what we have realized
> Through these obscure words,
> They will be explained in parables.
>
> Your mind is profound and deep
> Yet, in the Mudrā posture listen,
> And reason on what we sing.
>
> In the East, in the auspicious gate of China,
> A Chinese woman weaves a silken web;
> If she makes no mistakes
> Through chattering with her sisters,
> The wind without will not harm her work.

Therefore, to weave with care
Is of great importance.

In the North, lies the country of the Mongols;
Their brave and powerful troops are quick to fight.
If no revolt takes place inside the country,
They fear not even the men of King Gesar.[8]
Therefore, to rule the people well and wisely
Is of great importance.

In the West, at the steep gate of King Tazee [Persia]
Stands the gate of the secret-sign,
In shape resembling a fleshy shell;
If the forged iron bolts within it do not break,
No cannon-ball from outside can shatter it.
Therefore to fasten tight the inner portal
Is of great importance

In the South lies Nepal, the land of rocks and thunder.
If the natives with their axes
Cut not the healing tree of sandalwood,
The Mon intruder will not harm them.
To preserve the woods among compatriots
Is of great importance.

In this quiet place near the Drin River
You, Milarepa, meditate correctly.
If the thought of demons
Never rises in your mind,
You need not fear the demon hosts around you.
It is most important to tame your mind within;
Do not cherish any doubt there,
Oh ascetic Yogi.

Upon the hills of the Void Dharma-Essence
You should guard the castle of firm Samādhi.
If you wear the clothes of Bodhi-Mind
And hold the sword of Wisdom-and-Compassion,
The army of Four Demons cannot hurt you.
If you harbor not subject-object thinking,
No demons can e'er harm you.
Even if you are surrounded by the hosts
Of Yama, they cannot defeat you!

The attractions and inducements
In the world outside are great;
The drowsiness and distractions
Within are powerful;
Passions and attachments ever follow you like shadows.
E'en though you may absorb yourself in transcendental
        Wisdom,
It is still hard for you to conquer
The illusions of the demons and ghosts within —
For extremely quick and clever are these Nhamdog.[9]
On the steep path of fear and hope
They lie in ambush
With their ropes and snares,
Waiting for a chance to trap you.
The sentinel of vigilance
Should therefore be posted
To guard your inner citadel!

This melodious song with four
Parables and five meanings,
Is precious as a pearl.
A mirror of illumination,
It lights up the mind.
Please think of it with all attention,
Oh well-gifted Yogi!

Milarepa then replied, "As a rule, all trouble-making demons and Devas in the outer world are creations of the delusory thoughts of the
clinging [mind], which grasps forms and deems them to be real. What
you have said may all be very true. Nevertheless, we yogis do not consider obstacles as entirely evil and pernicious. Whatever forms and visions the demons may conjure we accept as helpful conditions and gracious gifts. Like the crack of a horsewhip, these demonic obstacles are
very good stimulants for indolent beginners. An unexpected shock will
undoubtedly sharpen one's awareness. Also, these demonic obstacles are
the very causes that will aid one's body and mind in devotion, and quick-
en the arising of Samādhi; to those advanced yogis who have already
reached stability on the Path, these obstacles become the nourishment
of Wisdom. Such hindrances will also deepen the clarity of the Light-
of-Awareness and improve one's inner Samādhis. Through them supreme
Bodhi-Mind will arise, thus enabling the yogi to better his devotion in
a rapidly progressive way. Today I have witnessed the fact that all the
Devas and demons have become Guardians of the Dharma. By the

merit of seeing these Guardians as the Transformation Body of Buddha, I shall achieve many more accomplishments. I have thus transmuted the obstacles into aids for spiritual growth and turned the evils into virtues. Now, all the Nhamdog — those distracting, illusory, and confusing thoughts — appear as the Dharmakāya itself. Thus you have actually given me all the assistance [necessary] for devotion on the Path. Insofar as the Ultimate, or the true nature of being is concerned, there are neither Buddhas nor demons. He who frees himself from fear and hope, evil and virtue, will realize the unsubstantial and groundless nature [of thoughts].[10] Saṃsāra will then appear to be the Mahāmudrā itself; all turbulent, distracting thoughts will vanish into the Dharmadātu — the so-called non-gathering and non-separating Dharmakāya."

The Jetsun again expounded these points as follows:

> Upon this earth, the land of the Victorious Ones,
> Once lived a Saint, known as the second Buddha;
> His fame was heard in all the Ten Directions.
> To Him, the Jewel a'top the eternal Banner [of Dharma]
> I pay homage and give offerings.
> Is He not the holy Master, the great Medripa?
>
> Upon the Lotus-seat of Medripa
> [My Father Guru] places his reliance;
> He drinks heavenly nectar
> With the supreme view of Mahāmudrā;
> He has realized the innate Truth in utter freedom.
> He is the supreme one, the Jetsun Marpa.
> Undefiled by faults or vices,
> He is the Transformation Body of Buddha.
>
> He says: "Before Enlightenment,
> All things in the outer world
> Are deceptive and confusing;
> Clinging to outer forms,
> One is ever thus entangled.
> After Enlightenment, one sees all things and objects
> As but magic shadow-plays,
> And all objective things
> Become his helpful friends.
> In the uncreated Dharmakāya all are pure;
> Nothing has even manifested
> In the Realm of Ultimate Truth."

He says: "Before Enlightenment,
The ever-running Mind-consciousness[11] within
Is shut in a confusing blindness
Which is the source of passions, actions, and desires.
After Enlightenment, it becomes the
    Self-illuminating Wisdom —
All merits and virtues spring from it.
In Ultimate Truth there is not even Wisdom;
Here one enters the Realm where Dharma is exhausted."

This corporeal form
Is built of the Four Elements;
Before one attains Enlightenment,
All illness and all suffering come from it.
After Enlightenment, it becomes the two-in-one Body
Of Buddha clear as the cloudless firmament!
Thus rooted out are the base [Saṃsāric] clingings.
In Absolute Truth there is no body.

The malignant male and female demons
Who create myriad troubles and obstructions,
Seem real before one has Enlightenment;
But when one realizes their nature truly,
They become Protectors of the Dharma,
And by their help and [freely-given] assistance
One attains to numerous accomplishments.

In Ultimate Truth there are no Buddhas and no demons;
One enters here the Realm where Dharma is exhausted.
Among all Vehicles, this ultimate teaching
Is found only in the Tantras.
It says in the Highest Division of the Tantra:
"When the various elements gather in the Nāḍīs,
One sees the demon-forms appear.
If one knows not that they are but mind-created
Visions, and deems them to be real,
One is indeed most foolish and most stupid."

In time past, wrapped up in clinging-blindness,
I lingered in the den of confusion,
Deeming benevolent deities and malignant
Demons to be real and subsistent.
Now, through the Holy One's grace and blessing

I realize that both Saṃsāra and Nirvāṇa
Are neither existent nor non-existent;
And I see all forms as Mahāmudrā.

Realizing the groundless nature of ignorance,
My former awareness, clouded and unstable
Like reflections of the moon in rippling water,
Becomes transparent, clear as shining crystal.
Its sun-like brilliance is free from obscuring
    clouds,
Its light transcends all forms of blindness,
Ignorance and confusion thus vanish without trace.
This is the truth I have experienced within.

Again, the foolish concept "demons" itself
Is groundless, void, and yet illuminating!
Oh, this indeed is marvelous and wonderful!

In this manner Milarepa showed his faithful obedience to his Guru's
instructions and his decisive understanding of the Dharma. Whereupon
the eighteen Great Demons and the other Devas and ghosts all addressed him with deep respect: "You are a yogi who has reached the
stage of stability. Unaware of this, we came to insult you and make
many troubles for you. Now we feel very sorry and regretful. Henceforth, we shall follow all your commands and serve you." Having taken
this oath, the innumerable demons and ghosts prostrated themselves before him like mud splashing and falling in heavy rain. Then the Devas
and demons all returned to their own abodes.

This is the story of how the great Repa, the indescribable Laughing
Vajra, met the five worldly Ḍākinīs, and replied [to their attacks upon
him] in song. This story is told by Bodhi Radsa, the Master of Ngan
Tson, from his indelible memory of the original account. It is written
in a poetic style called "The Rosary of Pearls."

NOTES

1 According to Tantrism, most of the visions that a yogi sees in his meditation are brought about by the "concentrating" of a particular Prāna, either the
Prāna of earth, water, fire, or air, in a specific "psychic" center of the body.

2 Yamāntaka (T.T.: gÇin.rJe.): one of the most wrathful deities in Tantrism, a sublimation of Yama, the King of Death.

3 Bha Wo and Bha Mo (T.T.: dPah. Wo, dPah.Mo.). The latter appears in the Tibetan text here as "Dakima." Bha Wo and Bha Mo are male and female deities, especially those associated with the teaching and practice of Tantrism.

4 Skandhas, or the Five Skandhas: the five constituents that made up a man, i.e., form, feeling, perception, impulses, and consciousness.

5 The Heaven of Conjuration (T.T.: lHa.dWañ.Phyug.): the Heaven of Iśvara.

6 The Three Identifying Exercises: to identify one's mind with the manifestation, with the body, and with the Dharmakāya.

7 Since one has been reincarnating for innumerable ages on every plane, and must have had two parents in each incarnation, he has thus inevitably built a parental relationship with all sentient beings. It is out of this conviction of the kindred relationship of all beings that the Bodhi-Mind and the great Compassion of the Bodhisattva were brought forth.

8 Gesar (T.T.: Ge.Sar.): The name of a legendary king of ancient Tibet whose romantic and literary adventures, as well as his military and religious achievements, have been the fountainhead of inspiration and imagination to Tibetan minds. The *Book of Gesar* (T.T.: rGyan.Druñ.) is a great Tibetan epic comparable to the Mahābhārata and the Iliad. It has been one of the most beloved and widely read books in Tibet. The exact number of volumes composing this book is almost indeterminable because of its many complex versions and editions, but it is generally believed to contain about 15 large volumes, totaling more than a million words. The professional Tibetan troubadours, whose knowledge is confined almost entirely to this one great book, are called by the Tibetans the "wandering story-tellers of King Gesar."

9 Nhamdog here implies the volatile and capricious aspects of the mind. See also Story 4, Note 4, and Story 1, Note 12.

10 The literal translation of this phase should be: "The confusion has no ground or substance" (T.T.: hKhrul.Pa.gShi.Med.).

11 The phrase "Yid.Gyi.rNam.Çes.", appearing in the original text, is tautological. It has therefore been translated here as "Mind-consciousness."

THE CONVERSION OF
THE GODDESS TSERINMA

Obeisance to all Gurus

> Crowned with the adornment of the
> Transformation Body of Tathāgata
> Is the Supreme One, the translator Marpa.
> From His face flows
> The nectar stream;
> From His Whispered Lineage
> Comes to birth the Innate-Born.
> Grown out of this pure Wisdom
> Is He, the famous Yogi, Mila.
> To you is paid sincerest homage
> Father Repa.

. . .   .

On the border between Nepal and Tibet, at the left shoulder of the misty snow mountain, Queen of the Azure Heights, under floating golden clouds lay the blessed place, the Valley of Medicine. Close to the bank of the celebrated Lodahan [Lohida?] River, it was encircled by a crystal range of snow hills. There dwelt the renowned great Repa Yogi Mila, who kept his unbounded mind absorbed in the teaching of the Supreme Vehicle, and perfectly consolidated in the limitless Bodhi-Mind. When the "Up-going Bliss"[1] reached the Throat-center of Enjoyment, the Song of Vajra flowed spontaneously from him. Blessed by an uninterrupted wave of grace, he had transformed his base consciousness into Wisdom, and, through Tantric Madness[2] had conquered all the demons and evil spirits. He was a yogi of great power and might.

Tranquilly absorbing his mind in the original state of Dharma-Essence, he occasionally demonstrated, with great compassion, the Samādhi resulting from the conquering of the Elements,[3] now concealing and now manifesting his powers to subdue evil spirits. While residing there, for the benefit of faithful human beings as well as devoted spirits and Devas, he also performed numerous and wondrous miracles.

On the eleventh night of the summer month in the year of the Water Snake, five bewitchingly lovable maidens came to [visit] him. They greeted him and circumambulated him many times. Then they said, "We have brought you some yogurt made from wild ox [Ba Men][4] milk." Saying this, they offered Milarepa a [big] blue-gem spoon filled with yogurt. Then they sat one by one on his left and said, "We five girls beg you to take us to your heart and permit us to make our Vow-for-Bodhi before you." The Jetsun thought, "I have never seen such a precious and unique spoon, nor is there in the world any food comparable to this wonderful yogurt! [As to these girls], their manner of prostration, their reverse way of circumambulation, and their other unusual behavior prove that they are heavenly beings." But in order to find out whether they would speak the truth, the Jetsun pretended to be ignorant. He looked at them and asked, "Who are you? Where did you come from?" And then he sang tunefully:

> For the sake of several well-destined disciples,
> The Holy Dorje-Chang, the essence of Four Bodies,
> At a time of dispute and corruption,
> Incarnated as Marpa, the Translator,
> In the mountainous Country of Snow, Bar Dha Na,[5]
> In the northern part of Tsamlin.
>
> With the voice of a roaring lion,
> He, the Supreme Being, rode the Supreme Vehicle.
> By merely hearing His Voice one will
> Be saved from falling into the Lower Paths.
>
> I pray to you great Marpa, for those who seek me —
> Pray grant them your blessing and accomplishment.
> Oh Father, with the power of your compassion,
> I pray that their minds with ease may be converted,
> That within them the buds of Enlightenment may sprout.
>
> In the Pure Land of the Void
> Abide the Buddhas and their Sons.
> With your sunlit compassion,

Pray send forth your rays of light
To shine o'er the Wisdom-lotus
In the hearts of your disciples,
And make them blossom.
Pray make the anthers
Of the Four Infinities grow today.

I have something to ask you
Lovely maidens sitting on my left.
There is nothing special I want to know —
Just tell me, are you human beings,
Or heavenly angels?
For this is the first time I have seen you.

Oh you five attractive damsels
With such fine and charming bodies,
In the dazzling light of magic
Your enchanting elegance
Glorifies the splendor of your beauty!

Oh you radiant maids from Heaven,
He who sees you at a distance seems
As in a dim evening fog to see five
Young maidens shopping in the town.
But when he looks more carefully,
He sees no tangible or steady image,
Only a hazy, flickering silhouette.
Thus am I much bewildered and perplexed.

When I venture on the road,
I see you run like rolling pearls,
Chatting gaily with much laughter.
But behind your coquettish charms and glamor,
Like the morning star shining in the east
You slowly fade away.

Seeing that you disperse and assemble e'er in groups,
I suspect that you are Devas or else fairies.
When one looks at your eyes a'twinkle,
One cannot help but smile!
I wonder to myself, "are you magic Ḍākinīs?"

The Buddhist way of circling in obeisance

Is from left to right,
But yours from right to left,
So you must Devas be, or fairies.

The usual way to render "Eye Obeisance"[6]
Is from left to right,
But yours from right to left,
So you must fairies be, or Devas.

You shake the upper body when you bow;
In every nine prostrations you ask of my welfare thrice;
You nod and shake your heads
When you make the "Eye Obeisance" once;
Only heavenly ladies prostrate in such a way,
But though you imitate, you are not really like them!

In every eight prostrations you ask of my welfare twice
After the fashion of all Devas;
You bend your knees to earth —
The form of your obeisance is unusual.

This spoon that's made with gems of blue
With various jewel ornaments that you gave me,
From Heaven came: it is not of this world.

I come from a distant country,
And have traveled in many different lands.
I have eaten many sorts of food
And many wondrous things have I seen and heard.
Compared to others, my experience should be not less,
        but more;
But in all my life I have never tasted
Such delicious yogurt made from wild ox milk,
Nor have I ever seen such wondrous things.
This is food from Heaven,
It is not of this world.

What you have said, oh happy fairies,
Is indeed a cause for wonder,
Especially your request to know the Bodhi-Mind.
Judging by your faith and fondness for the Dharma,
In past lives you must have had
Deep affiliation with the Doctrine.

I cannot but be pleased and most delighted.

Listen to me, my good young women.
I have more questions still to ask.
I shall make no false remark,
But only utter sincere words.

From whence did you come this morning,
And whither will you go this afternoon?
Where is your home and what your family?
What do you do with your magic powers?
What magic power can you bestow?
How came you to know of me?
Was it through hearsay, or have we met before?
Let no hesitation block your speech.
Please answer me with honest words.

The fairies replied, "You are the Jetsun, the supreme being. In your past lives you must have accumuulated many merits. Thus you were able to meet a unique and accomplished Guru. With a heart full of the nectar-like Dharma, you have fully realized the fallacy and illusiveness of worldly pleasures and desires. Thus, great compassion and benevolence arose in the depths of your heart, and a determination to cross the perilous, rolling river of Saṃsāra was established. Through great hardships and austerities you have devoted yourself to the practice of Dharma. Having perfectly mastered the illuminating Samādhi within, you also attained great miraculous powers by means of which you are able to see people's private affairs and thoughts [clearly and vividly] like images reflected in a mirror. Although you are perfectly aware of our families, lineages, and other things, still you pretend [not to know], and ask us about them. Surely, we shall be glad to tell you the full truth. Great Jetsun, please give us your attention for a moment, and listen to our song." And they sang melodiously together:

At this sad time of Five-defilements
Near Pakshu in Tibet, the home
Of the red-faced demoness, was born
A rare man in Snow Valley,
Surrounded by evil, icy hills.
Is he not the great Yogi, Mila?

Because of your worthy deeds in previous lives
You have met an accomplished Guru,

And are blessed by the divine Lineage.

Bathed in the Nectar Stream of Grace,
You have transformed your mind.
Thus you see all pleasures and glories
As phantom-like delusions.

Having left this world so hard to leave,
Diligently you persist in your devotions
Allowing nothing to distract you.
So you have become a heavenly yogi
Forever dwelling in the Realm of Dharmakāya.

Staying on the plane that is "Away-from-Playwords,"
You can use the power of that Samādhi, transforming
Into many forms —
A reward for conquering all the elements.
Yet even without it, all evils have you conquered.
Seeing the miracles that you have wrought,
Your faithful disciples were inspired and heartened;
Filled with wonder, and with joyful hearts,
Their hair stood up and their tears ran down.

Oh, you are the Jetsun, the Pearl of the Crown.
To you, all homage and offerings should be made.
You are the Jetsun Yed Pa,[7] Buddha's son,
The refuge of all sentient beings.

We, the five sky-going maidens
From a non-human tribe,
Who now sit beside you,
Are low in birth and lesser still in merit.
Pray, take pity on us with your great compassion!

From the clouds of your grace,
We pray the rain of nectar soon will fall
Whereby the obstinate passions — the cause of all evils
[In the world] — will be appeased,
And the precious bud — the supreme Bodhi-Mind — will
    flower.

You are the master of Yoga,
The majestic Yogi of Forbidden-Acts.

Through cultivation of awareness in Samādhi,
You know well the minds and the capacities,
The lineages, and Dharma-relationships of all men.
Though you know them clearly without error,
You pretended ignorance, and asked about us.

We are Nu Yin, worldly demonesses,
Ahdsidharata is our family line.
We are ghosts who wander in graveyards,
Worldly Ḍākinīs,[8] who magic make.
Many powers and accomplishments
Can we bestow and grant.

This morning in the house of Heaven,
We opened the cloud gate,
Rode the sun's rays, and came.
This evening we are bound for India
To attend the sacramental feast
In Cool Garden Cemetery.

On the right side of this valley,
Fashioned like a triangle,
Stands a high snow mountain.
On the summit of the central peak we dwell.
The crowning ornament of our house
Is a crystal-like ice-mirror
Reflecting rays of sun and moon.
Half way up the mountain
Lies a vase-shaped lake;
The hovering clouds above it roof
Our house, below lies the base,
Forever wreathed in fog.
This is Blue Queen Snow Mountain,
The famous place, our home.

First we saw you in the summer
When we came to harm and to insult you.
But you harbored neither anger nor resentment.
In return, you bestowed on us the rain of Dharma.
Thus for our evil-doing we all repented.
Having tasted the nectar of your Dharma,
We felt yet more thirsty and yearned for more to drink.
So to-day we come to visit you,

The supreme Being who gives refuge.

We pray you, the perfect man,
To let us quench our thirst and satisfy
Our yearnings at your nectar-stream.

Milarepa then said, "Formerly, you were very malicious and resentful. You have repeatedly threatened me in wrathful shapes, and tried to harm and revile me. But I have fully realized that all manifestations are plays of the mind, and that the Mind-Essence is illuminating yet void. Therefore, I have never had the slightest fear or concern about delusory hindrances caused by demons. Observing this, you should sincerely repent of the damage and harm you have inflicted upon people and devoted yogis. With deep remorse you should confess all your sinful deeds and should not commit any more, or harm other beings. You must first take an oath on this. If you do so, I can then admit you and grant you the prayer of Taking-the-Three-Refuges, and initiate you into the Raising of Bodhi-Mind. Otherwise, if you have not made yourselves handmaidens of the profound Teachings and of the Supreme Precepts, it will be like 'throwing a yak cow into the abyss,' or like 'dragging the nose of a corpse to the place of lament.' Now, pay the strictest attention and listen to the song of this old man":

> On this auspicious evening when midnight is
>   drawing nigh,
> A silvery light gleams brightly in the East
> Chasing the darkness back across the sky.
> Is that not the lucid, crystal-pure moonlight?
>
> Riding on the glittering rays — your horses,
> You five maidens came
> Clad in shrouds of light.
> Are you not the five earth-bound Ḍākinīs?
>
> Near the bank of Lodahan River
> Is a delightful and quiet cell,
> Where lives a mad ascetic
> Who knows not disgrace and shame.
> Naked, he knows not bashfulness
> And feels nor heat nor cold.
>
> Absorbed in the mind-transcending Essence,
> Undistracted for even a single moment,

He contemplates the nature of the Void.
Is he not Mila, the great meditator?

You five maids of magic have sung a song to me;
I, the cotton-clad Yogi, sing in return for you.
We have shared some vows and Karma in the past;
'Til now you have of this been unaware.
How happy must you be to know it now!

In the late spring of last year
You caused all ghosts and Devas
To come here and afflict me.
As the flags unfurled
And the demon-soldiers drew up in array,
All four armies showered missiles down
And tried to harm me in all sorts of ways.
But since I had already realized
That all form is of the mind,
While the mind itself is void,
I was never frightened
By these demonic shadow-shows.

By merely seeing you poor sinful beings,
An unbearable compassion, quite beyond control,
Rose of itself within me.
In return I showered on you
The mercy-rain of Dharma.
You were thus converted
To faithful be, and pious.

To-night as five lovely maids you came;
Once more with your dazzling beauty
You circled and bowed many times before me,
Folding your hands upon your breasts
To show sincere respect.
With your melodious song
You asked me for the Dharma, saying:
"Pray, gather and precipitate the clouds of Bodhi-Mind,
And shower down on us the Dharma-nectar."
Since you have such earnest faith
[I will give you the teaching
And so fulfill your wish].

Upon the lotus-seat a'top my head[9]
Sits my precious Guru —
The great Translator, matchless Marpa!
Like the immaculate Sambhogakāya,
He sits gracefully upon my head.

From the radiant moon of His sweet compassion,
Cloudless and resplendent,
Emanates bright light,
Shining upon the hearts of His disciples;
It freshens the awakening anthers
And brings quick to blossom
The water-lily of their minds.
You bewitching sorceresses,
Have you ever seen these things?
If not, the reason is your sins.
You should thus confess, without reserve
All that you have e'er done wrong
Since time without beginning;
Else you can ne'er receive my teaching
And may fall into the wretched Realms once more.

Before, you were malignant and were bitter,
Accustoming yourselves to vice;
For you to take an oath meant nothing,
Nor would it have helped the Doctrine.
He who does not respect the Law of Karma,
[Will fall] into the dread Realms of Misery.
You should, therefore, take heed
Of even the smallest sin.

He who knows not the faults of wordly pleasures,
And from his depth of heart does not renounce them,
From the prison of Saṃsāra can ne'er escape.
He should know that the world is but illusion,
And work hard to subdue his desires [Kleśas].

If for the wrongdoings
Of all sentient beings
In the Six Lokas
One has great pity,
He will avoid the Hīnayāna path;
With a great compassion

He should strive hard to emulate a Bodhisattva!

Oh Ḍākinīs of the Mahāyāna Path,
If you can accept this beneficial preaching
Which I have just imparted to you,
Brothers and sisters, then, we may tread the Path
     together,
Entering at last the Pure Land of Happiness.
There we will consummate all merits and good works,
There without doubt we will meet once more.

Milarepa continued: "We are living in a time of defilement. Corruption and vice abound everywhere, people are voracious and harbor strong desires and passions [Kleśas]. This is a very difficult time for one to subdue all his desires at once; therefore one should examine himself, and see what precepts he may take and live up to."

The Ḍākinīs then said to Milarepa, "Yes, indeed, Lord. It is only because you are so compassionate that you have preached for us the truth of Karma and called our attention to morality and virtue. This is all very wonderful, but we have heard this kind of preaching before. In the great cemetery of Sinhala, the Wisdom Ḍākinī, the outstanding Earth-Protecting Goddesses, such as the Lion-faced one, Damala Richroma, the Dumo Ngosungma, and the accomplished yogini, Bhina Betsar, have already preached to us the merits and glory of the Bodhi-Mind. We have heard many sermons on morality and discipline. Therefore, please do not merely preach to us these [fundamental and preliminary] teachings. As to our demonstration of malignant and wrathful forms before you a while ago,[10] it was to make a crucial test of your Realization. Since we are protectors of Dharma, we would not do anything truly harmful to people. But now we pray you to give us the [Precept] for raising the Bodhi-Mind."

The Jetsun replied, "Why not, since you ask with such sincerity and earnestness? Of course I will give the Precept to you. Now, prepare your offerings and Maṇḍala for the ceremony. I would like to tell you this, however: I am not a person who cares for worldly goods and pleasures, but each of you may now offer your special worldly accomplishments[11] to me, and also tell me your true names."

Whereupon, with great enthusiasm and respect, the Ḍākinīs sat in a row with folded hands to make their offerings. The first said, "I am the leader in this group. My name is Auspicious Fair Lady of Long Life [Drashi Tserinma]. I now offer you the accomplishment of protecting and increasing one's progeny." The Ḍākinī who sat on the right side of the leader said, "My name is Fair Lady of the Blue Face [Tingeyalzun--

ma]. I now offer you the accomplishment of divining with a mirror."
The Ḍākinī who sat to the right of Tingeyalzunma said, "My name is
Crowned Lady of Good Voice [Jupan Drinzonma]. I now offer you the
accomplishment of refilling a storehouse with jewels." The Ḍākinī who
sat to the left of the leader said, "My name is Immutable Fair Lady of
Heaven [Miyo Lonzonma]. I now offer you the accomplishment of
winning food and prosperity." The remaining Ḍākinī, who sat to the
left of Miyo Lonzonma said, "My name is Fair Lady of Virtue and Action [Degar Drozonma]. I now offer the accomplishment of increasing
livestock."

Thereupon, the Jetsun imparted to them one by one the teaching of
Taking Refuge, the Code of Morals, and the raising of the Bodhi-Mind
of Wish and of Action, explaining them in general terms as well as in
detail. Whereupon, the magical Ḍākinīs were very much pleased and
fascinated. They said to Milarepa, "Although we will not be able to
practice these teachings in as perfect a manner as you have so edify-
ingly instructed us, we will try not to violate these principles and will
never forget the gratitude that we owe you." They then expressed their
sincere thanks to the Jetsun by bending their bodies towards him,
laying their foreheads upon his feet, circling round him, and prostrating before him many times. Then they all flew into the sky and
vanished in the far distance in a blaze of light.

One evening, later in the month, the hostile and insolent demons of
the Eight Divisions who had come before, returned to Milarepa with
their servants and sons. From the low regions also came many lovely and
coquettish worldly Ḍākinīs [including the five who had come before],
wearing splendid silk garments which fluttered lightly in the breeze, and
adorned with jeweled bracelets, necklaces, and various other ornaments
of precious stones. Together with their retinues and associates, these
Non-men spirits all came to Milarepa, filling the sky before him. They
then began to rain flowers upon him, to play all kinds of musical instru-
ments, to burn fragrant incense, and to offer abundant food and drink.
They said, "Pray relate to us your experience of Final Enlightenment —
the utmost understanding of all Buddhas in the Three Times, and the
absolute consummation of the Path. Pray preach for us the Final Truth
of Dharma." In response to their request Milarepa sang a song called
"The Understanding of Reality," in which he illucidated the essence of
the Final Truth and the Ultimate Reality:

On the border of Tibet and Nepal
Lies Dinma Drin, a wonder town.

There lives the Medicine Deva, protectress of the
    natives.
On the splendid Snow Queen Mountain, the beauty
    of this land,
Dwells the great Auspicious Lady of Long Life —
She is the lady with the braided hair,
Her life is lasting as a diamond.

At the left side of the mountain,
Covered by clouds throughout the year,
Are pasture lands and ranges of snow hills
Where gently flows a winding river;
Close by is Medicine Valley.

With great earnestness, I,
The Yogi Milarepa,
Meditate alone in this quiet place.
You, proud worldly demons —
Thieves who steal yogis' lives —
Who came here once before to insult and scorn me,
Have returned today.
Are you not the same group
Who afflicted me before?
Late last evening, close to midnight,
Five lovely maids came here.
They vowed to raise the Bodhi-Mind,
Offering wish-fulfilling accomplishments,
And then they disappeared.

Tonight, while the clear moon
Shines o'er the earth serene,
You five charming maidens, gay and skittish,
Come once more.
The silk scarfs round your lovely bodies
Sway and flutter, your jewels
Sparkle in the light.
You have been conjured to perfection,
Enchanting and most beautiful.
At the Goddess Leader's call, the proud
Devas and spirits of the Eight Divisions
Have come with you, filling all the sky.
They all offer me delicious food,
And play such charming tunes.

Since you have asked for the utmost Truth and Final
    Teachings,
You should heed most carefully, and give your
    full attention.

Sentient beings in the Three Kingdoms
Possess different Passion-Bodhis.[12]
Among them there are many kinds of egoism
And many types of behavior;
They have a myriad ways of ego-clinging.
To suit the minds of ignorant men,
The Buddha said, "All things are existent."

But in [the realm of] Absolute Truth
Buddha Himself does not exist;[13]
There are no practices nor practisers,
No Path, no Realization, and no Stages,
No Buddha's Bodies and no Wisdom.
There is then no Nirvāṇa,
For these are merely names and thoughts.
Matter and beings in the Universe
Are non-existent from the start;
They have never come to be.
There is no Truth, no Innate-Born Wisdom,
No Karma, and no effect therefrom;
Saṃsāra even has no name.
Such is Absolute Truth.

Yet, if there are no sentient beings, how
Could Buddha in the Three Times come to be?
For if there is no cause, there will be no effect.
Therefore Buddha says, "In Mundane Truth,
All Saṃsāric and Nirvāṇic things exist."
In Ultimate Truth, manifestation and the Void,
Existence and non-existence,
Are the same, being one in "taste"![14]
There is no difference, such as "this" and "that."
All Dharmas are two-in-one in the Greatness.
This is understood by those enlightened ones
Who see no consciousness but Wisdom,
Who see but Buddhas, and no sentient beings.
Who see no Dharma-forms, but Dharma-Essence.
Spontaneously a great compassion

Flows out from their hearts.
Their powers and virtues ne'er decline.
They possess all merits and wish-granting powers.
They have realized all virtues and the Truth.

Oh, you ghosts and Devas here assembled,
[When you approach the preachers]
You hear not the profound Dharma
But hark to pagan ranting;
When you reach the country of Ahbhira,
You do not visit wise men,
But go to mad instructors.

Wolves and foxes wandering in graveyards
Are frightened when they hear a lion's roar.
Should there be a gifted one in this assembly,
Through hearing this, my preaching,
He will in time be liberated.
Most joyful now am I;
May you also be gay and happy.

After singing this song, he said to the visitors, "The Buddha has preached numerous Dharmas, commonly known as 'The Eight Thousand Groups.' All these various teachings are given to different people, in accordance with their needs and capacities. However, the [utmost Truth is One] and the final destination [to which all paths lead] is One. This sole, absolute Foundation [of all] is the unaltered [unacted-upon and untouched] real nature of being. *By merely understanding this Truth, one will not be able to liberate himself. He must proceed on the Path. Only thus can he actually realize what he has understood.* The essence of the Path is the Two-in-One Voidness-Compassion, and though there are myriads of different paths or doctrines, they all lead to the Two-in-One Realm of Wisdom and Means, or the realization of the non-distinction of the Two Truths."[15]

Then the five Ḍākinīs who had come to Milarepa the night before to take the oath of Bodhi-Mind, rose from the assembly and, standing to the left of the Jetsun, sang together a song of praise, "We See His Merits":

Beneath the bright light in the sky
Stand snow mountains to the North.
Nigh these are auspicious pasture lands,
And fertile Medicine Valley.

Like a golden divan is the narrow basin,
Round it winds the river, earth's great blessing.

At this time of defilement and corruption
Came you, the ascetic Yogi, full of wonders.
The food you eat is nectar of Non-thought,
The drinks you quaff are natural secretions.
In your mind, there is no disgrace or shame;
In your mind there is nothing clean or filthy.
You act like a madman leading an ascetic life.

For the sake of testing your ability,
We came last summer to this river bank —
To the left of Lashi Mountain —
And found you in Sendentsema Wood
With your naked body indifferent to shame,
Amusing yourself with the lesser fairies.

We saw you in the mirror silvered thick,
We saw your meditation powers and your wondrous feats,
We saw your body vanish in the sky.
By these wonders we were so amazed
That in midautumn we returned.
You were then meditating in the Tsonlung Cave,
Absorbed in deep Samādhi. We crept in
And saw you wearing clothes of sun and moon
With a precious garland on your head.
Your body was besmeared with ash of cinnabar,
And in your hands, the canopy and victorious banner.

We saw you riding a fierce animal, flying
Through the firmament to vanish in the sky.
Thus we had no chance to harm you.

We came again last summer to put you to the test,
Intending to disturb your meditation.
But your mind was like the ocean,
While your body burned with fire.
Poisonous snakes were writhing round your head
As an adorning diadem.

Leaning on the blade of a sharp knife,
You sat in the lotus posture on a spear.

We saw you play a'top a wish-granting
Ball, and swallow a whole mountain.
Thus were we fascinated and bewildered too!

You are a yogi who has mastered Mind-awareness,
And like Indra, you can conjure and dissolve
Your body and perform countless miracles.
In your mind there is no pride, no thought.
You are free of doubt, of hope and fear.

You are a yogi like unto a lion,
For you fear not and have no misgiving.
You are a yogi like a great elephant,
For you will ne'er be frightened by any obstacle.
When one sees you, his heart is full of joy
And the hairs of his body stand on end.
By merely touching and beholding you,
All obstacles are cleared away,
All altruistic deeds accomplished.

You are the Wish-fulfilling Gem,
You are the Yogi, as the heavens great.
Since you have realized what "beyond-words" means
And never would be swayed by thoughts,
Demons can ne'er disturb you!

When we found we could not harm you,
It seemed it was ourselves whom we were mocking.
Thus we have changed our hostile stand,
Conjuring wondrous and delightful visions for you.
You also preached to us the Dharma,
And led us to the harmonious Path and Peace!

On that auspicious night last month
You sowed in us the Buddha-Seed.
The priceless buds in our hearts have grown.
You are the supreme teacher for the Path that no
     one can mistake,
You are the shelter and refuge of all beings.

Later, when you go to the Pure Land of Joy[16]
Where stands the palace of Mijurpa Buddha,
All the great Bodhisattvas will come to greet you.

The Ḍākinīs above, on, and beneath the earth,
Together with the meritorious Devas
Will also come to greet you. They will bring
Victorious banners and great canopies
And play melodious music for your welcome.
They will make you splendid offerings,
Showing you the way to the Pure Land.
Let us, who have seen you and heard you preach,
Both human beings and Non-men,
All become your servants
And follow you to the Pure Land!

Thus they sang, offering their sincere wishes and expressing their admiration.

Milarepa thought, "These worldly Ḍākinīs are very arrogant and incorrigible. They still have to be subdued and disciplined." So he said, "Fair ladies, it is indeed wonderful that you have such faith and respect for me and have expressed your sincere, pure wishes for the future. I have shown you the Path leading towards Buddhahood, and granted you the Precepts of the Bodhisattva. Now I am going to give you the Instructions and Precepts of the Diamond Vehicle, which abounds with skills and means; it is the easiest, fastest, and most versatile Path leading towards Buddhahood. Now you should prepare the offerings, and also surrender to me the quintessence of your lives."

The Ḍākinīs were thrilled with great joy. Immediately they arranged oblations on a grand scale, prostrated themselves before the Jetsun, and circumambulated him many times; and finally they offered him their lives. They then sat round him, as before. Thereupon, Milarepa vouchsafed them the Initiation called "Demonstrating the Awareness of Drol Ma," and the Initiation of the Goddess Kurukullā, together with the teaching of the Reciting-the-[words-of-] Essence. He admonished them to observe the discipline strictly, and instructed them to visualize their Guru sitting on their heads at all times. He taught them that whatever the crisis they might encounter, good or bad, they should look only to the Three Precious Ones for guidance and help. Never should they put their trust in pagan gods. The Jetsun then said, "You should know that the outer world is, in essence, identical with the Beyond-measure Palace of the Buddhas; all sentient beings are, in essence, identical with the Patron [Yidham] Buddhas. Whoever you meet, you should respect him and love him. Not even for a single moment should you have any malignant and hostile thoughts towards anyone, nor should you revile or hurt him in any manner. In all circumstances and at all times you should not forget the Self-Buddha Pride." [17]

The five goddesses then said to Milarepa, "Oh Jetsun, the teaching of Tantra is indeed the fastest, easiest, and most resourceful of all teachings. We are very grateful that you bestowed it and its precepts upon us. We impure sentient beings have been driven by deep-rooted habitual thinking since beginningless time in Saṃsara. We women, especially, are low of birth and inferior in intelligence. Though we cannot really understand that which you have imparted to us, we shall try our best to learn and practice it. Though we may not be able to perceive that all sentient beings are Buddhas, we shall not harm them in any manner. We will give assistance and service to the followers of Dharma, and will try our utmost to give special protection and help to the followers of your Lineage. We will provide them with all they need for their devotions and assist them to obtain all the favorable conditions they require. We will serve them as their servants." Swearing thus, they bowed down to Milarepa and circumambulated him many times. Then they all disappeared into the sky.

This is the story of how the indescribable great Yogi Milarepa, the Laughing Vajra, met with the five worldly Ḍākinīs, including their leader, the Auspicious Lady of Long Life. Also found in this story is the song which answered the Ḍākinīs' inquiry about the principle of raising the Bodhi-Mind. This event was recorded by the well-gifted, virtuous Repa Shiwa Aui on the peak of the Auspicious Mountain of Tuntin, by the left side of Dinma Drin market. In recording this story, Shiwa Aui has carefully and repeatedly inquired, and discussed [the matter] with the Auspicious Lady of Long Life in person. Afterwards, he met the Jetsun himself three times, the Jetsun also giving him, with approbation, some needed information. In that quiet, delightful, and accomplishment-granting place, the Meritorious Forest of Ahom Chun, Shiwa Aui and Ngan Tson Dunba Bodhiradza, in consideration of benefiting some destined persons in the future, have faithfully put the Jetsun's words down without adding to or abridging the original narrations and events. Their rhetorical and well-arranged writing [deserves to be called] the Illuminating and Nectar-like Rosary of Words.

NOTES

1 "Up-going Bliss": According to the supreme Bliss-Void Yoga, a great bliss will arise if a yogi can lift his life-energy from the lower part of the Central Channel

to a higher position. The consummation of this bliss is achieved when the life-energy reaches the Cakra at the top of the head.

2 It is said that when a Tantric yogi reaches a very advanced stage of Enlightenment, he should practice the Tantric Madness or Act-of-Insanity by behaving like a lunatic, to completely emancipate himself from all conventional thoughts and habits and thus reach final and perfect Enlightenment.

3 Lit.: The Saṃādhi of "Elements-Exhaustion" (T.T.: Zad.Pa.hByuñ.Bahi.Tiñ. Ñe.hDsin.): Having completely mastered the art of Dhyāna, the yogi is said to be capable of working miracles by manipulating the Prāṇa in various ways within his mind-body complex. He is thus able to conceal or bring into manifestation the power of each Element for a specific performance or purpose.

4 Ba Men, the wild ox of Tibet: Some say this is another name for the Tibetan yak.

5 T.T.: Bar.dHa.Na.: This seems to be another geographical name for Tibet.

6 The Tibetan word, "sPyan.Phyag," means literally "eye obeisance." The translator presumes that this term refers to a certain eye-gesture (mudrā) performed for the purpose of veneration. This may still be used in India, but is no longer extant in Tibet.

7 Yed Pa (T.T.: bShad.Pa.): Milarepa was given the name of Yed Pa Dorje (the Laughing Vajra) by his Guru, Marpa, when he was first initiated.

8 Worldly Ḍākinīs (T.T.: hJin.rTen.mKha.hGro.Ma.): Khandroma, or Ḍākinīs, the sky travelers, are not all more holy than, or spiritually superior to, ordinary sentient beings. According to traditional Tibetan beliefs, there are two kinds of Ḍākinīs: one is the holy, or transcendental type, and the other is the worldly kind. Tārā, Dorje Paumo, etc., belong to the former category, for they are fully enlightened Buddhas manifesting in female form. The worldly Ḍākinīs, such as Tserinma, are still bound by Saṃsāric desires and ignorance despite their superhuman powers.

9 Lit.: " . . . at the upper end of my three Nāḍis."

10 A while ago: See Story 28.

11 Worldly, or mundane accomplishments: miraculous performances and superhuman powers which are still of a Saṃsāric nature.

12 Passion-Bodhis (T.T.: hDod.Bahi.Byañ.Chub.): This is a very rare term seldom seen in the general Buddhist scriptures. Literally it means the "Bodhi of Kleśas." Although, according to the principle of Tantrism, it is permissible to say that human passions and desires (Kleśas) are *in essence* identical with the merits and wisdom of Buddhahood, it is incorrect to say that the two are absolutely identical in every aspect. Passion-Bodhis, or the Bodhi of Kleśas, should therefore be treated as an exceptional term reflecting a certain special Tantric thought outside the general framework of Buddhist orthodoxy.

13 This sentence as it appeared in the Tibetan text (Folio 151a, line 6) is as follows: "bGegs.Pas.Sañs.rGyas.Ñid.Kyañ.Med." The translator believes that "bGegs. Pas.," meaning "because of hindrances," is a misprint, otherwise it would be very difficult to explain, and to fit into this context.

14 T.T.: Ro.gCid., lit.: "one-taste." A freer translation is "at-one-ment," or "the great one identity." "Ro.gCid." is a very widely used term in Tantric literature, denoting the all-identical or non-differentiated nature of beings.

15 Two Truths: They are, first, the Mundane Truth (T.T.: Kun.rDsob.bDen. Pa.), and second, the Transcendental Truth (T.T.: Don.Dam.bDen.Pa.). The former can also be rendered as the "conditional, dependent, or expedient Truth," and the latter as the "absolute or final Truth."

16 The Pure Land of Joy (T.T.: mÑon.dGha.): the land of Buddha Mijurpa (T.T.: Mi.hGyur.Pa.; Skt.: Akṣobhyā): His position among the five Dhyāna Buddhas is in the East.

17 Self-Buddha Pride (T.T.: lHahi.Ña.rGyal.): A Tantric yogi should, in all daily activities, always remember his Patron-Buddha-Identification "feeling" which he has gained during his Arising Yoga practice. This Patron-Buddha-Identification Yoga is designed for the transformation of all worldly, empirical experiences into a higher order that may be described as corresponding to that of perfect Buddha-hood. Thus, in the practice of this Yoga, the yogi is taught to think and to visualize his body as becoming the Buddha's body, his words as the Buddha's preaching, and his thoughts as the Buddha's all-manifesting Wisdom. The meditation exercise of "Identification-with-Buddha" is also called the "Arising of Self-Buddha Pride."

GUIDING INSTRUCTIONS
ON THE BARDO

Obeisance to all Gurus

> The God of gods,
> Lord of Ḍākinīs,
> Marpa the great Translator —
> Blessed is he by the Transmission Gurus.
>
> A pearl radiates waves of grace
> From the crown he ever wears —
> Blessed is he, the great Repa Mila.
>
> Delivered and matured is he
> Who has completed his devotion.
> To him, the Laughing Vajra, the gifted Repa Jetsun,
> I pay sincerest homage!
>
> To help the ignorant
> I now relate this story
> Of Mila's answer to the fairies,
> Wherein is given the pith of the instructions
> On guidance through the perilous Bardo.

When Marpa the Translator was imparting the Initiation to Milarepa, the Buddha Saṃvara and other deities of the Maṇḍala, together with the thirty-two Guards of Dharma and Ḍākinīs, and the sixteen Heavenly-Ladies-of-Offering, all revealed themselves in the upper sky. Milarepa saw this vision clearly for a moment. He was then given the name, "Laughing Vajra," by his Guru and the Ḍākinīs.

Urged by Marpa, Milarepa devoted his life to meditation. Because of his extreme asceticism, he had gained the Tantric Accomplishments and Merits by [mastering] the [inner and outer] causations. Through his physical body he had attained the rainbow-like Body-of-the-Mind[1] and so became the great Jetsun — one who had achieved the Ultimate Realization of Mahāmudrā.

Now, Milarepa was residing [in a green valley] to the east of the wondrous [market] town of Dinma Drin, bordering on the Mon region west of the lower Khum Bu. Beneath dark clouds, above the gate to the passage of the black planet Rāhu and to the left of a snow mountain perpetually wreathed in clouds, lay this pasture land, Medicine Valley, where flourished emerald-like meadows, jasmine flowers, and various kinds of herbs. Gently flowing by were two rivers — the Auspicious Milk, and the Nectar and Power. [Milarepa's hut] was in a quiet and blessed spot known as the "Virtuous Palace Hermitage of Chu Bar." He was then completely absorbed in the Universal Realm of the Absolute Essence — the realm of departing-from-all-playwords, the illuminating realm of no-arising and no-extinction.

It was in the autumn of the year of the Wooden Horse, while the 24th Constellation was declining, that the inhabitants of Dinma Drin were afflicted with the white and black smallpox, [and with] vomiting of blood, dizziness, fever, and many other severe and contagious diseases.[2] Many livestock and human beings had died.

In the late afternoon of the eleventh day of the second month of that autumn, when the declining sun looked like a fireball, a young girl [whom Milarepa recognized as a Ḍākinī] came to see him. Beautiful, charming, and radiant, she was dressed in a white silk robe of magnificent design, edged with jewel-like lace, and having an apron of exquisite silk with gorgeous tassels. She bowed down at Milarepa's feet, circled him seven times, and made nine more prostrations. She then said, "Oh Jetsun, our people are very, very sick. Please be kind enough to come with me to the other side of this snow mountain [to help us]." Milarepa replied, "It is better that we go tomorrow. You may stay here tonight." The girl said, "If we go by the Road of Miraculous Light, through Manta Tsari [?] there will be no hardship. Oh please, please come! You must come today!" "This old man has never seen such a road before," replied Milarepa, "nor do I know where it is. But because of your earnest request, I shall go with you. It is better if you go ahead and show me the way." The girl then produced a woolen blanket, and lifting it up toward the sky, said to the Jetsun, "Let us ride on this blanket — it will carry us there at once." As soon as Milarepa stood upon the blanket, it rose in the air, and quick as lightning, they reached their destination on the other side of Queen of the Azure Heights Snow Mountain.

On the left slope stood a white silk tent with a golden covering. The ropes and pegs were inlaid with precious stones of magnificient quality. In this tent lay another beautiful girl, wrapped in many bedcoverings, and with a long tassel, which almost reached the ground, in her hair. Her eyes were flame-colored [as if she had a fever]. As the Jetsun entered, she made an effort to lift her head up a little, crying, "I am very sick. Please help me!" Milarepa asked, "How did you catch this disease? How long have you been ill? What are your symptoms?" The girl answered, "Last summer some shepherds came and lit a big fire near here. I was caught in the flaming smoke, which made me very sick at the time. Since last autumn I have not been feeling at all well, and today I feel extremely ill.[3] Therefore I had to send for you. The vapors from our mouths have caused many people in this area to contract many diseases." Milarepa thought, "That's why so many people here have caught the pestilence. I cannot consent to cure her right away; first I must admonish her." Then he said, "Fair lady, not long ago you came to me and took the Bodhisattva's Vow, and also received the teachings of the Patron Buddha. I preached to you at length on the virtues and Karma, but instead of following my instructions, you have violated them all. You have never given the slightest consideration to your moral obligations and the precepts! You could not even endure such a slight discomfort as that caused by the shepherds, and in revenge you have spread the worst kind of pestilence among innocent people, causing them great suffering and misfortune. Since you have violated the precepts, you well deserve such punishment. In view of what you have done, I can no longer trust you. If you will immediately heal all the people in this area, I shall then see whether or not I can help you. If you do not promise to do so, I shall leave at once. Since you, the She-ghost, have broken your own oaths and violated the precepts, you will surely be damned!"

Hearing this warning from the Jetsun, the Ḍākinī was very frightened and immediately clutched Milarepa's feet and said, "We are blind and wicked beings. Because of our ignorance we have spread illness in this region. But please do not talk to us like this! As a rule, if the pure Devas and spirits from the higher ranks do not afflict *us*, we will never attack them first. Expecially, in consideration of your [former] admonishment, I have not harmed any people or sent others to afflict them. In the last month of this summer the river here overflowed, and all the narrow and precipitous places were flooded. [Taking advantage of this], some of our retainers, associates, and kinsmen, together with many flesh-eating and blood-drinking servants of ours, went about afflicting people. I will stop all the contagious diseases as soon as I get better. Therefore, please look after me and have pity on me." Thus she earnestly besought the Jetsun.

Milarepa then performed for her the Hundred-Words Cleansing Ritual[4] and prayed for her to the Gurus and the Precious Ones many times. He also increased her longevity by performing the ritual of the Victorious Mother of the Crown.[5] The next morning she was able to get up from her bed and make obeisance to him.

During the next seven days the Jetsun continuously blessed her with the power of Illuminating-Awareness, and the girl was then completely cured. She became even more healthy and vigorous than before. After this Milarepa said to her, "Fair lady, as you have completely recovered, now is the time for you to go to the villages and help the people. Tell me what offerings you would like them to make to you? What rituals should be performed to cure the sick?" She replied, "According to the reciprocal-relation principle of the Law-of-Causation, when we recover from a disease, so will the people. It is the common oath of all wordly Ḍākinīs[6] that if one of us has been made unwell or unhappy, we are all offended and the Devas and spirits support us, throwing the world into confusion. Therefore, if one wants to convalesce quickly, he should recite the quintessential Mantra of Buddha Tsudor many times, read the profound Mahāyāna Sūtras, perform the Ritual of Cleansing with Vase-Water, mark a circle round the village and confine people in it, offer white and red oblations and huge Dormas,[7] deck the altars, dedicate the merits to all, and then make his wish. He who does all these things will soon be cured."

Milarepa then went to Drin and said to the villagers, "I have had indications from a dream that the pestilence now prevailing in this area was caused by the local goddesses who are angry with you because you offended and injured them by the fires you kindled. In revenge they have spread the diseases. You should now perform suitable rituals and make various offerings."

Thereupon, the villagers all prayed to the Gurus, the Buddhas, and the Guards of Dharma, offering them many oblations and huge Dormas, and dedicating these merits to the Devas and spirits. Through the infallible power of these prayers and blessings, the pestilence completely disappeared within a short time.

On the 29th day of that month, the five Auspicious Ladies of Long Life, together with many of their followers and local deities, came to visit the Jetsun. They brought delicious food and excellent wine in jeweled beakers and offered them to Milarepa. After they had made obeisances to him and circled him many times, they stood in a row and said, "It is you, the Jetsun, who have saved our lives and cured our illnesses. You have been most gracious to us." Whereupon, with sweet voices they sang:

He who can foretell the fall of rain
Knows how to observe the sky.
When one sees that dark clouds gather,
And the dragon thunders,
He knows that the Dragon King will soon give rain
To nourish all sentient beings.
When slowly the rain drizzles,
It shows that moisture and heat
Are in balance on the earth.
When the deafening thunder peals,
It indicates the clashing conflict
Between heat and cold.

Under the flying clouds
Stands a great snow mountain with three peaks —
The central one is highest.
A crown of crystal
Is her head ornament;
Starlight, soft and glimmering,
Surrounds her in the serene night;
The rays of sun and moon gleam upon her.
Beauteous and resplendent was she fashioned.
There our noble castle stands!

By the left slope of the snow mountain
Are the wondrous pastures of Medicine Valley.
A canopy of rainbows ever hangs above it,
Reflecting beams of glowing light.
Lovely are the herbs grown in the valley,
Here dance and play the local gods,
Here lies the land of crops and fruit —
A garden full of lovely flowers.

Your hut stands by the river bank,
A place of great blessing,
Where the great Yogi Mila dwells.

Through the merits of your previous lives
You receive a precious human body.
By sloth unhindered
You meditate without diversion.
Thus, you have realized Mind-nature, the Unborn,
And mastered the magic gestures.

No obstacles and distractions can frighten you.
Unshakeable as a mountain,
You are a yogi of stability.
Having mastered Prāṇa to perfection,
You have no need of clothing,
Exposing your body freely.
By your grace and your devotions
Many beings have been saved.
At a time of defilement and distress
You came to the red-faced country [of Tibet]!
You are the glory of the world,
Our shelter and our pride!

[The leader of the four Ḍākinīs continued to sing]:

On the eleventh of this month
I was hurt and sullied by smoke and fire.
With great pain was my body wracked —
The unbearable torment tore at me.
So I became most angry and malignant.
Then I asked your help, and graciously you
    blessed me,
Performing the Ritual of Cleansing.
Also, you enlightened me
On the Mind-Essence which is beyond both life
    and death.
Of a sudden, I came to realize the Truth.
Like clouds that vanish in the sky
All my hurt was cleared away,
My mind became fresh and alert,
My body light as wool,
So comfortable and well.
The fevers left, health was restored,
And my failing breath regained its strength.
Thus the peril of death was overcome!

Failing to complete their missions
The agents of Death went back with shame.
A great debt of gratitude I owe you, oh great Yogi!
Though my birth is low and great my ignorance,
My compassion small and inferior my mind,
How can I forget he who saved my life?
Till the end of it,

I shall ne'er forget this boon!

Showing my deepest thanks
I now offer you my magic powers.
With loyalty confirmed
I shall obey your teaching.
From now until I win perfect Buddhahood
I will consort with you;
By the power of this sincere wish
May I never leave you even for a second.
As a shadow, may I follow in your steps.
Like the five first disciples of Gautama Buddha,
May we be the first disciples in your Pure Land,
When you reach perfect Buddhahood.
May we be the first to drink your nectar
And become the children of Dharma.
May we gather the clouds of the Four Actions[8]
And rain down heavenly waters
To nourish ignorant beings!

Thus, in making their pure wishes, the Auspicious Fair Lady of Long
Life led her four Ḍākinī-sisters in singing this song. The Jetsun thought,
"Now these malicious goddesses have shown their gratitude to me for
healing their sickness. If I give them the preliminary Instructions of the
Arising and Perfecting Yoga, they may be able to practice them." Then
he said, "Fair ladies, with great sincerity you have now shown me your
deep gratitude for the recovery of your health. Your words and attitude
seem to have met the requirements for Tantric teaching. I intend to
give you an Instruction, through which you may forever free yourselves
from sufferings on the perilous path of Saṃsāra. But will you be able to
practice it?" Milarepa then sang them a song, "The Growth of Joyful-
ness":

Under the canopy of sunlight in the East
Towers the propitious peak of Mount Menlha;[9]
Like the head of a crystal eagle
It reflects the glowing golden beams.
The floating clouds are like a roof,
And arched above it shines the rainbow.
On the mountain's waist
The gem-like rocks are girdled in dense fog.
Is this not the great snow mountain, Queen of
        the Azure Heights?

Residing on it are there not five wondrous ladies?
In an enchanting voice
One has just sung divinely.
Is she not the Fair Lady of Long Life,
Most sparkling and most glamorous?

This time you are really frightened,
For you have lost your pride!
Your body was torn with agonizing pain,
And your mind was full of grievances!
Your breath was failing like a thinning mist,
And your life was nearly at an end.

All this was due to your past sinful deeds —
A bitter retribution of the Ripening Karma.
If from these sinful deeds you do not refrain,
Into the great Hell you may fall perchance.
That is more dreadful than any sickness!

That you did not die is fortunate,
Praiseworthy that your seed of faith has grown.
With great compassion have I blessed you.
Through the great power of Tantra
Have I saved you from the hand of Death.

All despair and misfortune
Has turned to good and boon.
In joy you thanked me with deep gratitude,
Which in many others would be lacking.
In a charming voice
You have sung sweetly with good meaning.
Hearing it, I too feel glad and joyful.

If you would follow my instruction
Please listen and remember well:
Painful is the path of Saṃsāra,
Perilous and hard to cross
Are the Four Rivers.[10]
Dismal is the "forest" of Eight Strivings,
Hard to escape are the triple Bardo's dangers.
To live under the constant threat
Of Four Devils[11] is distressing.
But here is a path of no-fear —

An escape from all miseries,
Leading to the Land of Bliss Eternal.

I may not be superb,
But my Lineage is supreme.
From the great Dorje-Chang, the Sixth Buddha,[12]
To my teacher, the Translator Marpa,
All the Transmission Gurus are Nirmāṇakāyas.
Never has a commoner corrupted the Lineage.
Cherish then and value all my teachings!

The stories of Medripa and Nāropa are well known;
You also must have heard their names before,
As their fame is known all over India.
Blessed by these two accomplished beings
Is my father Guru, Marpa.
Like a shadow to its body,
I stayed close to him for six years and eight
          months.
By following his orders faithfully,
Joy and aspiration filled my heart.

The profound Tantra Hevajra, the gracious Dem-Chog,
The quintessential Tantra of Mahāmāya,
The lofty Tantra of Sungdue,
The concealed Tantra of Den Yi,
And the Nirmāṇakāya of the Skull —
All these vital Tantras
And their commentaries, deep as the ocean,
Were bestowed on me,
A gift of precious gems.

The Key-Instructions, essential and most pithy,
Must be taught intimately, face to face.
To master them one also needs to practice;
Like an apprentice to a master goldsmith,
One must learn the art of melting and alloying
Gold, and how to stoke the fire.
The vital teachings of Tantra
Are also taught by word of mouth.

Witnessed by Ḍākinīs, I was given
The Pith-Instructions of the Lineage.

To my father Guru, I am forever grateful!
To repay him, I practice meditation.
By hard and steady work
I have mastered the Five Prāṇas;
With confidence I can perform the Action of
        Equality.[13]
No longer do I fear the pains of sickness.
Oh my daughter-disciples,
If you also want to attain such joy
Follow my words and footsteps.
Enter now the Path,
And you will soon be happy!

The human body is beset with sickness,
And trying to free one's mind from grief
Often leads to more distress.
By the force of Karma and the senses
All self-made confusions are created.
They are but dreams passing in a flash;
Even Hell with all its torture through the aeons,
Does not exist.
From evil and habitual thoughts [within]
Arise the pains without.
This is the Final Truth
Buddha Gautama preached to Dorje Ninpo.
The whole Universe is but "imagination,"
All in all, it is but a shadow-show
Of one's own mind.
If one knows not this truth
He may possess the world of Brahmā
But never can he win true happiness.

The Four Dhyānas[14] that for kalpas last
Are on the lower path;
Never can they bring one to Omniscient Buddhahood.
Only through cultivating Bodhi-Mind
And contemplating on the Void
Can Karmas, troubles, hindrances, and habitual
        thoughts be killed.

Oh well-endowed fair ladies,
It is our lot to meet here today.
Wear the armor of zeal

And abjure distraction!
Your wishes for good soon will be fulfilled.

Milarepa then said to the Ḍākinīs, "Please think carefully about this song and its meanings and practice Dharma at once. You may think that the Four Bodies of Buddha are something beyond yourself, an exterior object or goal that you should strive to reach. But, in fact, there is no Buddha to be found outside of one's own mind. The Light-of-Death [or, the Light that shines at the moment of death] is the Dharmakāya; the [pure manifestation of] Bardo is the Sambhogakāya; the different births one takes are the Nirmāṇakāyas; and the inseparable unity of the Trikāya is called the Body-of-Essence.[15] They are with us all the time, yet we are unaware of them. To unfold them, one must rely on the profound Pith-Instructions from an accomplished Guru of an uninterrupted Lineage."

The Fair Lady of Long Life then said, "When our Guru Padmasambhava first came to Tibet from India, we all went to afflict him, but we were subdued by his powers and mighty gestures. Then we obeyed his orders and offered him our lives and service. We also besought him for the essential teachings of Tantra. From him we received instructions on the truth of Karma and other Dharmas and Sūtras. At the Dark Noisy Cemetery[16] in India we received great Initiations and Vajrayāna teachings from Guru Shojigocha,[17] and the Black Performer.[18] Therefore, perhaps we may consider ourselves to be qualified to receive esoteric instructions. This time we have suffered greatly from illness. This painful lesson was so real and so frightening that we are convinced once and for all that never would we be able to endure the torment of Hell for a moment. The warnings in your song also impressed us deeply. So, pray protect us from these fears, cleanse us from all sins, and show us the way to Buddhahood." Whereupon, they sang:

Floating in the bright firmament,
The golden clouds by magic and wonder are created
To adorn the Nagas' crowns.
Under them, the lesser Devas, the Non-men,
And the Fragrance-eating She-ghosts
Dance and gaily sing, enjoying
Sensuous pleasures with much laughter.

Beneath those flying clouds
Lies the lucky valley of Dinma.
Its upper region is circled by snow ranges,

Its lower part abounds in springs and brooks.
In the center of this valley
Grows a luxuriant meadow
Where Devas sport and play.
This brilliant Medicine Valley
Is the Nagas' treasure house,
Filled with fruit and honey.
This is where four-footed creatures thrive —
A land of pastures, quiet and delightful.

Near the river bank is a hut
Wherein a wondrous yogi dwells.
By merely hearing of his name,
Or seeing his splendrous body,
One's hindrances and sins are cleared.
He works all miracles and Mudrās.
Having realized the Omniscient Mind,
With mastership of Dharma-Essence,
He preaches Voidness with compassionate voice.
To him all Devas and spirits
Should pray and give homage.
Trust and reliance should one place in him.
He is the son of Buddha,
Who grants us all our wishes.

Driven by deep-rooted ignorance,
We worldly, magical Ḍākinīs
Wander in Saṃsāra from time without beginning.
First, we must take an earthly birth —
We have no other choice.
Then we think we can live for long,
But suddenly we hear the call of Death
And our hands are tied —
We cannot escape.
Dizzy are our heads and dark our thoughts.

Without freedom from death, we must fade,
And with us all our beauty and our splendor.

When the living organs cease to function
The awesome play of Bardo must begin.
Along the fearful Bardo path
Wanderers, confused and desolate,

Are chased by merciless demons.
They are torn apart
By anxiety and fear;
By sinful acts and habitual thoughts
They are driven away.
Then, regardless of their wishes,
They are reborn in a strange and foreign land.

In the rolling ocean of Saṃsāra we repeat
The round of birth, old-age, sickness, and of death;
No one yet has rescued us from drowning.
Today you have given us the raft of Bodhi-Mind
On which we shall escape the witch-land of desires,
And elude the dreadful monster of the deep.
Riding the gale of wrong thoughts
We shall arrive safely
In the Happy Land.
From despair and weariness
We shall revive;
With hope and guidance,
Will our wishes be fulfilled.

In Saṃsāra's dark and fearful woods
Roam ghostly beasts, our passions.
Seeing them, in panic do we tremble.
In this dark and thorny forest
We have lost our way;
Pray show us the path
And deliver us in safety.
As the bright autumn moon
Illumines the great earth,
Enlighten, pray, our ignorance
And grant us your guidance.
In the dread Bardo path,
Perilous and inescapable,
Point out the dangerous traps.

We have been enslaved by the Devil's band,
And fettered in a dungeon by our acts;
From this dread imprisonment
We could not escape.
But today we have met you,
The Savior Guru whom none dare dispute.

With your guidance and protection
We will surely cross the road.

Pray show us the way to Dharmakāya
Through recognizing the Death Light.[19]
Pray show us the way to Samboghagakāya
Through recognizing Bardo's phantom forms.
Pray show us the way to Nirmāṇakāya,
Thus letting us incarnate at our will!

Beyond the fearful realm of the Three Bardos[20]
Lies the Pure Land of No-regression.[21]
Much have we heard of it
But we have never been there.
Oh compassionate Guru, savior merciful,
Pray guide us to it now!
Pray answer the cry for help
From those in despair and grief.
Pray now reveal to them
The Fourfold Body of Buddhahood!

Then they offered the Jetsun a silver mirror Maṇḍala decorated with a golden lotus and various gems. The Jetsun said, "Since you have petitioned me so earnestly, I shall now bless you in the tradition of my Lineage. Please prepare a sacramental feast for the occasion."

That evening the five Ḍākinīs offered a Maṇḍala filled with sixty different kinds of food to the Jetsun. He blessed and initiated them into the order of the Inborn Mother[22] of the Whispered Lineage, and then sang a song in which he gave them the instruction for identifying the perilous Bardo with the Trikāya, by means of which one delivers himself [forever from Saṃsāra] to the Pure Land of Great Bliss:

In the land of India,
In the center of this earth,
There is a great monastery, Bidrama[23] called.
A university is found therein
Whence springs the fountain of all learning.
There the professor of the Northern School
Is the peerless Paṇḍita, lion of men,
A mighty champion who has
Defeated every heretic.
Is he not the great Nāropa,
Master of the four Tantras,

Master of both the mundane and the ultimate
    Accomplishment?

The foremost son of this great Paṇḍita
Is my Father Guru, the Translator Marpa,
A man with strong will and perseverance,
A man of great fame, thunder-like.

He said, "At the time of defilement,
When declines the Buddha's teaching,
Lives will be short and merits poor.
Evils and hindrances, in myriad forms,
Will o'ershadow all the world;
Leisure and long life will become most rare;
Knowledge will [expand] to a point
Too stupendous to comprehend;
Proofs and conclusions will be hard to reach.
To understand the truth of Tantra will be
    most difficult.
Therefore, my son, try nothing else,
But work hard at the practice!"

Following this injunction,
I abjure indolence, and meditate
With perseverance in my hermitage.
Thus I have gained a few Experiences.

Destined fair ladies, now listen with attention!
Along the Path of the Three Existences[24]
There is no end of wandering in Samsāra!
Know then that the Six Dharmas of Bardo
Are the root of all.
[The following parables,
Will explain the teaching of Bardo.]

Three traveling [merchants], on a long journey,
When in a perilous place sent out for help.

When they saw their guides return with
    native welcomers
They were o'erwhelmed with joy.
Without reliable guides they would have lost
Their way and fallen into the hands of enemies.

If merchants go abroad without these three good
    guides[25]
Fear and misgiving fill their minds;
By false prophesies and revelations
Three Devils lead them
To a bandits' ambush.

Thus wanderers in the dark Sidpa Bardo
Will freeze and burn for nine and forty days,
Driven by the force of Karma
To Saṃsāra's prison to return.
If from this prison you would escape
You should contemplate the Oneness
Of the Saṃsāra-Nirvāṇa Bardo,
And meditate on the Root-principle,
Truth Absolute, the Mahāmudrā.

The Bardo of Birth-and-Death
Is a good ground on which to drill the illuminating
    mind.
Upon it one should practice the Arising and
    Perfecting Yogas.

The essence of the Bardo-of-the-Path
Is that of Innate Wisdom.
The Whispered Lineage practice will unfold it.

The Bardo of Dream-and-Sleep is best
To convert habitual thinking into Wisdom;
Within it one should practice the Yogas
Of Light and of the Phantom Body.
At the end of the Sidpa Bardo
The Three Bodies of Buddha will appear.
This is the time to enter the Three Pure Lands.[26]

If in Bardo one fails to realize Trikāya
And time elapses till the Incarnation-Bardo[27]
    comes,
By his faith and purity
He can still be born in a land of fortune,
His body well endowed with leisure.
Because the Law of Causation never fails to bring
    what one deserves,

By waking from past Karma
And perfecting meditation,
He will gain Liberation soon!

To you five wondrous maidens
Who asked with sincerity and faith
Is given this important Bardo teaching.
Even if the Jetsun Marpa should Himself come here,
He could give you no instruction more profound
    than this!

The five Ḍākinīs then prostrated themselves before the Jetsun and circumambulated him seven times. They offered him a Maṇḍala made of precious stones; praised his body, word, mind, and merits; and finally made him the supreme-bliss-void offering of the Wisdom-of-Four-Blisses produced through the ecstasy of union. Then they said, "Your instructions on the Bardo are clear and comprehensive. Now please give us the pith of this teaching to make it easier for us to practice," and they sang:

We pay homage to you, gracious Guru,
The refuge of all sentient beings.
With the teaching of the Whispered Lineage
You have transformed our pains to joy,
As by [a magician] iron is turned to gold.
Pray, most holy Buddha,
Always pity and protect us.

Above the immaculate lotus
Untarnished by Saṃsāric soil,
Your throne, oh Jetsun Guru,
Illuminates the Void!
A myriad Ḍākinīs cloud around you;
The sun and moon shine down on you,
Illumining the absence of wavering thoughts!

For your handsome face and radiant
Body we feel insatiable,
And desire to look once more.
Beautiful, with well-proportioned features,
You are like the son of the Victorious Ones.
Seeing you, one feels joy and happiness.
To the tune of Dri Za[28] we sing
A song of praise to you.

Your voice is like the roaring
Of a lion, great and mighty,
Like the Dharma, clear yet void.
Your voice frightens the devils and pagans
And fulfills the wishes of the gifted ones.
In the Ten Directions your fame will spread afar.

Like a diamond, your mind cannot be broken;
Like space it embraces all.
From the sky of No-conception
Shines the light of your Bodhi-Mind
Emancipating disciples from darkness.

Your body, word, and mind are like those of Buddhas —
From them spring all Accomplishments.
If one thinks of you, the Wish-fulfilling Gem,
All one's wishes will be fulfilled.
If one worships you with earnestness,
As the adorning crown-of-grace
Upon his head, all his hopes will be fulfilled.
If one prays to you wholeheartedly night and day
Like a mighty king, you will grant
All his requests.
To you, the precious Jetsun,
We pay homage and give praise.

From the clouds of your compassion
Falls the nectar rain of blessing;
When the destined disciple drinks it
He will conquer all his desires
In this very life, and the seed
Of Enlightenment will sprout within him.
Reaching the Thirteenth Stage,[29]
He will become the great Dorje-Chang.

With your teachings, wisdom, and performance
May all beings become filled and happy!
May the flower of perfection bloom in joy!
May we serve you as escorts on the Path,
Till we reach the Ultimate Enlightenment.
May we attain final Samādhi
Through normal worldly rapture.
By the Wisdom-of-Four-Blisses

May we stabilize the bliss-void Samādhi.

As women of intelligence we are convinced
Of the truth of the Middle Way.
With joy we shall obey your orders,
Pray grant us permission to serve you.

At the close of this song we ask
You for concise teaching on the Bardo.
Pray grant us the instruction for realizing
    Buddha's Four Bodies
At the time when death calls us.

Nourished and fostered by your grace,
May we win merits like yours.
In this very life
May we all attain perfect Enlightenment.

The Jetsun continued: "Fair ladies! Driven by the three desires and
flowing thoughts, sentient beings have been wandering down the endless
road in the Three Realms, forever subjected to the Eight Deprivations.
This journey is so long and hazardous that one feels very weary and exhausted. There are three different kinds of travelers on this road. The
first have received, followed, and practiced the Instructions; the second
have also received but have not practiced them; while the third have not
even the Instructions. The first kind do not fear or worry about the
dangers of the road nor about the traps of demons, because by practicing the Dharma they are able to vanquish all these fears. The third
kind are ordinary people who spontaneously enter the perilous path, and
are automatically seized by the devils-of-Karma. They will undergo all
the pains of birth and death, and wander in the Three Realms of Saṃsāra forever. The second kind have the same fears and hazards as the
third. But they have received the Instructions and have learned to recognize and fight against evil influences; and so, if they have an unshakeable faith towards [Buddha] and an understanding and aspiration for the Dharma together with the armor of unyielding diligence,
they may slowly and gradually recognize the Trikāya of Buddha by
observing carefully how the senses and elements subside [at the time.
of death]. You ask me about the teaching of realizing the Trikāya.
You should know that at the time of death, when the outer and
inner elements successively subside, the [consciousness] of the dying
man will be [temporarily] set free from the string of Kleśas. The
absolute Reality, the essence of the voidness of Dharmadhātu beyond

all thought, will unfold itself, shining bright as the sun and moon in the sky. This is the Light-of-Death, or the Dharmakāya itself. One should recognize it as it is. But to do so at the time of death, a man must first understand the nature of Mind in the way his Guru pointed out during his lifetime, and also practice the Illuminating Light-of-the-Path.[30] In the perilous path of the Sidpa Bardo, the wanderer will be pursued and attacked by 'executioners' who are, in fact, created by his own previous Karmas and thoughts. These 'mind-created body-forms' are luminous, their organs are complete, and they possess the miraculous powers of a mundane karmic nature, which include the ability to pass through material objects, [telepathy,] and so forth. The Bardo body of this stage is, in fact, identical with the Sambhogakāya. At this time one should invoke the magic-like two-in-one Buddha Body [to replace and purify] the karmic Bardo body created by habitual thoughts, and thus recognize the Sambhogakāya as it is. To recognize this Sambhogakāya in the Bardo stage, one should practice the Arising Yoga and clearly visualize the Patron Buddha's Body during his lifetime, and also practice the Dream Yoga, to master the [manifestation] of the Phantom Body. At the final stage of Bardo, driven by the winds of Karma and Blindness and having no choice whatsoever, he searches for somewhere to incarnate. When he watches sex intercourse between [his future] mother and father, hate [towards one] and lust [toward the other] rises in him. But if at this time he can remember the Pith-Instructions, and enter the void-bliss experience [of Samādhi] and remain there, then karmic and worldly thoughts will not arise again. When he intends to incarnate he should think and observe that all he sees are manifestations of the Nirmāṇakāya Buddha, and recognize the Nirmāṇakāya as it is.

"In order to be able to recognize the Nirmāṇakāya, one should, in his present life, endeavor to arouse [transcendental] Wisdom through practising the Heat Yoga of the Liberation Path and the Karma Mudrā of the Path-of-Love. Only then will he be able to realize the full meaning of the Third Initiation[31] and thus vanquish [instinctive] jealousy. In brief, one must know well the different stages and times [in the Bardo state] in order to realize the fruit of the Trikāya. Even the ultimate Pointing-out Instruction of the Whispered Lineage — the core of the Skillful Path, the most cherished prize in Marpa's heart — can give you no profounder instructions than this. I have no better and no more convincing teaching than this to rely on and confide. So, fair ladies, appreciate what I say, follow, and practice it."

The Fair Lady of Long Life, the leader of the [Four] Ḍākinīs, was greatly inspired by these profound Instructions of the Skillful Path, and her faith was confirmed. She bowed down at the feet of Milarepa and said, "Oh Jetsun! From now on I will follow you and practice Karma Mudrā with you until I have consummated my Experience and Realization of this quintessential Bardo instruction. Please always remember and look after me." Praying to him with great sincerity and earnestness, the Ḍākinī again made obeisances and circumumbulated him many times. Then she returned to her own abode.

This is the story of the Great Repa Mila, the Laughing Vajra, and his meeting with the five worldly, magical Ḍākinīs, including the songs of inquiry and answer known as the "Golden Rosary," in which are found the instructions for emancipation from the perilous Bardo.

. . .   .

This is the story of the gracious Guru,
The accomplished, Gem-like Repa,
His meeting with five worldly Ḍākinīs of low birth,
And their songs of inquiry and his answers.
It is written with garlanded words
As a song containing
The profound hidden teaching of the Toagal.[32]

I have not added to this story
For fear of losing and forgetting it;
But for the benefit of disciples in the future
And to inspire their joy,
I have written this tale
In my Guru's words.

Three times did I seek my Guru's permission
To write this book.
He smiled at me, [but] did not grant it
Until the third time.
I dare not violate the rules
Because the Ḍākinīs are most severe and strict.

My Guru says this story should be told
Only to great yogis in the future
As a reference for their devotions;
But from others it must be secret kept.

Lest I violate the Ḍākinīs' rules and wishes
I now sincerely pray to them

To conceal this story from those
[Who cannot profit by it],
And never let it widely spread.

When Buddha Sākyamuni won Enlightenment,
In the latter part of the [month)
In which he worked miracles,
I, Auijee Thajan, and the Guru Bodhi Radsa,
In a tamarisk grove where wild beasts roam,
Asked our Elder Brother, perfect in the Tantric
    precepts,
In detail about this story,
And wrote it down in words.
It is "The Song of the Golden Rosary"
On how to free oneself from the perilous Bardo.
I now dedicate the merit of writing it
To the emancipation of all beings
From fear and danger in the Bardo.

At the request of the five Shajhamas,[33] the Fair Lady of Long Life
and her sisters, the instruction for freeing one from the perilous path
of Bardo was given by the peerless Yogi, the great Milarepa. After
careful discussions, the two Repas put it down in words as a service
and offering to the Dharma.

NOTES

1 Rainbow-like Body of the Mind (T.T.: hJah.Tshon.lTa.Buhi.Yi.Kyi.sKu.):
This term is not an established or often-used term in Tibetan Tantrism. It was
perhaps created by the author to denote the illuminated "mental body" of an accomplished yogi, usually known as hJah.Lus. — the Rainbow Body.

2 These are free translations of the diseases' names. Because of their obscurity, it is difficult to identify the equivalent medical terms.

3 The Tibetans believe that smoke caused by a forest or mountain fire will
usually injure or afflict the local deities. Thus, in revenge these deities will spread
germs of disease in the region.

4 The Hundred-Words Cleansing Ritual (T.T.: Yi.Ge.brGya.Pahi.Khrus.Chog.):
This is the cleansing ritual of the Vajrasattva whose main Mantra consists of one
hundred words.

5 The Victorious Mother of the Crown (T.T.: gTsug.Tor.Nam.Par.rGyal.
Ma.): a Tantric goddess who can bestow great powers of attraction.

6 Worldly Ḍākinīs (T.T.: hJig.rTen.mKhah.hGro.Ma.): Ḍākinīs are not nec-essarily all enlightened and benevolent beings. Worldly Ḍākinīs are local goddess-es, or fairies who, like ordinary human beings, are still bound by desires and passions. They are by no means holy or divine. See Story 29, Note 8.

7 Dormas (T.T.: gTor.Ma.): In making the various oblations for Tantric rit-uals, Tibetan lamas have developed a highly sophisticated art of making these ob-lation objects from baked flour dough. Using this material as the main ingredient, together with additional decorative articles and figurines, Tibetan lamas can make up a great variety of oblations called Dormas.

8 Four Actions (T.T.: bsDus.Wa.rNam.bShi.; Literal translation: "Four Co-operative Acts"): These are the four Bodhisattva's virtues (Skt.: Catuh-saṁgraha-vastu). They are (1) to give the things that others like to receive; (2) to say the pleasant words that others like to hear; (3) to do profitable deeds for sentient be-ings; and (4) to adapt oneself under all circumstances for the benefit of sentient beings.

9 Menlha (T.T.: sMan.lHa.): a holy place in Tibet.

10 Four Rivers: a symbolic term denoting the pains of birth, old-age, sick-ness, and death, that, like hazardous rivers, are difficult to cross.

11 Four Devils: the Devils of Illness, of Interruption, of Death, and of De-sires.

12 Sixth Buddha: Counting clockwise, the first four Buddhas in a Maṇḍala, starting from the East, are (1) Buddha Vairocana, East; (2) Buddha Ratnasam-bhava, South; (3) Buddha Amitābha, West; and (4) Buddha Amoghasiddhi, North. The fifth Buddha, Vajrasattva, occupies the center place, and the sixth, Vajradhara (Tib.: Dorje-Chang) sits in the center above Vajrasattva. Dorje-Chang is the source and center of all the other five. Chronologically He is the First Buddha. The so-called Sixth Buddha is, therefore, a very misleading term created because of the Oriental habit of counting in the direction starting from the East.

13 Action of Equality (T.T.: Ro.sÑoms.Kyi.sPyod.Pa.): When a yogi reaches the advanced stage he is able to "equalize" fear and hope, joy and pain, evil and vir-tue, etc. He is then no more affected by polarity, and begins to equalize and unify the opposing forces as manifested in dualism.

14 The Four Dhyānas: These denote the Four Formless Dhyānas, i.e., the Dhyānas of Infinite Space, of Infinite Consciousness, of Nothingness, and of Neith-er Consciousness nor Non-Consciousness.

15 Body-of-Essence (T.T.: Ño.Wo.Ñid.Kyi.sKu.): The complete name for this term should be "Body of the Universal Essence" (T.T.: Chos.dWyiñ.Ño.Wo.Ñid. Kyi.sKu.), which is the unity, or the indivisible aspect of the Trikāya. This term seems to be found only in the Tantric literature, and is criticized by some Buddhist scholars as senseless and redundant, since its characteristics have been well cov-ered by the tenets of the Dharmakāya.

16 Dark Noisy Cemetery (T.T.: Mun.Pa.sGra.sGrogs.).

17. Guru Shojigocha (T.T.: sLob.dPon.Phyogs.Kyi.Go.Cha.).

18 Black Performer (T.T.: sPyod.Pa.Nag.Po.).

19 Death Light (T.T.: hChi.Bahi.Hod.Zer.): the light of the Dharmakāya that shines forth at the time of death.

20 The Three Bardos: (1) Chikhai Bardo (the Bardo at the moment of death); (2) Chönyid Bardo (the Bardo of Reality); (3) Sidpa Bardo (the Bardo of Rebirth). See "The Tibetan Book of the Dead," 3rd ed., edited by W. Y. Evans-Wentz, Oxford University Press, 1957.

21 The Pure Land of No-Regression: Buddha's Pure Land is said to be immune from all adverse conditions that may pull one back from his progress on the spiritual Path, therefore it is also known as the Pure Land of No-Regression.

22 Inborn Mother (T.T.: lHan.Cig.sKyes.Ma.): another name for Dorje Pagmo, who symbolizes the Inborn Wisdom of Buddhahood.

23 Bidrama (T.T.: Bi.Kra.Ma.): This is probably a corruption of the word Vikramasila (Monastery).

24 Three Existences: These are the Existences of Life, of Death, and of Bardo.

25 The names of the so-called "three guides" are not mentioned in the text, and the translator is not certain about them.

26 The Three Pure Lands: Judging from the context, the Three Pure Lands in question seem to be the Pure Lands of the Dharmakāya, of the Sambogakāya, and of the Nirmānakāya. But this locution is rather unusual, and lacks sufficient reason. It is acceptable in Mahāyāna Buddhism to say that there is a Pure Land of the Sambhogakāya or a Land of the Nirmānakāya, but it would be difficult to accept the idea of a Land of the Dharmakāya, which is formless and void. The translator presumes that this locution is merely an embarrassing sacrifice to style, caused by the Procrustean approach of the trisymmetrical form adopted in this song.

27 The Incarnation-Bardo (T.T.: sKye.gNas.brGyud.Pahi.Bar.Do.): commonly known as the Srid.Pa. Bardo.

28 Dri.Za.: the Smell Eater. It is said that most of the spirits, or metamorphosis-born beings, are fed on odors. This is true of Devas, Asuras, and ghosts.

29 The Thirteenth Stage: Generally, Mahāyānists accept only ten progressive enlightenment stages of a Bodhisattva, known as the Ten Bhūmis; passing the tenth stage, Buddhahood is then reached. Therefore, Buddhahood is considered as the eleventh stage. But according to some Tantrists, the Supreme Vajra-Buddhahood is still two steps beyond the general eleventh stage. Thus, the stage of Dorje-Chang is considered as the Thirteenth Stage — a very controversial topic in Tantric Buddhism.

30 The Illuminating Light-of-the-Path (T.T.: Lam.Gyi.Hod.Zer.): This is the Wisdom-Light a yogi sees on the Path (or during his meditation practice). Altogether there are three kinds of "Lights": (1) The Light of Origin, or the Mother Light (T.T.: Mahi.Hod.Zer.); (2) The Light of the Path, or the Light of the Son (T.T.: Lam.Gyi.Hod.Zer.); and (3) The Light of Fruit, or the Light of Union (T.T.: hBras.Buhi.Hod.Zer.).

31 The Third Initiation: Third Initiation is also called the Wisdom Initiation (T.T.: Ye.Çes.Kyi.dWan.) During this initiation the disciple is shown the truth of the unity of bliss and voidness by the symbol of sexual union.

32 Toagal (T.T.: Thod.rGal.): This is the advanced teaching of the Great Perfection of the Ningmaba School, which is quite different and unique in comparison with the Yogic teachings of the New Schools of Tibetan Tantrism. This is a type of "Light Yoga," stressing the functional or manifestating aspect of the "Innate Light." Literature of this Yoga has so far never been translated into any Western language.

33 Shajhama (T.T.: Phyag.rGyag.Ma.): the female yogi who helps one in the practice of the Third Initiation Yoga.